Learn PHP By Examples

Practical Approach to Web Application Development

Second Edition

WINFRED YAOKUMAH

Learn PHP by Examples

Practical Approach to Web Application Development

Second Edition

ISBN: 1541203720

ISBN-13: 978-1541203723

Printed by CreateSpace, An Amazon.com Company.

Available from Amazon.com, CreateSpace.com,

and other retail outlets.

DEDICATION

To my wife, Peace and children: Daniel, Joshua, Joseph, Eunice, and Esther.

PRACTICAL APPROACH TO WEB APPLICATION DEVELOPMENT

Learn PHP By Examples

Work diligently. Work hard. Focus. Perform as if you are at the Olympics.
One day, unexpectedly, it will start paying off.
By Joan F. Marques

CONTENTS AT A GLANCE

PART I

PART I: PHP LANGUAGE FUNDAMENTALS

Learn PHP By Examples

A great deal of talent is lost to the world for want of a little courage.

By Sydney Smith

CONTENTS AT A GLANCE

PART II

GETTING INVOLVED IN ADVANCED TOPICS

Contents

Acknowledgments

I am indebted to many people for their contributions in the development of this book and would like to acknowledge them here.

I am grateful to many students over several semesters and years in my undergraduate web technologies courses who used preliminary versions of this book. I appreciate not only their helpful suggestions but also their patience and support of this work. Two students in particular, David Okumi and Francisca Mens, did a good work to review and edit some of the solutions in this book. I am grateful to the following reviewers of preliminary versions or portions of this book: Joshua Kissiedu, Teaching Assistant at the Information Technology Department of Pentecost University; Kwesi Debrah, former IT Head of Department at the Bank of Ghana; Simons Augustine, IT Head of Department at Ghana Stock Exchange; Dr. George Ofori Dwumfuo, Dean of the Faculty of Computing at the Wisconsin University College.

I am particularly grateful for the help of Rebecca Amponsah, who provided tremendous assistance, spent long hours solving questions and reviewing the materials in this book, and offered insightful suggestions. Many thanks to Nana Yoofi Takyi for reviewing this book. Thanks also to Apostle Prof. Opoku-Onyina (Chairman of the Church of Pentecost), Apostle Alfred Koduah (Former General Secretary of the Church of Pentecost), Rev. Apostle Daniel Walker (Rector of Pentecost University College) and Prof. Kwame Omane-Antwi (Vice Rector of Pentecost University College) for their words of encouragement and mentoring. Their many years of experience and wise counsel have been a source of inspiration to me when the going got though.

I wish to thank my wife, Peace. She has been instrumental in the success of this book. Her love and relentless support allowed me to spend many late nights working on this book. Most important, I acknowledge the Almighty, the giver of life, knowledge and wisdom, without whose abundant grace I could not write this book. My thanks also to the publisher and others – that assisted with the publication of this book. I want to apologize to any person who contributed but I have overlooked at this time.

Finally, I hope that you will derive value from this book. Any shortcomings, errors, omissions, or inconsistencies attributed to the book are the sole responsibility of me.

Preface

Introduction

Welcome to the exciting world of the most popular scripting language used in web application development, PHP. This book, *Learn PHP by Examples*, shows you how to build skills that you need in developing web applications that have global accessibility running on the Apache web server. It also explains key points for the understanding of how to develop better and faster web applications.

The Intended Audience of This Book

Learn PHP by Examples is intended to be used by individuals who want to learn PHP and be able to apply it in writing programming logic for the web. It can be used by universities and colleges as a single term course in Web Technologies. *Learn PHP by Examples* is written primarily for undergraduate and college students who want to quickly master PHP and become expert developers. Because web application development is relatively new compared to desktop applications, developers can read this book to expand their scope in catching up with the current trend in application development. I recommend that you have basic knowledge in HTML prior to reading this book. You can find useful tutorials on HTML at www.w3school.com. In addition, experience with programming languages such as C/C++ or Perl would contribute to a better understanding and appreciation of programming in PHP.

Why I Wrote This Book

My sole goal for writing this book is to provide my own students with in-depth and practical hands-on experience with web application development. The numerous feedbacks I have received on earlier drafts of this book from my present and former students (sometimes from their supervisors at the work places who saw and used the book) have encouraged me to pursue its formal publication so that other students and people who want to learn and master PHP may benefit from it as well. Many students find the materials in this book very useful and applicable when developing their project work as many students' projects were geared toward web application development.

On the Bibliography and Internet Sources

This book relies on earlier contributions by many authors. To facilitate reading, the discussion of sources appears in most cases not in the course of the discussion, but in the Bibliography section at the end of the book. Make sure you read those sections, so as to understand the origin of many ideas and find out where to learn more. Again, this book makes extensive use of electronic sources (Internet related sources) such as World-Wide-Web pages, discussion groups, and other Internet sources. Electronic sources undoubtedly provide much useful, comprehensive and relevant information. Sources used are presented under Internet Sources in the Bibliography section.

I am always eager to receive feedback and suggestions from readers of my book. Please send your suggestions and comments about this book to **winfred91@gmail.com**.

Contents of This Book

Included in this Book:

- Step-by-step teach yourself approach to quickly master PHP.
- Comprehensive examples that provide solid foundation to develop dynamic websites.
- 170 well-explained PHP scripts to help you speedily grasp PHP basic concepts.
- 30 detailed questions and solutions.
- 45 real-world and practical programming questions to try out.

The materials in this book have been arranged so that you can either read it from start to finish or read any topic that interests you. This book is divided into two major parts of the 21 chapters. Part 1 (Chapter 1 to 11) deals with PHP language fundamentals and Part 2 (Chapter 12 to 21) addresses advanced topics. The following is a brief description of each chapter.

Chapter 1: Installing and Configuring the Web Server

Talks about how to install, configure, and test PHP, MySQL server, and Apache Web server. The chapter helps you to understand how PHP, MySQL, and Apache Web server work together.

Chapter 2: Writing Your First PHP Scripts

Discusses how to use various PHP tags, write basic PHP scripts, and display PHP contents using **print** and **echo** keywords. It also illustrates how to embed PHP into HTML and run simple scripts.

Chapter 3: Variables

Discusses data types, variable naming convention and assignment, type-casting, string concatenation and interpolation, single and double quoted strings, etc.

Chapter 4: Constants

Explains how to define and assign values to constants, helps you to differentiate between constants and variables, and also discusses the use of magic constants in your scripts.

Chapter 5: Operators

Talks about different types of operators as well as the use of operator precedence in PHP.

Chapter 6: Decision Structures

Discusses programming decision structures such as **if, if … else**, **switch … case, break** and **continue** keywords that enable a programmer to construct rich logical program segments that are based on decisions.

Chapter 7: Performing Repetitive Tasks

Illustrates iterative programming, which enables the programmer to perform repetitive tasks by the use of **while … loop, do … while, for ..loop, and foreach … loop** and apply the use of **break** and **continue** keywords in looping statements.

Chapter 8: Functions

Identifies both in-built and user-defined functions, which enable the reader to apply the concepts of functions and how to call a function, pass parameters to functions and return values from functions. Moreover, the chapter consists of a host of pre-defined functions such as mathematical, error, email, file, and ODBC functions.

Chapter 9: Arrays

Covers the concept of arrays and how they are defined in PHP. It distinguishes between numeric and associative arrays, and as well as the use of one, two, and three-dimensional arrays.

Chapter 10: Fundamentals of Object-Oriented Programming

Introduces the new trend of PHP – OOP; it gives the programmer the basic object-oriented programming concepts and its fundamental principles. The chapter discusses with thorough examples the use of classes, objects, properties, methods, access specifiers (public, private, and protected), and how to embed constructors and destructors in programming codes.

Chapter 11: Basic Form Processing

Discusses the basics of HTML form creation with form control (textbox, radio buttons, checkbox, command buttons, optgroups, fieldset, file upload, etc) tags and the use of $_POST, $_GET, $_REQUEST global variables to gather form data.

Chapter 12: Sessions

Discusses the concept behind session management and gives examples on how sessions can be applied. Talks about how to track user activities on web pages.

Chapter 13: Cookies

The chapter discusses the concepts behind cookies, how it works and how to apply cookies in scripts to track user activities.

Chapter 14: File and Folder Manipulation

Demonstrates the use of PHP scripts to create files and folders. It furthermore discusses file and folder management using PHP scripts (to open, read, write, rename, delete files) and how to access and modify the contents of files and folders.

Chapter 15: Uploading Files

Talks about how to write PHP scripts to upload files (including images, pictures, etc) to the web server. It also discusses writing scripts to upload multiple files with one submission and identifies the possible error tracking techniques in file upload.

Chapter 16: Sending Automated E-Mails

Discusses how to send simple automated email and to setup Windows and Linux platform for sending automated emails.

Chapter 17: Server-Side Form Validation

This is a critical chapter as far as web design is concerned. It talks about server-side validation using PHP, which enables the programmer to apply server-side validation techniques to form data, including letters, numbers, email, date, and empty fields.

Chapter 18: Client-Side Form Validation

Talks about client-side validation using JavaScript. It enables the programmer to apply client-side validation techniques to form data including letters, numbers, email, date, and empty fields.

Chapter 19: PHP Errors and Exceptions Handling

Introduces the advanced techniques that most PHP programmers eventually want to use, including error-handling and major causes of errors in programming, particularly, as they relate to PHP. Discover how to use simple **die()** and **exit()** functions to track errors, and work with custom error handling techniques. The chapter also explains object-oriented way of dealing with exceptions.

Chapter 20: Introducing PHP and MySQL Interaction

Discusses PHP functions for working with MySQL database. It enables the programmer to use scripts that dynamically interact with MySQL database. The chapter shows how to write scripts to connect to and close MySQL server, create, truncate, and drop databases and tables from within PHP scripts.

Chapter 21: Insert, Update, Select, Delete Records

This chapter discusses how to perform record insertion, updating, retrieving, and deletion in your PHP script.

Apendix A: Deprecated Functions

Lists some of the deprecated extensions, functions, and statements in PHP 7

Apendix B: XAMPP Installation Procedure

Shows you the step-by-step instructions for installing XAMPP server on your computer.

1

Installing and Configuring the Web Server

The only people who have anything to fear from free software (open source software) are those whose products are worth even less.
By David Emery

Learning Objectives

After studying this chapter, you should be able to:

- Understand what Apache Web server, MySQL database server, and PHP are and how they work together.
- Install and test Apache Web server, MySQL database server, and PHP.
- Understand how to configure Apache Web server, MySQL database server, and PHP for efficient performance.

Introduction

The first part of this chapter provides basic information about the benefits of using Apache Server, MySQL and PHP. The second part provides an in-depth step-by-step procedure as to how to install the web servers and PHP interpreter (MySQL, Apache Server, PHP). The final part takes you carefully through how to configure and fine-tune your web servers for higher performance. What you will learn in this chapter will help you administer web servers and offer you solid understanding of how web servers work.

PHP, MySQL and Apache Web Servers

What is PHP

PHP stands for Hypertext Preprocessor. PHP is a powerful server-side scripting language for creating dynamic and interactive websites. PHP is the widely-used, free to download, and an efficient alternative to other scripting languages such as ASP (Active Server Pages) and JSP (Java Server Pages). PHP is perfectly suited for Web development and can be embedded directly into the HTML (Hypertext Markup Language) code. The PHP syntax is very similar to Perl and C. PHP is often used together with Apache web server on various operating systems such as Linux, Unix, Mac, and Windows.

A PHP file may contain text, HTML tags and scripts. Scripts in a PHP file are executed on the server and hence referred to as server-side scripting language. Apart from PHP, ASP and JSP are also server-side scripting languages. But the HTML tags are rendered on the client machine and are therefore referred to as client-side language. Other examples of client-side scripting languages are JavaScript and CSS (Cascading Style Sheet).

As already noted above, PHP is a server-side scripting language (executed on the Web server and the output sent in HTML to the browser). This means that the scripts are executed on the Web server. One advantage of PHP is that it supports many major databases such as MySQL, Informix, Oracle, Sybase, Solid, PostgreSQL, and many others. PHP is also an open source software (OSS). This simply means that PHP is free to download and use without having to worry about copyright laws.

A typical PHP file may contain a combination of text, HTML tags and scripts. When you run a PHP file, the file is returned to the browser as plain HTML. You cannot view the PHP source code by selecting "View source" in the browser. You will only see the output from the PHP file, which is in plain HTML. This is because the scripts are executed on the server before the result is sent back to the browser.

As you create your PHP file, it is important to save the file with a file extension "**.php**". For example you can name your file **`helloworld.php`**.

PHP 7 New Features

As stated in current PHP documentation, PHP 7 comes with several new features and the most significant ones are listed below:

- Improved performance – Uses new Zend Engine 3.0 to improve application performance. It is almost twice faster than PHP 5.
- Lower memory consumption – PHP 7 utilizes lesser memory resources. It is reported to have 50% better memory consumption than PHP 5.6.
- Scalar type declarations – The parameter and return types can now be enforced.
- Return and scalar type declarations – Support for return type and parameter type added.
- Consistent 64-bit support – Provides support for 64-bit architecture machines.
- Improved exception hierarchy – Exception hierarchy is improved.
- Coverts many fatal errors to exceptions – Range of exceptions is increased covering many fatal errors converted as exceptions.
- Secure random number generator – Introduction of new secure random number generator application program interface (API).
- Deprecated SAPIs and extensions removed – Various old and unsupported SAPIs and extensions are removed from the latest version.
- Null coalescing operator (??) – New null coalescing operator is added to PHP 7.
- Anonymous classes – Support for anonymous classes added.
- Zero cost asserts – Support for zero cost assert added.

The new features will be illustrated with examples to show you how they can be used. Some of the deprecated extensions, functions, and statements are presented in Appendix A.

What is MySQL Server

MySQL is a database server. MySQL provides all the basic features and objects found in other database management systems such as tables, views, procedures, triggers, events, transactions, and cursors. It is ideal for both small and large applications. MySQL supports standard SQL (Structured Query Language) and compiles on a number of platforms including Unix, Linux, and Windows. Also MySQL is free to download and use because it is open source software.

Why Use PHP and MySQL Combination

The major advantage of combining PHP and MySQL is that they are cross-platform. This means that you can develop the website in Windows and deploy it on a Linux platform. The following features make PHP and MySQL the preferred choice when developing web applications: They

1. run on many different platforms (Windows, Linux, Unix, etc.).
2. are compatible with almost all web servers used today such as Apache, IIS (Internet Information Server), etc.
3. are free to download from the official PHP (**`www.php.net`**) and MYSQL (**`www.mysql.com`**) sites.
4. are easy to learn.
5. run efficiently on the server side.

What is Apache Server

Originally developed for Unix environments, Apache Web server has been ported to Windows, OS/2 and other operating systems. Apache is generally recognized as the world's most popular Web server, the HTTP (hypertext transfer protocol) server. The Apache Web server provides a full range of Web server features, including CGI (common gateway interface), SSL (secure socket layer), and virtual domains. Apache also supports plug-in modules for extensibility.

How to Get Started

In order to start writing your scripts, you need to install the following. These files can be downloaded from the websites indicated below:

- Install an Apache server (**www.apache.org**) on a Windows or Linux machine.
- Install PHP (**www.php.net**) on a Windows or Linux machine.
- Install MySQL (**www.mysql.com**) on a Windows or Linux machine.

Instead of installing and configuring Apache, PHP and MySQL separately, the three have been bundled together as a package. This facilitates ease of installation and setup. Some of these packages are EasyPHP, LAMP (Linux, Apache, MySQL, and PHP), WAMP (Windows, Apache, MySQL, and PHP), and XAMPP which stands for Cross-Platform (X), Apache (A), MariaDB (M), PHP (P) and Perl (P). This book uses XAMPP. You can download the current version of XAMPP from **https://www.apachefriends.org**.

Installing XAMPP (PHP, MySQL Server, and Apache Server)

The steps involved in installing XAMMP Server are shown in Appendix B. Some of the screens are not shown, but during the installation, read and follow the setup wizard carefully. After the installation, you can test the web server.

Testing the Installation

After installing XAMPP, the XAMPP Control Panel is created as an icon. You can use it to **start**, **re-start** or **stop** the servers. Moreover, if you make any changes to the configuration settings, for changes to take effect, it is required to restart Apache and/or MySQL. In XAMPP, if the Apache and MySQL servers are already running, stop them and start them again as shown in Figure 1.1.

Figure 1.1: XAMPP Control Panel settings.

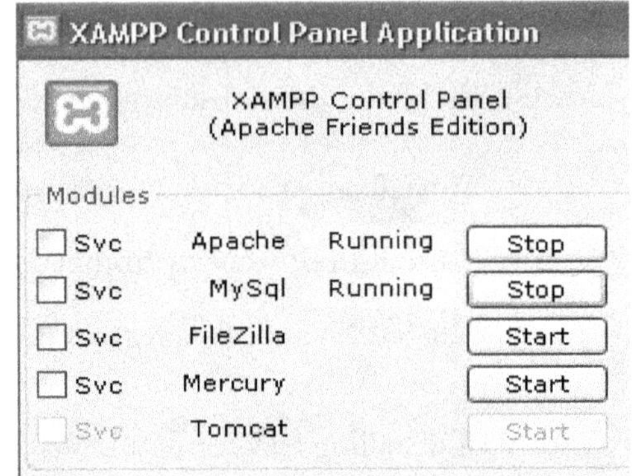

Steps:

- On the desktop, from the start menu, or in the system tray, double-click the XAMMP Control Panel icon.
- Click on **Stop** buttons of both the running Apache and MySql to stop the server.
- Click on **Start** buttons of both Apache and MySql to restart the servers

Once you have started Apache in the control panel, type **http://localhost** in your web browser's address bar. This would bring you a web page that lists XAMPP related details. This indicates that your PHP is running.

Knowing Your XAMPP Directory Structure

Figure 1.2: Major folders in the XAMPP installed folder

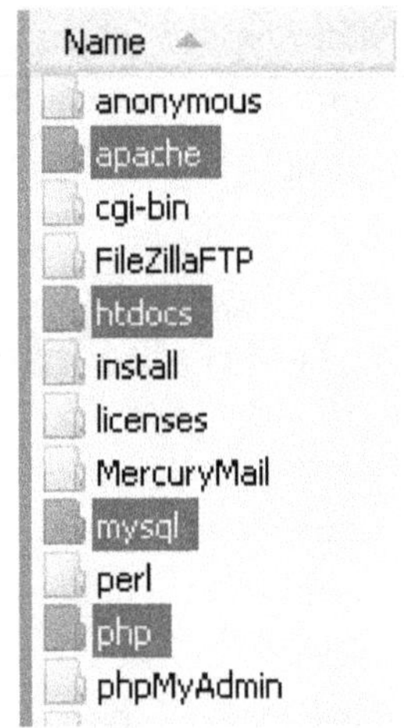

The XAMPP directory structure (Figure 1.2) contains important folders representing the three main components of the package: these are **php**, **mysql**, and **apache**. One other important folder is **htdocs**. This is where you should put your website related contents.

By default, all web files run from within **htdocs** folder when using XAMPP. The location may differ depending on the package being used. For example, when using EasyPHP, your web folder will be **www**.

You may want to run many websites on the web server. To do this, for each website you want to host, it is better to create new folders inside **htdocs** folder and then put the contents into the respective folders to separate the websites. For an example, you can create a folder called **tutorials** inside **htdocs** folder and put welcome.php inside it. Then you can access it via the URL (Uniform Resource Locator).

```
http://localhost/tutorials/welcome.php
```

or

`http://127.0.0.1/tutorials/welcome.php` (using the loopback IP address)

Similarly, you may also create a folder called **phpscripts** within the **htdocs** folder and put **helloworld.php** into it. To run this file you will use

```
http://localhost/phpscripts/welcome.php
```

or

```
http://127.0.0.1/phpscripts/helloworld.php
```

Root URL and Display of Home Page Content

In the example above, the root URL (Uniform Resource Locator) of your web site is **http://localhost/tutorials/.** However**,** it is generally expected that we see the home page (**welcome.php**) of the website once the root URL is typed in the web browser, for instance **http://localhost/tutorials**/. Usually web servers have been configured to look for an **index** file (can be **index.htm, index.html, index.php,** etc) in the root of the website folder (**htdocs** or **www**) and show its content as the home page of the site. So, if you have a file called **index.php** inside **phpcodes**, you would see its output once you typed **http://localhost/phpcodes/**. So, you have to name the page you intend to be your home page as **index.php** or **index.html**.

It is important to make sure you have only one **index** file in your website to avoid conflicts. If you have more than one (say **index.html, index.php**), the required file will be chosen based on the order defined in your web server's configuration settings (will be discussed in the following sections). On the other hand, if you give another name to your home page, which is different from **index.html** or **index.php**, say **welcome.php**, then add **welcome.php** to the configuration file **(httpd.conf).** This will be discussed in the following sections.

Locations of Configuration Files

Based on your requirements, sometimes you would need to change default settings of your Web and database servers or your PHP compiler. Usually, this is done by altering directives in their configuration files. In the XAMPP folder, Apache, PHP and MySQL configuration files are located in the following locations (This assumes XAMPP is installed on drive C and in **xampp** folder, **C:/xampp**). Table 1.2 shows the location of the main configuration files.

Table 1.2 Configuration Files

Configuration File Type	File Name	Location
Apache configuration file	`httpd.conf`	**`C:/xampp/apache/conf/httpd.conf`**
PHP configuration file	`php.ini`	**`C:/xampp/apache/bin/php.ini`**
MySQL configuration file	`my.cnf` or `my.ini`	**`C:/xampp/mysql/bin/my.cnf`**

In XAMPP, some Apache configuration settings have been moved to sub configuration files under **xampp/apache/conf/extra**

In the sections that follow, we will discuss how to configure MySQL, PHP and Apache Server.

Configuring MYSQL (`my.cnf` or `my.ini` File)

You can change settings of MYSQL in **my.cnf** or **my.ini** file. It is, however, not likely you will need to edit the **my.ini** file unless you need to do some more advanced MySQL setting. It is in the **my.ini** file that the buffer sizes, mysql dump sizes, directory locations, and database options are set. Other changes you may wish to make include changing the port (*defaults to 3306*), disabling the **innodb** table type, or opening it up to be accessed from other computers. None of these changes are recommended for beginners.

To start editing **my.ini** files, open it in NotePad++, NotePad or any text editor. NotePad++ is recommended because it displays the line numbers. You can download NotePad++ on the Internet (it is free). Locate **my.ini** file in **C:/xampp/mysql/bin/my.ini** (can be any other drive depending on where you installed XAMPP). When you open the file, you will see its content similar to Figure 1.3. You may scroll up and down to view the contents.

Figure 1.3: Displays the contents of **my.ini** configuration file

```
17  # The following options will be passed to all MySQL clients
18  [client]
19  #user          = your_username
20  #password      = your_password
21  host           = .
22  port           = 3306
23  socket         = "MySQL"
24  
25  # Here follows entries for some specific programs
26  
27  # The MySQL server
28  [mysqld]
29  basedir                  = "E:/xampp/mysql/"
30  datadir                  = "E:/xampp/mysql/data/"
31  port                     = 3306
32  socket                   = "MySQL"
33  skip-locking
34  key_buffer               = 16M
35  #max_allowed_packet       = 1M
36  max_allowed_packet       = 256M
37  table_cache              = 64
38  sort_buffer_size         = 512K
39  net_buffer_length        = 8K
40  read_buffer_size         = 256K
41  read_rnd_buffer_size     = 512K
42  myisam_sort_buffer_size = 8M
43  
44  default-time-zone        = "America/Los_Angeles"
45  
```

Knowing the Log Files

On or near line 46 and 49 (line numbers may differ on your computer) you will find the error and activity log files. It may not be necessary to change these. You can open their contents to view errors and general system logs. The **E:/xampp/mysql/data/mysql.err** means that XAMPP has been installed on drive E.

```
log_error              = "E:/xampp/mysql/data/mysql.err"
general_log_file       = "E:/xampp/mysql/data/mysql.log"
```

Setting Maximum Packet Size

On or near line 153 you will find setting for maximum packet size. The packet size becomes very important when you take and restore backups. If it happens that any of your database object (e.g. table) is bigger than the maximum size stated in the setting, you cannot be able to restore your backup. The restore will terminate when copying the file and and error message will displayed. You can choose to increase your **max_allowed_packet** to 1024M.

```
151 [mysqldump]
152 quick
153 max_allowed_packet = 512M
154
```

Moreover, in **my.ini,** you may change the port number, buffer sizes, and other settings. But these may not be necessary in most circumstances.

Configuring PHP (`php.ini`) File

This is a PHP initialization file which is responsible for configuring many of the aspects of PHP's behaviour. Though the file comes with default settings, many developers will probably wish to make some changes to the default PHP configuration so that it acts more like the production server. Most of PHP's options are editable within the **'php.ini'** file. Below are some common settings which you may or may not wish to change. It would be a good idea of taking a backup of this file before making any changes.

Open the **php.ini** file in Notepad++ or any text editor from:

```
C:/xampp/apache/bin/php.ini
```

This file is over 2000 lines long, so it is recommended to use a good editor with line numbers such as NotePad++ to edit the file. When you open the file, you will see its content similar to Figure 1.4. You may scroll up and down to view the contents. It is also recommended that you first read through the comment section which includes information about this file and some of the important settings. Any line with a semi-colon (;) in front is a comment and will not be executed.

The **`php.ini`** file is divided into sections, namely

- Language Options
- Resource Limits
- Error handling and logging
- Error Reporting
- Data Handling
- File Uploads
- Email Settings

We shall now discuss the various sections and learn how they can be set. You will notice that php.ini file is well-documented and most of what you may want to do are well-explained. As such, here we will give brief explanations to the settings.

Language Options

These are directives (commands) directly related to the language (PHP) interpreter.

Set PHP Engine

This directive enables the PHP scripting language engine to be set **off** or **on**. Turning the engine off means that PHP code will not be parsed (executed) by the Web server. It is advisable you leave the engine directive **on**.

```
; Enable the PHP scripting language engine under Apache.
; http://php.net/engine
engine = On
```

Setting the Short Tag

The **short_open_tag** directive controls whether the parser (interpreter) should recognize the shortcut **<?...?>** tags in your script, as well as the standard **<?php...?>** tags. Turning this option **off** means that scripts **<?...?>** will not be interpreted. You may turn the option **off** if you want to apply strict syntactical rules to your PHP code. In this case, all your scripts must conform to the standard **<?php...?>** tags

```
; http://php.net/short-open-tag
short_open_tag = Off
```

Setting ASP Tag

This directive allows or disallows ASP-style **<% %>** tags. When set to **on** ASP (Active Server Pages) style is allowed. ASP style is disallowed when set to **off**.

```
; Allow ASP-style <% %> tags.
; http://php.net/asp-tags
asp_tags = Off
```

Setting the Number of Significant Digits

With this directive, you can set the number of significant digits to display in floating decimal numbers. In the settings below, it has been set to 14.

```
; The number of significant digits displayed in floating point numbers.
; http://php.net/precision
precision = 14
```

Setting the Output Buffer

Output buffering is a mechanism for controlling how much output data PHP should keep internally before pushing that data to the client. Sessions, cookies or HTTP header data in a PHP script are normally sent before any output is generated by the PHP script (when the buffer is **off**). When output buffering is **on**, PHP stores the output of your script in a special memory buffer and sends it only when explicitly told to do so. This allows you to send special HTTP headers and cookie data anywhere within your script. This, however, marginally degrades system performance.

```
; http://php.net/output-buffering
output_buffering = Off
```

Figure 1.4: Display of some contents of `php.ini` file.

```
;;;;;;;;;;;;;;;;;;;
; Resource Limits ;
;;;;;;;;;;;;;;;;;;;

; Maximum execution time of each script, in seconds
; http://php.net/max-execution-time
; Note: This directive is hardcoded to 0 for the CLI SAPI
max_execution_time = 120

; Maximum amount of time each script may spend parsing request data. It's a good
; idea to limit this time on productions servers in order to eliminate unexpectedly
; long running scripts.
; Note: This directive is hardcoded to -1 for the CLI SAPI
; Default Value: -1 (Unlimited)
; Development Value: 60 (60 seconds)
; Production Value: 60 (60 seconds)
; http://php.net/max-input-time
max_input_time = 120

; Maximum input variable nesting level
; http://php.net/max-input-nesting-level
;max_input_nesting_level = 64

; Maximum amount of memory a script may consume (128MB)
; http://php.net/memory-limit
memory_limit = 128M

;;;;;;;;;;;;;;;;;;;;;;;;;;;;;;
; Error handling and logging ;
```

Resource Limits

The resource limit section handles the settings of resource availability to your PHP scripts. This directive specifies how long it takes a **PHP** script to execute before it times out. The maximum execution time of each script is stated in seconds. Here, the maximum execution time is set to 120 seconds.

```
; Maximum execution time of each script, in seconds
; http://php.net/max-execution-time
; Note: This directive is hardcoded to 0 for the CLI SAPI
max_execution_time = 120
```

Setting Maximum Input

This directive indicates the maximum amount of time each script may spend parsing request data. It is recommended that you limit this time on production servers in order to eliminate unexpectedly long running scripts. Here, it is set to 120 seconds.

```
; http://php.net/max-input-time
max_input_time = 120
```

Setting Maximum Memory for a Script

This directive signifies the maximum amount of memory a script may consume. The default size is 128MB.

```
; Maximum amount of memory a script may consume (128MB)
; http://php.net/memory-limit
memory_limit = 128M
```

Error Handling and logging

PHP errors are classified into four categories: parsing errors, notices about code bugs such as uninitialized variables, warnings (non-fatal errors), and fatal errors. Normally, when PHP encounters either a parsing, non-fatal or fatal error, it displays the error. If the error is fatal it stops script processing at the point where the error occurs. You can alter this behavior with the *error_reporting* variable, which accepts a bitfield of error codes and only displays errors matching those codes (error level constants). The recommended way of setting values for this directive is through the use of the error level constants and bitwise operators (& for AND, | for OR, and ~ for NOT). The error level constants are shown below in Table 1.2.

Table 1.2: Error Level Constants

Error Constants	Description
`E_ALL`	all errors and warnings (includes E_STRICT as of PHP 6).
`E_ERROR`	fatal run-time errors.
`E_RECOVERABLE_ERROR`	almost fatal run-time errors.
`E_WARNING`	run-time warnings (non-fatal errors).
`E_PARSE`	compile-time parse errors.
`E_NOTICE`	run-time notices (these are warnings which often result from a bug in your code, but it's possible that it was intentional (e.g., using an uninitialized variable and relying on the fact it has been automatically initialized to an empty string).
`E_STRICT`	run-time notices, when enabled, PHP suggests changes to your code which will ensure the best interoperability and forward compatibility of your code.
`E_CORE_ERROR`	fatal errors that occur during PHP's initial startup
`E_CORE_WARNING`	warnings (non-fatal errors) that occur during PHP's initial startup.
`E_COMPILE_ERROR`	fatal compile-time errors.
`E_COMPILE_WARNING`	compile-time warnings (non-fatal errors).

Continuation of Table 1.2: Error Level Constants

Error Constants	Description
E_USER_ERROR	user-generated error message.
E_USER_WARNING	user-generated warning message.
E_USER_NOTICE	user-generated notice message.
E_DEPRECATED	warn about code that will not work in future versions of PHP.
E_USER_DEPRECATED	user-generated deprecation warnings.

Setting Error Reporting

By default, PHP will display all errors, notices and warnings to the screen. A notice error can occur during the normal running of a script, such as when an undefined variable is used (when developers fail to pre-define variables before using them). In the listing below, that is on or near line 514 you will find a setting for error reporting. Error reporting directive controls which errors PHP cares about, and whether they are shown to the screen or not.

In the example below, error reporting is set to display all errors (E_ALL), but should not display notices (~E_NOTICE) and deprecated key words (~E_DEPRECATED).

```
511 ; Development Value: E_ALL | E_STRICT
512 ; Production Value: E_ALL & ~E_DEPRECATED
513 ; http://php.net/error-reporting
514 error_reporting = E_ALL & ~E_NOTICE & ~E_DEPRECATED
```

Another example is

```
error_reporting = E_ALL & ~E_NOTICE
```

This means that all errors should be shown, except for notices and coding standards warnings

```
error_reporting = E_ALL | E_STRICT
```

This also means that all errors, warnings and notices including coding standards should be shown

Setting Display Errors

With display errors set **on,** all errors are displayed on the screen anytime they occur in your script. On the other hand, when display errors are set to **off**, error messages are not shown on your screen when they occur. It is recommended you leave display errors **on** unless you are running a production server.

```
; Default Value: On
; Development Value: On
; Production Value: Off
; http://php.net/display-errors
display_errors = Off
```

Setting Startup Errors

The display of errors which occur during PHP's startup sequence are handled separately from **display_errors**. By default, PHP suppresses the display of errors that may occur during the system startup process from clients. You can set the startup errors on or near line 542. Turning the display of startup errors **on** can be useful in debugging configuration problems. But, it is strongly recommended that you leave this setting **off** on production servers.

```
538 ; Default Value: Off
539 ; Development Value: On
540 ; Production Value: Off
541 ; http://php.net/display-startup-errors
542 display_startup_errors = Off
```

Setting Error Log

In addition to displaying errors to the screen or suppressing the errors, you can also log errors to locations such as a server-specific log, or a location specified by the error_log directive. On production servers it is recommended you do not display the errors to the screen. Instead, write all the errors into the log file which may help you to monitor system activities.

```
; http://php.net/log-errors
log_errors = On
```

If you want to write errors to a custom log file instead of the system logger, you should assign the name of your log file to the *error_log* variable. For instance, the directive below logs errors to *mylog.txt* file.

```
log_errors = "mylog.txt"
```

And always remember to check the log file regularly to monitor what is happening inside your application.

Setting Maximum Length of Error Log File

You can also set the maximum length of your log file. The default is 1024KB. When set to 0 any maximum length is allowed.

```
; http://php.net/log-errors-max-len
log_errors_max_len = 1024
```

Setting Repeated Errors

You may want to prevent the system logging repeated messages. Repeated errors must occur in same file on same line unless *ignore_repeated_source* is set **on**.

```
; http://php.net/ignore-repeated-errors
ignore_repeated_errors = Off
```

Similarly, you can ignore source of message when ignoring repeated messages. When this setting is **on,** it will not log errors with repeated messages from different files or source lines.

```
567 ; http://php.net/ignore-repeated-source
568 ignore_repeated_source = Off
```

Data Handling

You can enable or disable super global variables such as $GET, $POST, $REQUEST. This directive determines which super global arrays are initialized (registered) when PHP starts up. If the *register_globals* directive is enabled (set to **on**), you can also determine the order the variables should be populated into the global space. G,P,C,E and S are abbreviations for the following respective super globals: $GET, $POST, $COOKIE, $ENV and $SERVER. You may choose to set **off** the *register_globals,* but this is not recommended (see line 696). On line 672, the super global variables are loaded in the global space ordered as GPCS ($GET, $POST, $COOKIE, $SERVER).

It should be noted however that system performance is marginally degraded when super global variables are set to **on**.

```
671 ; http://php.net/variables-order
672 variables_order = "GPCS"
```

```
695 ; http://php.net/register-globals
696 register_globals = Off
```

Setting Maximum Size of POST data

On or near line 733, you can also set the maximum size of POST data that PHP will accept.

```
731 ; Maximum size of POST data that PHP will accept.
732 ; http://php.net/post-max-size
733 post_max_size = 128M
```

File Uploads

Uploading files are important in web application development.

Setting File Upload

However, you can allow (**on**) or disallow (**off**) file upload (see line 877).

```
875  ; Whether to allow HTTP file uploads.
876  ; http://php.net/file-uploads
877  file_uploads = On
```

Temporary File Upload Location

On line 882, the temporary directory for HTTP uploaded files is specified (this may vary from the system you are using).

```
881  ; http://php.net/upload-tmp-dir
882  upload_tmp_dir = "E:\xampp\tmp"
```

Setting Maximum File Upload

Here on line 886, you can set the maximum allowed size for your uploaded files.

```
884  ; Maximum allowed size for uploaded files.
885  ; http://php.net/upload-max-filesize
886  upload_max_filesize = 128M
```

Email Settings

On or near line 1102 you'll find a setting for SMTP (Simple Mail Transfer Protocol) which is used by PHP mail functions to determine your outgoing mail server. By default, this is set to localhost, however unless you are running your own mail server (*unlikely*), you need to change this to be the same as your ISP's SMTP server.

```
1100  ; For Win32 only.
1101  ; http://php.net/smtp
1102  SMTP = localhost
```

If you subscribe to mail services, you can contact your ISP (Internet Service Provider) to obtain your ISP's outgoing mail server. Most of the times, it is of a format **'mail.ispname.com'**.

If you are connected to the internet via a modem, you need to be online before PHP can send your email.

You can now change SMTP directive to:

```
SMTP = mail.yourisp.com
```

In addition to the above SMTP server setting, you can optionally set the **'sendmail_from'** directive. It is important to place a real email address here; otherwise your script's email may not be accepted.

```
sendmail_from = your@real_email_address.com
```

Configuring Apache Server (`httpd.conf`)

The main configuration file for Apache is the **'httpd.conf'** file. This is the main Apache HTTP (Hypertext Transfer Protocol) server configuration file. It contains the configuration directives that give the web server its instructions. There is not much to set in the apache configuration file for the beginners. But there are a few key options you may want to configure or know more about. It is best to keep a backup of this file before editing it.

The **httpd.conf** file is located on the directory path shown below (the path may vary based on where you install the package).

C:/xampp/apache/conf/httpd.conf

When you open the file, you will see its contents similar to Figure 1.5. You may scroll up and down to view the contents. It is recommended that you read through the first comment section which includes information about this file. And note that any line with a '#' on the left is a comment. Below are some common settings which you may or may not wish to change.

Figure 1.5: Displays the contents of `httpd.conf` file.

```
# ServerName gives the name and port that the server uses to identify itself.
# This can often be determined automatically, but we recommend you specify
# it explicitly to prevent problems during startup.
#
# If your host doesn't have a registered DNS name, enter its IP address here.
#
ServerName localhost:80

#
# DocumentRoot: The directory out of which you will serve your
# documents. By default, all requests are taken from this directory, but
# symbolic links and aliases may be used to point to other locations.
#
DocumentRoot "E:/xampp/htdocs"

#
# Each directory to which Apache has access can be configured with respect
# to which services and features are allowed and/or disabled in that
# directory (and its subdirectories).
#
# First, we configure the "default" to be a very restrictive set of
# features.
#
<Directory />
    Options FollowSymLinks
    AllowOverride None
    Order deny,allow
    Deny from all
</Directory>
```

Listen to the Outside World

On or near line 47 there is a Listen statement, which indicates the IP (Internet Protocol) the web server is running. The IP address of 127.0.0.1 is the default and the port number of 80 (TCP – Transmission Control Protocol) is specified. You may set this command to an IP address of your local machine (the server) by specifying the IP address as **Listen 192.168.1.1:80**

```
45 #Listen 0.0.0.0:80
46 #Listen [::]:80
47 Listen 80
```

Setting the Server Name

The **ServerName** setting gives the name and port number that the server uses to identify itself. This can often be determined automatically, but it is recommended that you specify it explicitly (see line 181) to prevent problems during system startup process.

```
181  ServerName localhost:80
```

If your host does not have a registered domain name service (DNS) name, you can enter its IP address here. For example, you can have

```
ServerName 196.168.1.1:80
```

For development purposes you can probably leave this as **'localhost'**; however if you have people viewing the server from other computers, and if you have a fairly static IP address, it would be worthwhile to change the value to your public IP address.

Changing the Port Number

You can edit Apache's default port. You can change the port number that Apache listens to from the default of 80 to another as long as it is not in use by your computer. This could allow you to run multiple web servers on the same computer. For example, IIS (Internet Information Services) might have port 80 and Apache could be assigned port 8080.

To do this, you can change the following:

```
Listen:8080

ServerName localhost:8080
```

Once you have changed the port number to 8080, you would access the server by using the following url: **http://localhost:8080/**

Setting the Document Root

The document root is the directory in which you will keep your web documents to be accessed by the web clients. By default, all requests are accessed from this directory (see line 188), but symbolic links and aliases may be used to point to other locations.

```
188 DocumentRoot "E:/xampp/htdocs"
```

The value points to the location on the server's hard drive where the Website's root should be. All website files would be stored there (unless you use virtual directories).

If you wish, you can change this setting to point to another location on your drive, say

```
DocumentRoot "C:/mydocs/www"
```

If you change the **DocumentRoot**, you must also change the **"<Directory ...>"** directive on or near line 215 to <**Directory "C:/mydocs/www"**> so that they match.

```
213 # This should be changed to whatever you set DocumentRoot to.
214 #
215 <Directory "E:/xampp/htdocs">
```

Setting Default Documents

On or near line 250 you will find where you can change the default documents, which Apache will search for and load as your homepage file. This is done using the **'DirectoryIndex'** directive.

The order in which the documents are listed here are the same order Apache looks for them (*starting with index.php, index.pl, etc*). Apache loads the first document it finds. If none is found, Apache will show the directory index instead (if enabled).

```
249 <IfModule dir_module>
250     DirectoryIndex index.php index.pl index.cgi index.asp index.shtml index.html index.htm \
251                    default.php default.pl default.cgi default.asp default.shtml default.html default.htm \
252                    home.php home.pl home.cgi home.asp home.shtml home.html home.htm
253 </IfModule>
```

Now, by typing **http://localhost/** in a browser address bar, any of the files listed in the **DirectoryIndex** and found in your **htdocs** folder would be accessed, but in the order in which they are specified. You may wish to change the order, remove non-used documents for speed, add new ones, or comment out the line completely with a '**#**'.

2

Writing Your First PHP Scripts

The most difficult things to accomplish in life are the simple things.
And the most important skills to develop are the basic skills.
- Scott Walker

Learning Objectives

After studying this chapter, you should be able to:

- Write and run simple PHP scripts.
- Understand the difference between **print** and **echo** keywords.
- Know how to display PHP contents using **print** and **echo** keywords.
- Discover how to embed PHP scripts into HTML and HTML tags into PHP.

Introduction

As discussed in Chapter 1, PHP is a server-side scripting language. This means that PHP scripts are executed on the Web server and the results are forwarded to the Web browser for display to the user. One major advantage of PHP is that it supports many major databases such as MySQL, Informix, Oracle, Sybase, Solid, PostgreSQL, and many others. It also provides support to connecting many databases via generic ODBC (Open Database Connectivity). For this reasons, PHP is used to develop complex and dynamic Web applications involving databases. PHP is also an open source software (OSS). This simply means that PHP is free to download and use without having to worry about copyright laws.

Parts of a PHP File

A typical PHP file may contain a combination of text: HTML tags and PHP scripts. When you run a PHP file, the file is returned to the browser as plain HTML. That is why in the browser, as you view the source code of a PHP file, you will only see HTML tags but not PHP scripts. You cannot view the PHP source code by selecting "View source" in the browser - you will only see the output from the PHP file, which are plain HTML tags. This is because the scripts are executed on the server before the result is sent back to the browser.

What to Know Before Learning PHP

Before you begin, it's important that you are familiar with the Windows environment. In addition, an appreciable working knowledge of HTML makes it much easier for you to learn PHP.

You should also be familiar with:

a. Basic word processing using any text editor (e.g. NotePad, NotePad++).
b. How to edit HTML tags.
c. Basic understanding of Internet browsing using browsers like Internet Explorer, Mozilla Firefox, Opera, etc.
d. How to create folders (directories) and files.

e. How to navigate through different folders.

Creating a PHP Script

Creating a PHP document is easy. To begin coding in PHP you need only two main things: a simple-text editor and a Web browser. Notepad or Notepad++ is the most basic of simple-text editors. Notepad++ contains automatic line numbers and alignment features that make your script readable. You can also use any HTML editor such as Dreamweaver. You can write your PHP scripts into your HTML codes.

Here are the simple steps to create a basic HTML and PHP integrated file:

1. Open **Notepad, Notepad++,** or another text editor.
2. At the top of the **Notepad** or **Notepad++** page, type **<html>**.
3. On the next line, indent five spaces and now add the opening header tag: **<head>.**
4. On the next line, indent ten spaces and type **<title> </title>**.
5. Move the cursor to the next line, indent five spaces from the margin and insert the closing header tag: **</head>**.
6. Five spaces from the margin on the next line, type **<body>**.
7. On the next line, type **<?php**.
8. Move the cursor to the next line and type **echo "Hello World!".**
9. On the following line, type **?>** to close the PHP.
10. Now move the cursor to another line and type the closing tag **</body>**.
11. Finally, go to the next line and type the closing **</html>**.
12. In the **File menu**, choose **Save As**.
13. In the **Save as Type** option box, choose **All Files**.
14. Name the file with an extension **.php** and save it into the **htdocs** folder within the Web server installation folder (eg., **xammp\htdocs**).
15. Click **Save**.

Now, following the above steps, we shall create a file, named **helloworld.php** using NotePad or NotePad ++ and save it in the Web server's root directory. In our example, we shall put the file into the **htdoc** folder of the apache folder (eg. **C:/xammp/htdoc**).

Note that as you create your PHP file it is important to save the file with a file extension of "**.php**".

Your PHP scripts execute from the directory (folder) in which the Apache server has been installed. If the server runs from a different directory, make sure your scripts are located in that directory.

Now, let's take our first example. Listing 2.1 shows how to embed basic PHP into HTML.

Listing 2.1: helloworld.php

```
<html>
<head>
<title>My first PHP script</title>
</head>
<body>

<!-- write php into html -->
<?php
      echo "Hello World!";
?>

</body>
</html>
```

It should be noted that the PHP script block (**<?php** and **?>**) can be placed anywhere in your HTML document, at any location that you want the script to produce and display its output.

Running Your PHP Script

In order to run PHP script and view the result, you must

a) Start the Apache Server in the Startup menu or double-click its icon on the desktop or in the Window's start menu (XAMMP for Windows → XAMMP Control Panel).

b) Open your browser (for example Mozilla Firefox, Internet Explorer, Opera).

c) Type into the browser's address bar

```
http://localhost/helloworld.php
or
http://127.0.0.1/helloworld.php
```

d) Press the **Enter** key.

Listing 2.1 will generate an output similar to the one in Figure 2.1.

Figure 2.1:
Output from PHP script

Hello World!

It is important to note that PHP files cannot run if you have not, first of all, started the Apache Web server. Also, you cannot run PHP script by opening it from the browser's File Open menu.

.

Opening & Ending PHP Tags

PHP code is normally mixed with HTML tags. PHP is an embedded language; this means you can write PHP scripts into HTML tags. In order to embed PHP script into HTML, PHP must be set apart using PHP start and end tags. PHP tags tell the Web server were the PHP code starts and ends.

The PHP parser (interpreter) recognizes four sets of start and end tags.

XML Style

The first set of PHP tags is referred to as the XML (eXtensible Markup Language) tag style and is the preferred style. This tag style works with XML documents. This style should be used when mixing PHP with XML or HTML documents. All the examples in this book use the XML tag format.

```
<?php
      PHP Code Block
?>
```

Short Style

The short style is the simplest; however, it is not recommended since it interferes with XML document declarations. You should avoid using the **short style** tags in your application especially if your site is meant to be distributed on other Web servers because it interferes with XML document declarations. Also, the short tags are not always supported on some Web servers. Moreover, the short tags are available only if **short_open_tag** value is set to **on** in the PHP configuration file, **php.ini**. The **php.ini** file is located in the **apache** folder of your installation.

```
<?
      PHP Code Block
?>
```

Script Style

This script style is the longest and is similar to the tag style used with JavaScript. This style is preferred when using an HTML editor that does not recognize the other tag styles. Since most new HTML editors recognize the XML tag style, this style is not recommended.

```
<script language="php"
     PHP Code Block
</script>
```

ASP Style

The ASP style tags is available only if the **asp_tags** value is set to **On** in the PHP configuration file **php.ini**. By default **asp_tags** is set to **Off**.

```
<%
     PHP Code Block
%>
```

All PHP codes in this book will use the XML Style, that is **<?php** and **?>.**

The following example illustrates the use of the four script formats.

Listing 2.2: hello.php

```
<?php

   // the XML style
   echo "The XML style";
?>

<?
   // the Short style
   print "The short style";
?>

<script language="php">
   // the Script style
   $myvar = "Script style";
   echo $myvar;
</script>

<%
   // the ASP style
   echo "The ASP style";
%>
```

The scripts above should display the following:

The XML style

The short style

Script style

The ASP style

The example above shows how to write PHP code. It also shows the **echo** statement used to output a string. You can see that the **echo** statement ends with a semicolon. Every command in PHP must end with a semicolon. If you forget to use semicolon and use colon instead after a command you will get an error message like this:

```
Parse error: parse error, unexpected ':', expecting ',' or
';' in c:\Apache\htdocs\examples\get.php on line 7
```

However, in the **hello.php** example above, omitting the semicolon would not cause an error. This is because the **echo** statement was immediately followed by a closing tag. A line immediately before the PHP closing tag needs not be terminated by a semi-colon.

Using Comments

A comment is a part of your PHP code that will not be translated (interpreted) by the PHP engine. You can use it to document your PHP scripts, describing what the code does. A comment can span a line or multiple lines.

PHP supports three kinds of comment tags:

- // This is a one line comment.
- # This is a Unix shell-style comment. It is also a one line comment.
- /* .... */ Use this multi-line comment if string more than one line..

Example on the use of comments is as follows.

Listing 2.3: comments.php

```
<?php

    echo "One line comment <br>";
    // you won't see me in the output
    // I'm a one line comment

    echo "Multi-line comment <br>";
    /*
    I'm multi line comment
    I'm multi line comment
     */

     echo "This is a Unix shell-style comment <br>";
    # this is a unix shell-style comment
    # you cannot see me

?>
```

Displaying Contents

PHP includes two basic statements to output text to the web browser: **echo** and **print**. Both **echo** and **print** statements are coded between the opening and closing PHP code block tags and can occur anywhere in the PHP documents. The **echo** and **print** statements appear in Table 2.1:

Table 2.1: echo and print Statements

Syntax	Description
echo	Used to output one or more strings.
print	Used to output a string.

The Listing 2.4 demonstrates the use and placement of the **echo** and **print** commands in a PHP document.

In most cases, it is necessary to display entire paragraphs in the browser window or create line breaks when displaying content. By default, the **echo** and **print** statements do not create automatic line breaks. With both the **echo** and **print** statements, it is necessary to use a **<p>** or **
** tag to create paragraphs or line breaks respectively. White space created in the HTML editor using carriage returns, spaces, and tabs are ignored by the PHP engine.

Listing 2.4: basic.php

```
<?php

    // the use of echo command
    echo "This is a basic PHP document <br>";

    // the use of print command
    print "Text to be displayed";

?>
```

In the example below, the HTML paragraph tag is included inside of the PHP **echo** statement. In PHP, HTML tags can be used with the **print** and **echo** statements to format output. In these cases, the output should be surrounded by double quotes (" ") to ensure that the browser does not literally interpret the tag and display it as part of the output string.

```
echo "<p>This is a basic PHP document </p>"

echo "<p>Text to be displayed </p>"
```

By including the paragraph tags, the statements are displayed as two separate paragraphs. The output will be display as below:

This is a basic PHP document

Text to be displayed

Without the use of the HTML paragraph tag, the preceding **echo** statements would render the content in the following format, putting the two lines on the same line, which may not be meaningful.

This is a basic PHP document Text to be displayed

The Difference Between echo and print Keywords

The basic difference between **echo** and **print** is that **echo** allows multiple, comma-separated variables or values. The **print,** however, does not allow for multiple variables, comma-separated variables or values. Both **echo** and **print** can use multiple variables when they are concatenated with dot (.) operator.

Consider the following script:

Listing 2.5: echoprint.php

```
<?php

// assign variables
$fname = "John";
$lname = "Baba";
$salary = "1000";

// echo can take a comma-separated list of variables.
echo $fname, $lname, $salary;

// break to next line
echo "<br>";

// print can take only one string or variable.
print $fname;
echo "<br>";

/* concatenation operator can be used to print multiple
strings with multiple variables. */
print $fname . $lname . $salary;
echo "<br>";

echo $fname . $lname . $salary;

?>
```

Embed PHP into HTML and HTML into PHP

So far we have seen how to embed PHP script into HTML. As a reminder, we used PHP tags **(<?php … ?>)**. However, to write HTML into PHP we will have to write HTML tags into double quotes (**" "**). Listing 2.6 illustrates this.

Listing 2.6: htmlphp.php

```
<html>
<head>
<title> PHP and HTML </title>
</head>
<body bgcolor="#f5f5f5">

<?php

    // write html into php using double quotes (" ")
    echo "<br>";
    echo "<hr>";
    echo "<table>";

    // write php only
    echo "PHP is fun!";
    echo "Hello World!";

?>

</body>
</html>
```

Listing 2.6 would output the following:

Figure 2.2:
Combining PHP and HTML

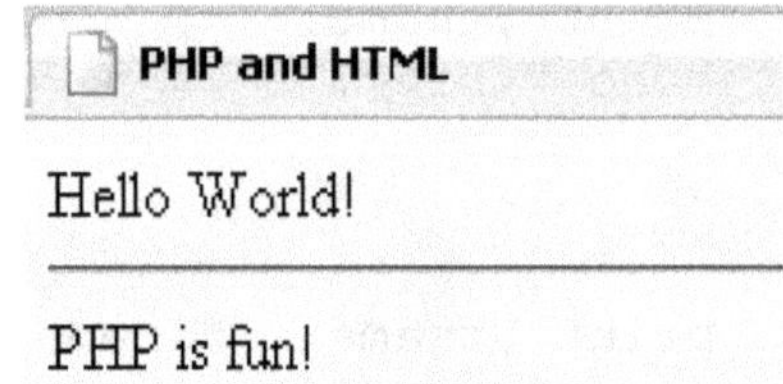

Instruction Terminators

Each statement in PHP must end with an instruction terminator, the semicolon (;). The instruction terminator is used to distinguish one set of instructions from another. Failure to include the instruction terminator causes the PHP interpreter to become confused and display errors in the browser window. Listing 2.7 shows a common instruction terminator error:

In this example, the first **echo** statement is missing the instruction terminator. Because PHP interpreter cannot determine the end of the first **echo** statement and the beginning of the second, an error would occur. Depending on the interpreter's error handling settings, an error will be displayed or the browser simply displays a blank page. The following is an example of a typical error that would be displayed when the instruction terminator is omitted:

```
Parse error: syntax error, unexpected T_PRINT in
C:\ApacheRoot\terminator.php on line 11
```

Listing 2.7: terminator.php

```
<html>
<head>
<title>A Web Page</title>
</head>
<body>

<?php

   /* there is no semicolon, this will generate an error
   message */
   echo "This line will produce an error, it has no
   instruction terminator"

   // this will not generate an error message
   echo "This line is correct, it has instruction
   terminator";

?>

</body>
</html>
```

As you can see, PHP error messages tend to be rather confusing in nature. The omission of the instruction terminator is common among developers new to PHP. You should remember to always check each line for an instruction terminator.

3

Variables

No one, after putting his hand to the plow and looks back, is fit for service in the Kingdom of God.
Luke 9:62

Learning Objectives

After studying this chapter, you should be able to:

- Understand variable naming rules, conventions and variable assignment.
- Be familiar with PHP data types, type-casting and string concatenation.
- Apply the concept of interpolation to your scripts.
- Distinguish the difference and use of the single and double quoted strings.
- Code and run scripts involving variables.

What are Variables

Variables are temporary placeholders used to hold values in PHP scripts. They represent locations in memory that store values. Variables are the means by which values are stored in memory. They can store text, string, images, floating point numbers, integer values, and many other types of data. Variables can be reused throughout your code instead of having to type out the actual values over and over again. The value stored in a variable can be changed by another statement during the cause of your program.

Naming Rules and Conventions

Variable naming rules and conventions that you need to follow when choosing a name for your PHP variables are important aspects of writing PHP scripts. There is a difference between the naming rules and the conventions. Variable naming rules cannot be violated as it will result in an error; that is the violation of language syntax (grammar). However, violation of variable naming conventions will not result in an error.

Variable naming conventions are generally accepted principles used to ease communication among programmers. Conventions foster uniformity, readability, and maintenance of programs written by different programmers. The following shows how to formulate variable naming rules and conventions:

Naming Rules

- PHP variables of all types (integer, string, etc) must begin with the dollar "$" sign.
- PHP variables must then be followed by a letter or an underscore "_".
- PHP variables may consist of alphabets, alpha-numeric characters, and underscores. That is a-z, A-Z, 0-9, or _.
- Variable names cannot contain special characters like +, - , %, (,), . , &, etc.
- PHP variable names are unique.

- Variable names are case-sensitive. There is a difference between $customerName and $CustomerName.

Naming Conventions

- Variables with more than one word should be separated with underscores, for example `$first_name`.
- Variables with more than one word can also be distinguished with capitalization, for instance `$firstName and $customerAddress`.

To place emphasis on the rules and conventions in formulating variable names, it is imperative to remember that if you forget to place the dollar sign ($) at the beginning of the variable, it will result in an error and your script will not work. This is a common mistake most new PHP programmers make.

Also, remember that variable names are **case-sensitive.** As such, you have to use the exact capitalization when using a variable. The variables, for instance, **`$firstname`,** **`$Firstname`,** and **`$FirstName`** are different in PHP.

In PHP we can declare and assign a value to a variable in the following forms:

```
$variable = value;          as in $number = 99;

$variable = expression;     as in $area = ½ * $base * $height;
```

Variable Types

Variable types refer to the type of data that the variable stores. A variable may store an integer, decimal numbers, a piece of writing , etc. In PHP, the type of a variable is determined by the value stored in it. PHP supports 8 primitive data types as follows.

The Four Scalar Types

Data Type	Description
Boolean	Expresses truth value, can only be TRUE or FALSE.
Integer	Whole numbers, both negative and positive (-5, 0, 123, 211, ...)
Float	Floating-point numbers or 'double' or numbers with decimal position (0.9283838, 23.0, ...)
String	Piece of data in quotes such as "Hello World" or 'PHP and MySQL'. They are put into single or double quotes. The difference between the single or double quotes will be explained later in this chapter.

The Two Compound Types

Data Type	Description
Array	This is a named and indexed collection of values. This data type will be discussed later in this book.
Object	This is an instance of programmer-defined classes, which can contain other kinds of values and functions that are specific to the class.

The Two Special Types

Data Type	Description
Resource	This is a special variable that holds references to resources which are external to PHP (such as database connections). One example is the return value of `mysql_connect()` function.
NULL	This is a special type of variable that has only one value: NULL.

Scalar and the NULL data types will be explained later in this chapter. Array, Object and Resource data types will be discussed in the later chapters.

Integers

Integers are whole numbers which are without a decimal point, like 123. They correspond to whole numbers, either positive or negative. Integers can be assigned to variables, or they can be used in expressions, like in the following script:

Listing 3.1: integer.php

```
<?php

    // declare the variable and assign value to it
    $int_var1 = 123;

    // assign an expression to a variable
    $int_var2 = $int_var1 + 123;

    // this will output 246
    echo $int_var2;

?>
```

Integers can be in decimal (base 10), octal (base 8), or hexadecimal (base 16) format. Decimal format (base 10) is the default, octal integers are specified with a leading 0, and hexadecimals have a leading 0x. For most common platforms, the largest integer is (2^{31-1} or 2,147,483,647), and the smallest negative integer is (-2^{31-1} or -2,147,483,647).

Floats

These are numbers with decimal points such as 3.14 or 0.1. By default, floats print with the minimum number of decimal places needed. For example, the following code (Listing 3.2) will print to 2 decimal places:

Listing 3.2: float.php

```
<?php

   // declare and initialize the variables
   $float_var1 = 123.904;
   $float_var2 = 123.016;

   // add variable1 to variable2
   $float_result = $float_var1 + $float_var2;

   // this will output 246.92
   print $float_result;

?>
```

Boolean

Booleans are data types that have only two possible values, either true or false. PHP provides two constants especially for use as booleans: **TRUE** and **FALSE**.

Interpreting Other Data Types As Booleans

Other data types can be interpreted or evaluated to **TRUE** or **FALSE**. The following are the rules for determining the "**truth**" of any value not already of the Boolean type.

- If the value is a number; it is FALSE if the value is exactly equal to zero and TRUE otherwise.
- If the value is a string; it is FALSE if the string is empty (has zero characters) and TRUE otherwise.
- Values of type NULL are always FALSE.
- If the value is an array; it is FALSE if it contains no values, and it is TRUE otherwise.
- For an object, containing a value means having a member variable that has been assigned a value.
- Valid resources are TRUE (functions that return resources will return TRUE when successful and will return FALSE when unsuccessful).

The Listing 3.2 illustrates the above rules. Each of the following variables has the truth value embedded in its name when it is used in a Boolean context.

Listing 3.3: Boolean.php

```
<?php

    /* these evaluate to TRUE because they hold some values */
    $true_num = 3 + 3.14;
    $true_str = "Welcome, new user!";
    $true_array[49] = "An array element";

    // array holding no value (element) will evaluate to FALSE
    $false_array = array();

    // null values evaluate to FALSE
    $false_null = NULL;

    // zero values evaluate to FALSE
    $false_num = 0;

    // empty strings evaluate to FALSE
    $false_str = "";

?>
```

NULL

NULL is a special data type that only has one value: NULL. To give a variable a NULL value, simply assign it as in the following two examples:

```
$my_var = NULL;

$my_var = null;
```

The special constant NULL is capitalized by convention, but actually it is case insensitive. A variable that has been assigned NULL has the following properties:

- It evaluates to **FALSE** in a Boolean context.
- It returns **FALSE** when tested with **`isset()`** function. The **`isset()`** function will be discussed in the later chapters.

Strings

A string is made up of a series of characters. In PHP, a character is the same as a byte. That is, for a byte there are exactly 256(2^8) different characters possible. It is not a problem for a string to become very large. Actually, there is no practical bound to the size of strings in PHP. As such, there is no reason at all to worry about storing long strings. String values can be used as literal or be assigned to variables. Simply put, literals are string values not assigned to variables.

In PHP, among others, a string literal can be displayed in the following ways:

- single quoted strings
- double quoted strings

To declare a string in PHP, you can use single quotes (' ') or double quotes (" "). In the following sections, we shall look at some differences you need to know about using single or double quotes. Below we demonstrate the use of single quoted and double quoted strings.

The following are valid examples of string data types:

Listing 3.4: string.php

```
<?php

   // a string with single quotes
   $string_var1 = 'Single quoted string';

   // a string with double quotes
   $string_var2 = "This is a string in double quotes";

   // a string with a number of characters
   $string_var3 = "This string has thirty-nine characters";
   echo $string_var3;

   // a string with zero characters
   $string_var4 = "";

?>
```

PHP 7 Scalar Type Declarations

A new feature, Scalar type declarations, has been added to PHP 7. Scalar type declaration has two options:

- **coercive** - coercive is the default mode and need not to be specified. It implicitly converts values held in variables according to their initial declaration. It forces the variable to take on its type declaration.
- **strict** - strict mode has to be explicitly specified. Variables cannot implicitly convert values according to their initial delaration.

The following types for function parameters (which are variables) can be enforced with the following variable type:

- int
- float
- bool
- string
- interfaces
- array
- callable

Now, let us take the following examples to let you better understand these concepts. Our first example is on the Coercive Mode.

```
<?php

// coercive mode, this does not need any explicit declaration
function sum(int ...$ints) {
        return array_sum($ints);
}

// call the function to print the result
 print(sum(10, '20', 30.4));

?>
```

In this example, the parameters of the function **sum** are ingeters. But when calling the functions (with **print(sum(10, '20', 30.4))**), an integer value (10), string value ('20'), and float value (30.4) were passed as the parameters. The function receives these values of different data types and implicitly converts them into integer.

Therefore, the script will produce the following browser output: **60**

Now, let us take an example on the Strict Mode.

```
<?php

// explicit declaration of variables in the strict mode
declare(strict_types=1);

// parameters received by this function must be of type int
function sum(int ...$ints) {
       return array_sum($ints);
 }

// call the function to print the result
print(sum(10, '20', 30.4));

?>
```

This example will produce an error message.

Fatal error: Uncaught TypeError: Argument 2 passed to sum() must be of the type integer, string given, ...

This is because the variables are all expected to be of type **int**. String and float values cannot be accepted when the function **sum(int ...$ints)** accepts only integers and the strict mode, **declare(strict_types=1**) has been set.

Single Quoted Strings

Single quotes provide the easiest method for working with strings. Using this method, strings are surrounded by single quotes (' '). If single quotes are needed as part of the display, they must be enclosed with the backslash ("\") character. While single quotes provide an easy method for working with strings, single quotes do not support the use of interpolation.

The concept of interpolation will be discussed later in this chapter. The examples below illustrate the use of single quotes.

Listing 3.5: single_quoted.php

```
<?php

    // a literal string displayed in the browser window
    echo 'PHP was developed in 1994 by Rasmus Lerdorf. ';

    // a literal string assigned to a variable
    $string = 'Since its development, PHP has become a popular
    Scripting Language.';
    echo $string;

    /* escaping single quotes. The output: The array contains the values
    '2,5,3,4'. */
    echo 'The array contains the values \'2,5,3,4\'.';

    /* attempt to expand a variable inside of a single quote
    string. Double quotes needed. */
    $name = "John Baba";
    echo 'The name is $name';

?>
```

Double Quoted Strings

PHP strings can also be displayed using double quotes (" "). If PHP strings are enclosed in double quotes, it is possible to take advantage of interpolation (a process of replacing a variable with its contents/values within a string). The following illustrates how this can be used.

Listing 3.6: double_quoted.php

```
<?php

    // a literal string displayed in the browser window
    echo "PHP is supported by Windows and Linux platform.";

    // the output: The user's name is John Baba.
    $name = 'John Baba';
    echo "The user's name is $name.";

    // the output: My favorite color is green.
    $colors = array('green', 'red', 'blue');
    echo "My favorite color is $colors[0].";

?>
```

Escape Characters

With double quoted strings, PHP also supports more escape characters. These characters are described in the Table 3.1 below. If you are using double-quoted strings, variables within the quotes will be expanded (processed). This means that the values stored in the variables will be printed but not the variable names themselves. Special characters such as line feed (\n) and carriage return (\r) are expanded too. However, with single-quoted strings the variables themselves will be printed but not its values. Let us take a look at the example in Listing 3.7 to see what this means.

Table 3.1: Escape Characters

Character	Description
\n	line feed (new line character)
\r	carriage return
\t	horizontal tab
\\	Backslash
\$	dollar sign
\"	double quote

Listing 3.7: escape_characters.php

```
<?php

   $fruit='apple';
   // this outputs: My favorite fruit is apple
   echo "My favorite fruit is $fruit <br>";

   // this outputs: I dislike apple
   echo "I dislike $fruit <br>";

   // this will print on two lines
   echo "\r\n This is the first line \r\n This is the second line
   <br>\r\n";

   // this will print on one line
   echo 'Though I use \r\n this string is still on one line
   <br>';

?>
```

The above script will print the result in Figure 3.1.

Figure 3.1

Note that the browser does not render newline characters (\r and \n) because they are in single quotes.

```
My favorite fruit is apple
I dislike apple
This is the first line This is the second line
Though I use \r\n this string is still on one line
```

Variable Concatenation

The dot (.) operator is used to concatenate (join or combine) strings and variables. Let us see the example in Listing 3.8.

Listing 3.8: concatenation.php

```
<?php

    $fname = "John";
    $lname = "Baba";

    // the output:  The user's name is John Baba
    echo "The user's name is " . $fname . " " . $lname;

?>
```

The string "The user's name is " is concatenated (by . operator) to the value of $fname (which is **John**) followed by a blank space - " " - and the value of $lname (which is **Baba**).

Interpolation

PHP also supports a process known as **interpolation** - replacing a variable with its contents within a string. Instead of concatenating variables and literals, they can be combined inside of double quotes (" "). Interpolation is a feature very useful in double quoting variables and literals. Variables and literals cannot be combined inside of single quotes (' '). However, with double quotes, the variable's value is displayed along with the literal. With single quotes, the variable name is "literally" displayed along with the rest of the string. The following example illustrates PHP's interpolation feature:

Listing 3.9: interpolation.php

```
<?php

    // declare and initialize the variables
    $fname = "John";
    $lname = "Baba";

    // the output will be: The user's name is John Baba
    echo "The user's name is $fname  $lname";

?>
```

This code produces the same output as the previous example under Variable Concatenation. Here the variables are combined with the literal strings surrounded by double quotes. In this case, concatenation is not required.

Figure 3.2. Interpolation example by the use of double quotes. There is no need for concatenation.

The user's name is John Baba

Variable Type Assignment

In PHP you do not need to explicitly specify the data type for variables. This is to say that variables need not be declared before use. But rather, a variable's type is determined by the context in which that variable is used. This means, if you assign a string value to a variable **$var** ($var = "Hello"), **$var** becomes a string. If you then assign an integer value to **$var** ($var = 99), it becomes an integer.

An example of PHP's automatic type conversion is the addition operator '+'. If any of the operands is a float, then all operands are evaluated as floats, and the result will be a float. Otherwise, the operands will be interpreted as integers, and the result will also be an integer. Note that this does NOT change the types of the operands themselves; the only change is in how the operands are evaluated. See this example in Listing 3.10.

Listing 3.10: variable_assignment.php

```
<?php

   // $var is string (ASCII 48)
   $var = "0";

   // $var is now an integer
   $var += 200;

   // $var is now a float
   $var = $var + 112.3;

   // $var is a string
   $var = 125 + "My Name";

?>
```

Variable Scope

The scope of a variable is the context within which the variable is defined. Basically, you cannot access a variable which is defined in different scope (within function) or scripts. Variables defined within different functions are regarded as being defined in different scope. Variables cannot be accessed directly outside the scope within which they were defined. Functions will be discussed in the later chapter. To understand variable scope, look at the Listing 3.11.

The script will not produce any output because the function **Scope()** declares no **$answer** variable. The `echo` statement looks for a local version of the **$answer** variable, and it has not been assigned any value within the function scope. Depending on the `error_reporting` value in **`php.ini`** the script above may print nothing or issue an error message as in Figure 3.3.

Figure 3.3

Variable not declared within the context within which it has been used will result in an error.

Notice: Undefined variable: answer in **C:\Program Files\EasyPHP 2.0b1\www\phpcodes\chapter2\variable_scope1.php** on line **15**

Listing 3.11: variable_scope.php

```
<?php

    // $answer is a global variable
    $answer = 1;

    // define a function Scope()
    function Scope()
    {
            /* try to print $answer, but $answer is not defined
            within this scope */
            echo $answer;
    }

    // call the function
    Scope();

?>
```

If you want your global variable (variable defined outside functions) to be available in function scope, you need to use the **$global** keyword. The code example below shows how to use the **$global** keyword.

Listing 3.12: variable_scope2.php

```
<?php

    // $a and $b are defined in global scope
    $a = 1;
    $b = 2;

    function Sum()
    {
         // now $a and $b are available in Sum()
         global $a, $b;
              $b = $a + $b;
    }

    // call the function
    Sum();

    // display the result
    echo $b;

?>
```

Pre-defined Variables

PHP provides a large number of predefined variables to any script which it runs. PHP also provides an additional set of predefined arrays containing variables from the Web server environment and user input. These new arrays are called superglobals. All the following variables are automatically available in every scope within your script.

Table 3.2: Predefined Variables

Variable	Description
$GLOBALS	Contains a reference to every variable which is currently available within the global scope of the script. The keys of this array are the names of the global variables.
$_SERVER	This is an array containing information such as headers, paths, and script locations. The entries in this array are created by the web server. There is no guarantee that every web server will provide any of these. See next section for a complete list of all the SERVER variables.
$_GET	An associative array of variables passed to the current script via the HTTP (Hypertext Transfer Protocol) GET method.
$_POST	An associative array of variables passed to the current script via the HTTP POST method.
$_FILES	An associative array of items uploaded to the current script via the HTTP POST method.
$_REQUEST	An associative array consisting of the contents of $_GET, $_POST, and $_COOKIE.
$_COOKIE	An associative array of variables passed to the current script via HTTP cookies.
$_SESSION	An associative array containing session variables available to the current script.

You can find how these variables are used in the later chapters.

Server variables: $_SERVER

$_SERVER is an array containing information such as headers, paths, and script locations. The entries in this array are created by the web server. Here we present some of the variables that are used with **$_SERVER** super global variable.

Table 3.3: Server variables

Variable	Description
`$_SERVER['PHP_SELF']`	The filename of the currently executing script, relative to the document root
`$_SERVER['SERVER_ADDR']`	The IP address of the server under which the current script is executing.
`$_SERVER['SERVER_NAME']`	The name of the server host under which the current script is executing. If the script is running on a virtual host, this will be the value defined for that virtual host.
`$_SERVER['REMOTE_ADDR']`	The IP address from which the user is viewing the current page.
`$_SERVER['SCRIPT_NAME']`	Contains the current script's path. This is useful for pages which need to point to themselves.
`$_SERVER['REQUEST_URI']`	The URI which was given in order to access this page; for instance, '/index.html'.

Below is an example of how to use the $_SERVER variable.

Listing 3.13: server_variables.php

```
<?php

    // to display the filename of the currently executing script
    echo $_SERVER['PHP_SELF'];
    echo "<br>";

    // to display the web server's IP address
    echo $_SERVER['SERVER_ADDR'];
    echo "<br>";

    // to display the web client's  IP address
    echo $_SERVER['REMOTE_ADDR'];
    echo "<br>";

    // to display the name of the web server
    echo $_SERVER['SERVER_NAME'];
    echo "<br>";

    // to display the current script's path
    echo $_SERVER['SCRIPT_NAME'];
    echo "<br>";

    // to display the URI
    echo $_SERVER['REQUEST_URI'];
    echo "<br>";

?>
```

Figure 3.4

Notice here that the Web server and the URL are all running and displaying from the local server (not a remote server).

```
/phpcodes/chapter2/server_variables.php
127.0.0.1
127.0.0.1
127.0.0.1
/phpcodes/chapter2/server_variables.php
/phpcodes/chapter2/server_variables.php
```

Type Casting

Type casting is a process of converting variable of one data type to another. To cast a variable, write the name of the desired type in parentheses before the variable which is to be cast.

The casts allowed are:

Casting	To
(int), (integer)	cast to integer
(bool), (boolean)	cast to boolean
(float), (double), (real)	cast to float
(string)	cast to string
(array)	cast to array
(object)	cast to object

See the following example.

Listing 3.12: type_casting.php

```
<?php

    // $abc is an integer
    $abc = 10;

    // $abc becomes a float
    $kml = (float) $abc;

    // $xyz becomes a boolean
    $xyz = (boolean) $abc;

    // display the values
    echo "abc is $abc and xyz is $xyz <br>";

?>
```

Detailed Examples

Q1. Stadium Seating

There are three seating categories at an athletic stadium. For a baseball, Class A seats cost $15 each, Class B seats cost $12 each, and Class C seats cost $9 each. Create a form that allows the user to enter the number of tickets sold for each class. The form should be able to display the amount of income generated from each class of ticket sales and the total revenue generated. The application's form should resemble the one shown below.

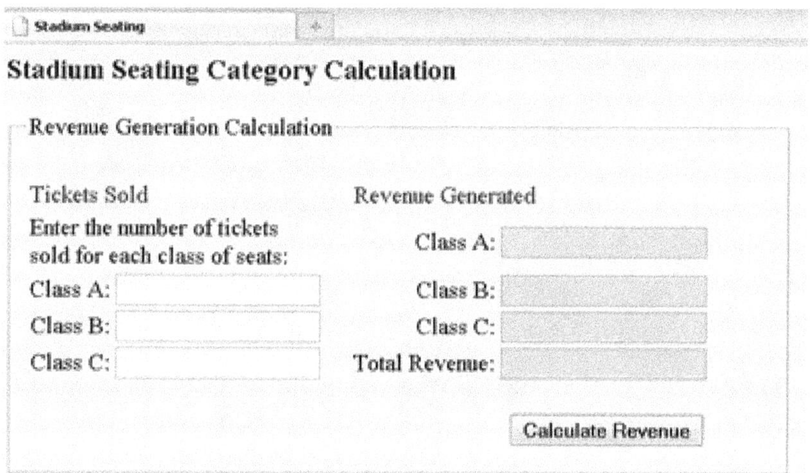

Suggested Solution:

Note that for this example, the HTML form tags have not been included. Chapter 11 teaches the use of form tags. In the later chapters, we will combine both the form tags and the PHP codes.

Listing 3.13: stadium_seating.php

```
<html>
<body bgcolor="f3f3f3">
<h3>Stadium Seating Category Calculation</h3>
```

Continuation of Listing 3.13: stadium_seating.php

```
<?php
//declare variables
$classATicketSold='';
$classBTicketSold='';
$classCTicketSold='';
$classAReveneGenerated='';
$classBReveneGenerated='';
$classCReveneGenerated='';
$totalRevenue='';

//initialize the amounts to the seat cost
$classAPrice = 15;
$classBPrice = 12;
$classCPrice = 9;

/* check whether the user clicks on the Calculate Revenue
button */
if(isset($_POST['calculateRevenue'])){

    // assign form values to variables
    $classATicketSold = $_POST['classATicketSold'];
    $classBTicketSold = $_POST['classBTicketSold'];
    $classCTicketSold = $_POST['classCTicketSold'];

    // calculate Revenue generated for each class, A, B, and C
    $classAReveneGenerated = $classATicketSold * $classAPrice;
    $classBReveneGenerated = $classBTicketSold * $classBPrice;
    $classCReveneGenerated = $classCTicketSold * $classCPrice;

    // calculate total revenue generated
    $totalRevenue =  $classAReveneGenerated +
                     $classBReveneGenerated +
                     $classCReveneGenerated;
}
?>

</body>
</html>
```

Q2. Test Average

Create a PHP application that allows the user to enter five test scores. The application should be able to calculate and display the average score. The form should resemble the one shown below.

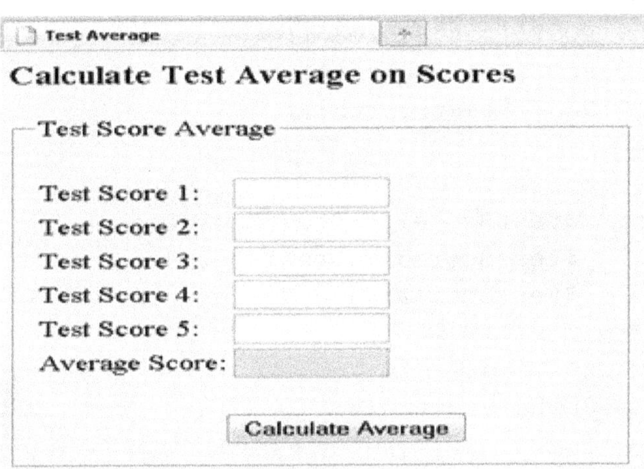

Suggested Solution:

Please, note that for this example also, the HTML form tags have not been included.

Listing 3.14: test_average.php

```
<?php

    // declare variables
    $testScore1='';
    $testScore2='';
    $testScore3='';
    $testScore4='';
    $testScore5='';
    $averageScore='';
```

Listing 3.14: test_average.php

```
    // if the user clicks on Calculate Average button
    if(isset($_POST['calculateAverage'])){

        // assign form values to variables
        $testScore1=$_POST['testScore1'];
        $testScore2 = $_POST['testScore2'];
        $testScore3 = $_POST['testScore3'];
        $testScore4 = $_POST['testScore4'];
        $testScore5 = $_POST['testScore5'];

        // calculate total score
        $totalScore  =   $testScore1 + $testScore2 +
                         $testScore3 + $testScore4 +
                         $testScore5;

        //calculate average score
        $averageScore = $totalScore / 5;
    }

?>
```

Programming Challenge

Q1. Write a PHP script segment to combine the following two variables:

a) $var1 = 'Welcome to ';
b) $var2 = 'pentvars.edu.gh';

Q2. Convert the following algebraic expressions into valid PHP expressions. A, B, C, D, and E are variable names, as such they must conform to PHP variable naming rules and conventions.

a) A + B
b) A2 + B2
c) A + B * C
d) $(A + B)^2$
e) A + [B * C – D] * E

Q3. Convert the following algebraic equations into valid PHP expressions. All the variables must conform to PHP variable naming rules and conventions.

a) $Z= (a+b)(c+d)(e+f)$

b) $H= a(b/c)$

c) $Q = -(a^2-b^2)$

d) $A = 4/3 \pi r^2$

e) $F= (cx + d)(bc + d^2)$, where c, x, d, b are variables.

f) $W = x^2 + x^2 + z^2$

g) $W = \dfrac{xy}{x^2 + y^2}$

h) $J = \dfrac{(-1)^{n-1} t^{n+1}}{1 + t}$

i) $MOM = S * \dfrac{1}{(1+R)^N}$

j) $PO = \dfrac{1-(1+R)^{-N}}{R}$

k) $PV = A + \left[\dfrac{A}{A-B} * (B - A)\right]$

l) $DF = \dfrac{1+M}{1+I}$

m) $IRR = 3\left(\dfrac{\frac{3}{4} \cdot T \cdot V}{I}\right)^{\frac{1}{3}}$

n) $R = \dfrac{D+P}{(1+I)^N}$

o) $B = (Y - 3^{X-1} + 2)^5$

p) $X = X^{I+1}$

q) $A = \sqrt{\frac{(X-A)^2}{S+4}}$

r) $BI = \sqrt{\frac{2CD}{H\left(1-\frac{D}{R}\right)}}$

Q4. Density

Write a script that computes the volume of an object. The script should ask the user to input the object's mass and density. The mass will be given in grams; the density will be in grams per cubic centimeter.

The relationship of mass, density, and volume of an object is given by

$$\text{Density} = \frac{\text{Mass}}{\text{Volume}}$$

Your program should output the volume in cubic centimeters.

4

Constants

I am not going to tell you what should motivate you; whether you wish to serve God, king, country, family, political party, to work for good causes, or to fulfill your duty is up to you. I only want to show that motivation - preferably an ambition to accomplish something that really satisfies you and hurts no one – is essential.
Hans Selye

Learning Objectives

After studying this chapter, you should be able to:

- To define and assign values to constants.
- Differentiate between constants and variables.
- Use magic constants in your scripts.
- Code and run scripts involving constants.

What is a Constant

A constant is a temporary placeholder in memory that holds a value. Constants just as variables are used to store information. Unlike variables, the value of a constant never changes within the program. That is to say that the value held in memory declared as a constant cannot be changed in the process of running the program. When a constant is declared, the **`define()`** function is used. The function requires the name of the constant and the value of the constant. They can be mathematic constants, passwords, paths to files, etc. By using a constant you "lock in" the value which prevents you from accidentally changing (overwriting) it in the program.

The Differences Between Constants and Variables

The following are the major differences between Constants and Variables:

1. There is no need to write a dollar sign ($) before constants, whereas in variables one has to prefix them with a dollar sign.
2. Constants cannot be defined by simple assignment, they may only be defined using the **define()** function. But, variables use assignment statement in their definition.
3. Constants may be defined and accessed anywhere within the program without regard to variable scoping rules. However, the scope of variables is the context within which they have been defined. That is, variables may be limited to the scope within which they are defined.
4. Once the constants have been set, they cannot be redefined or undefined anywhere in the program. On the other side, variables can be redefined and their contents can be changed.

Constant Syntax Definition

You can create a constant using the **define()** function as

```
define(CONSTANT_NAME, value);
```

The **define()** function accepts two arguments or parameters. The first must be a string. It represents the name which will be used to access the constant (i.e, the name of the constant). The name of the constant is case-sensitive. By convention, constant identifiers are always uppercase. A valid constant name starts with a letter or an underscore, followed by any combination of letters, numbers or underscores. The second argument of the **define()** function is the value of the constant. It can be a string or numbers and can be set explicitly or as the result of a function or an equation. PHP also has many pre-defined constants that can be used in your scripts. We will take a look at some of the pre-defined constants that are available in PHP so that you do not use the same names in constants that you create.

Some examples of constant declarations are demonstrated below:

```
define("STRING_CONSTANT", "This is my string.");

define("NUMERIC_CONSTANT", 5);

define("FLOAT_CONSTANT", 9.99);
```

It should be noted that only scalar data (boolean, integer, float and string) can be contained in constants.

Syntax 1: Declaring and Displaying Constants

The following code segment demonstrates how to declare constants, assign values to constants, and display the results in the browser window.

Listing 4.1: constant1.php

```
<?php

   /* declare and assign values to string, integer and float
   constants */
   define("STRING_CONST","PHP program is fun");
   define("INTEGER_CONST",200);
   define("FLOAT_CONST",21.25);

   // print the values stored in the constants
   echo STRING_CONST. "<br>";
   echo INTEGER_CONST. "<br>";
   echo FLOAT_CONST;

?>
```

In this example, three constants **STRING_CONST**, **INTEGER_CONST**, and **FLOAT_CONST** are declared and assigned values. Next, the **echo** statement is used to display the contents of the constants to the browser window (see Figure 4.1).

In addition to being echoed to the browser, constants can also be manipulated using PHP's mathematical and string functions.

Figure 4.1
Output from constant declaration and assignment.

```
PHP program is fun
200
21.25
```

Syntax 2: Declaring and Displaying Constants

Let us take a look at another example where we use the define function to set the initial value of a constant. Here, we also use the **constant** keyword together with the **echo** to display the result.

Listing 4.2: constant2.php

```
<?php

    // define a constant PASSWORD and assign admin
    define("PASSWORD","admin");

    // display the value of PASSWORD constant, i.e. admin
    echo (PASSWORD);

    // display the value of PASSWORD constant, i.e. admin
    echo constant("PASSWORD");

    // display the value of PASSWORD constant, i.e. admin
    echo "PASSWORD";

?>
```

The `constant()` Function

As indicated by the name, this function will return the value of the constant. This is useful when you want to retrieve a value of a constant, but you do not know its name. That is when it is stored in a variable or returned by a function.

Listing 4.3: constant_function.php

```
<?php

    // declare the constant
    define("TAX_RATE", 0.25);

    // the output: 0.25
    echo TAX_RATE;

    // same as the previous line, ie 0.25
    echo constant("TAX_RATE");

?>
```

PHP Magic Constants (Pre-defined Constants)

PHP also provides a number of built-in constants to any script which it runs. Many of these constants, however, are created by various extensions, and will only be present when those extensions are available, either via dynamic loading or because they have been compiled into the installation. For example, "**__FILE__**" returns the name of the file currently being read by the interpreter. "**__LINE__**" returns the line number of the file. These constants are useful for generating error messages. You can also find out which version of PHP is interpreting your script using the "**PHP_VERSION**" constant. These special constants are case-insensitive. A few "magical" PHP constants are described in Table 4.1.

Table 4.1: Magical Constants

Name	Description
`__LINE__`	The current line number of the file.
`__FILE__`	The full path and filename of the file. If used inside an **`include`**, the name of the included file is returned.
`__DIR__`	The directory of the file. If used inside an **`include`**, the directory (folder) of the included file is returned. This is equivalent to **`dirname(__FILE__)`**. This directory name does not have a trailing slash unless it is the root directory.
`__FUNCTION__`	The function name. This constant returns the function name as it was declared (case-sensitive).
`__CLASS__`	The class name. This constant returns the class name as it was declared (case-sensitive).
`__METHOD__`	The class method name. The method name is returned as it was declared (case-sensitive).
`__NAMESPACE__`	The name of the current namespace (case-sensitive). This constant is defined at compile-time.

Listing 4.4 shows the difference between **__FUNCTION__** and **__METHOD__**. The **__FUNCTION__** returns only the name of the function, while **__METHOD__** returns the name of the class along with the name of the function.

Listing 4.4: magic_constant.php

```
<?php

    // create a class model
    class model
    {
        function magicFunction()
        {
            echo __FUNCTION__;
        }

        function magicMethod()
        {
            echo __METHOD__;
        }
    }

    // create an object of the model class
    $obj = new model();

    /* call magicFunction function. It will
    output: magicFunction */
    $obj->magicFunction();
    echo "<br />";

    /* call magicMethod function. It will
    output:model::magicMethod */
    $obj->magicMethod();

?>
```

Figure 4.2

Notice that the **_FUNCTION_** displays the class name and function name, but **_METHOD_** shows only the function name.

magicFunctionmodel::magicMethod

Detailed Examples

Q1. FV Calculation

Write a PHP script that computes the future value (FV) of a given present amount. The formula for future value is

$$FV = PV * [1+(i/m)]^{m*y}$$

Where

PV is the present amount (take the present amount to be a constant of $3000).
i is the annual interest rate (i = 0.4)
m is the number of compounding periods per year (m = 4).
y is the number of years (y = 6).

Calculate and print the FV value.

Suggested Solution:

Listing 4.5: fv_calculation.php

```
<?php

  //declare PV as a constant and assign value.
  define("PV",3000);

  // assign value to the interest rate.
  $i = 0.4;
```

Continuation of Listing 4.5: fv_calculation.php

```
 // assign value to number of compounding periods per year.
 $m = 4;

 // assign value to number of years.
 $y = 6;

 /* break down the formulae into two in order to deal with
 exponentiation function (pow) */
 $number = 1 + ($i/$m);
 $exponent = $m * $y;

 //calculate and print the future value
 $FV = PV * pow($number,$exponent);

 /* format output to 2 decimal places.
  This outputs $29,549.20 */
 echo '$'.number_format($FV,2);

?>
```

Q2. Currency Conversion

Write a script that will convert U.S. dollar amounts to English pounds, German marks, French francs, and Ghana Cedi. The conversion factors to use are

1 dollar = 0.68 pounds
1 dollar = 1.7 marks
1 dollar = 5.82 francs
1 dollar = 1.5 Cedis

In your script, declare named constants to represent the conversion factors for the different types of currency. For example, you might declare the conversion factor for Cedis as:

CONST("CEDIS_FACTOR", 108.36);

Then, use the named constant in the mathematical conversion statement.

Suggested Solution:

The form and the script are listed below:

Convert From US Dollar To Other Currencies

Dollar Value

Enter Dollar Value : 95

Convert to other currencies

Pounds : 64.6
Marks : 161.5
Francs : 552.9
Cedis : 142.5
Convert

Listing 4.6: currency_conversion.php

```
<html>
<body bgcolor="f3f3f3">
<h4>Convert From US Dollar To Other Currencies</h4>
<?php

 //declare variables
 $pounds='';
 $marks='';
 $francs='';
 $cedis='';
 $dollarValue='';

 // define and assign values to the constants
 define("POUNDS", 0.68);
 define("MARKS", 1.7);
 define("FRANCS", 5.82);
 define("CEDIS", 1.5);
```

Continuation of Listing 4.6: currency_conversion.php

```
// when the user clicks the Convert button
if(isset($_POST['convert'])){

    // assign form values to variable
    $dollarValue=$_POST['dollarValue'];

    // calculate the converted amounts for other currencies
    $pounds = $dollarValue * POUNDS;   // calculates for Pounds
    $marks = $dollarValue * MARKS; // calculates for Marks
    $francs = $dollarValue * FRANCS;   // calculates for Francs
    $cedis = $dollarValue * CEDIS; // calculates for Cedis
}
?>

<!-- Start HTML form -->
<form action="currency_conversion.php" method="post">
<fieldset style="width: 25%; "><legend>Dollar Value</legend><br>

<table width="100%" border="0">
<tr>
      <td width="15%" nowrap>Enter Dollar Value :</td>
      <td width="85%"> <input type="text" name="dollarValue"
      value="<?php echo $dollarValue ?>" size="10"></td>
</tr>
</table>
</fieldset>
<br>

<fieldset style="width: 25%; "><legend>Convert to other
currencies</legend>

<table width="100%" border="0">
<tr>
      <td width="15%" height="24" nowrap>Pounds :</td>
      <td width="85%" > <input type="text" readonly="readonly"
      name="pounds" value="<?php echo $pounds ?>" size="10"></td>
</tr>
```

Continuation of Listing 4.6: currency_conversion.php

```
<tr>
      <td nowrap>Marks :</td>
      <td nowrap> <div align="left"> <input type="text"
      readonly="readonly" name="marks" value="<?php echo $marks
      ?>" size="10"></div></td>
</tr>
<tr>
      <td nowrap>Francs :</td>
      <td colspan="2" nowrap> <div align="left">
      <input type="text" readonly="readonly" name="francs"
      value="<?php echo $francs ?>" size="10"></div></td>
</tr>
<tr>
      <td nowrap>Cedis :</td>
      <td nowrap> <div align="left"><input type="text"
      readonly="readonly" name="cedis" value="<?php echo $cedis
      ?>" size="10"></div></td>
</tr>
<tr>
      <td>  </td>
      <td><input type="submit" name="convert" value="Convert">
</td>
</tr>
</table>
</fieldset>
</form>
</body>

</html>
```

Q3. Water and Sewer Bill

Write a program to compute a water and sewer bill. The input is the number of gallons consumed. A water and sewer bill are computed as follows:

- Water costs 0.021 cents per 100 gallons
- Sewer service is 0.001 cents per 100 gallons consumed.
- A service charge of 2 percent is applied to the total of the water and sewer service charges.

Suggested Solution:

The form and the script are listed below:

Miles Per Gallon Calculator

Number Analysis Information

Gallons of gas the car can hold: 78

Number of miles it can be driven on a full tank: 50

Miles per gallon: 0.6410256410

Calculate MPG

Listing 4.7: miles_per_gallon_calculator.php

```
<html>
<body bgcolor="f3f3f3">
<h3>Miles Per Gallon Calculator</h3>
<?php

//declare variables and assign empty value
$gallonsofGas='';
$numberofMiles='';
$milesPerGallon='';
```

Continuation of Listing 4.7: miles_per_gallon_calculator.php

```
// check whether the user clicks on the Compute Net Total button
if(isset($_POST['calculateMPG'])){

    // assign form values to variables
    $gallonsofGas = $_POST['gallonsofGas'];
    $numberofMiles = $_POST['numberofMiles'];

    // calculate miles per gallon
    $milesPerGallon = $numberofMiles / $gallonsofGas;
  }

?>

<!-- start HTML form here -->
<form action="miles_per_gallon_calculator.php" method="post">
<fieldset style="width: 30%; "><legend>Number Analysis</legend><br>

<table width="95%" border="0">
<tr>
      <td height="33" nowrap>Gallons of gas the car can
           hold:</td>
      <td width="65%"><input type="text" size="10"
           name="gallonsofGas" value="<?php echo $gallonsofGas
           ?>"></td>
</tr>
<tr>
      <td height="44" nowrap>Number of miles driven on a full
      tank:</td>
      <td><input type="text" size="10" name="numberofMiles"
      value="<?php echo $numberofMiles ?>"></td>
</tr>
<tr>
      <td>Miles per gallon:</td>
      <td> <input type="text" size="10" readonly="readonly"
      name="milesPerGallon" value="<?php echo $milesPerGallon
      ?>"></td>
</tr>
```

Continuation of Listing 4.7: miles_per_gallon_calculator.php

```
<tr>
      <td nowrap> </td>
      <td nowrap><input type="submit" name="calculateMPG"
      value="Calculate MPG"></td>
</tr>
</table>
</fieldset>
</form>
</body>

</html>
```

Q4. Monthly Sales Tax

A retail company must file a monthly sales tax report listing the total sales for the month, and the amount of state and county sales tax collected. The state sales tax rate is 4%, and the county sales tax rate is 2%. Write a script that allows the user to enter the total sales for the month. The application should calculate and display the following:

a. The amount of county sales tax
b. The amount of state sales tax
c. The total sales tax (county plus state)

In your script, represent the county tax rate (0.02) and the state tax rate (0.04) as named constants. Use the named constants in the mathematical statements.

Suggested Solution:

The form and the script are listed below:

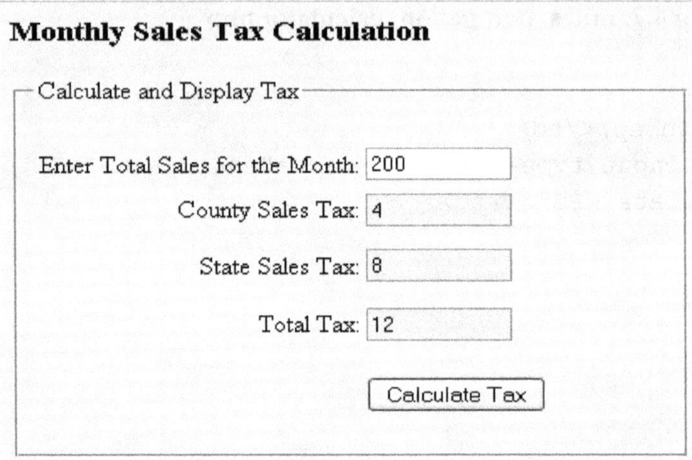

Listing 4.8: monthly_sales_tax.php

```
<html>
<head>
<title>Monthly Sales Tax</title>
</head>
<body bgcolor="f3f3f3">
<h3>Monthly Sales Tax Calculation</h3>

<?php

 //declare variables
 $totalMonthlySales='';
 $countySalesTax='';
 $stateSalesTax='';
 $totalSalesTax='';

 // define the constants
 define("STATETAX_RATE", 0.04);
 define("COUNTYTAX_RATE", 0.02);
```

Continuation of Listing 4.8: monthly_sales_tax.php

```
 // check whether the user clicks the Compute Net Total button
 if(isset($_POST['calculateTax'])){

     // assign form values to variables
     $totalMonthlySales=$_POST['totalMonthlySales'];

     // calculate county sales tax
     $countySalesTax = $totalMonthlySales * COUNTYTAX_RATE;


      // calculate state sales tax
     $stateSalesTax = $totalMonthlySales * STATETAX_RATE;

     // calculate total sales tax
     $totalSalesTax = $countySalesTax + $stateSalesTax;
}
?>

<form action="monthly_sales_tax.php" method="post">
<table width="100%" border="0">
<tr>
      <td width="16%" nowrap><div align="right">Enter Total
      Sales for the Month:</div></td>
       <td width="84%"> <input type="text"
       name="totalMonthlySales"
      value="<?php echo $totalMonthlySales ?>" size="10"></td>
</tr>
<tr>
      <td height="33" nowrap><div align="right">County Sales
       Tax:</div></td>
      <td nowrap> <div align="right"></div> <input type="text"
       readonly="readonly" name="countySalesTax"
       value="<?php echo $countySalesTax ?>" ></td>
</tr>
```

Continuation of Listing 4.8: monthly_sales_tax.php

```
<tr>
     <td height="38" nowrap><div align="right">State Sales Tax:</div>
     </td>
     <td nowrap> <div align="right"></div>
        <input type="text" readonly="readonly"
        name="stateSalesTax" value="<?php echo $stateSalesTax
        ?>" size="10"></td>
</tr>
<tr>
      <td height="37" nowrap><div align="right">Total
      Tax:</div></td>
      <td nowrap> <div align="right"></div>
      <input type="text" readonly="readonly"
      name="totalSalesTax"
      value="<?php echo $totalSalesTax ?>" size="10"></td>
</tr>
<tr>
      <td height="53">  </td>
      <td><input type="submit" name="calculateTax"
      value="Calculate Tax" ></td>
</tr>
</table>
</form>
</body>
</html>
```

Programming Challenge

Q1. Tuition Plan

A university uses the following tuition table to determine a student's semester tuition.

	Residence Status	
Class Standing	Local ($)	International($)
Undergraduate	450	780
Graduate	1250	3275
Professional	2300	5200

Assume that a variable called ***resStatus*** holds the value 1 for local students and the value 2 for international students. Also, assume that you have a variable ***classStanding*** that holds 1 for undergraduates, 2 for graduates, and 3 for professional students. Given this information, create a form that accepts student's class standing (***classStanding***) and residential status (***resStatus***) as inputs. Determine and output the appropriate tuition of the student based on the current ***classStanding*** *and* ***resStatus.***

Q3. Property Tax

Adenta Municipal Assembly (AMA) collects property taxes on the assessment value of property, which is 60% of the property's actual value. If an acre of land is valued at $10,000, its assessment value is $6,000. The property tax is then $0.64 for each $100 of the assessment value. The tax for the acre assessed at $6,000 will be $38.40. Write a script that displays the assessment value and property tax when a user enters the actual value of a property.

5

Operators

Nothing will ever be attempted if all possible objections must first be overcome.
- Samuel Johnson

Learning Objectives

After studying this chapter, you should be able to:

- Understand the different types of operators used in PHP, include Arithmetic Operators, Assignment Operators, Comparison Operators, Logical Operators and Conditional Operators.
- List operator precedence.
- Code and run scripts involving operators.

What are Operators

Operators are used to perform operations or actions on variables and constants. To explain this in a simpler term, consider the expression 2 + 3 which is equal to 5. Here 2 and 3 are called operands and + is called operator. Operators can be included in assigning a value to a variable, performing addition with variables, comparing the value of variables, and determining the status of a condition. In this chapter we shall discuss and demonstrate how to use different types of operators.

Classification of Operators

All the operators we are going to discuss can be classified into the following categories:

- Unary Operators, which precede or suffix a single operand such as ++$a and $a--.
- Binary Operators, which take two operands and perform a variety of arithmetic and logical operations such as $b+$c.
- Conditional Operators (ternary operators), which take three operands and evaluates either the second or third expression, depending on the evaluation of the first expression such as $b > $c.
- Assignment Operators, which assign a value to a variable such as $a=$b+$c.

Arithmetic Operators

They are used to perform basic mathematical operations. The following are arithmetic operators used in PHP: In order to illustrate their usage, assume that A holds a value of 5 and B holds 10.

Table 5.1: Arithmetic Operators

Operator	Description	Example
+	Adds two operands.	A + B will give 15
-	Subtracts second operand from the first.	A - B will give -5
*	Multiply both operands.	A * B will give 50
/	Divide the numerator by the denominator.	B / A will give 2
%	Modulus Operator; this is the remainder after an integer division.	B % A will give 0
++	Increment operator, increases integer value by one.	A++ will give 6
--	Decrement operator, decreases integer value by one.	A-- will give 4

The use of the Arithmetic Operators is shown in the script below. Try the following example to understand how the arithmetic operators work.

Listing 5.1: arithmetic_operators.php

```
<?php

    // declare and assign value to variables
    $sum = 12;
    $newsum = $sum + 4;

    // the addition operator. This will output 16
    echo "Addition operator: $newsum <br/>";

    // the subtraction operator. This will output 14
    $difference = $newsum - 2;
    echo "Subtraction operator: $difference<br/>";

    // the multiplication operator. This will output 42
    $product = $difference * 3;
    echo "Multiplication operator: $product<br/>";

    // the division operator. This will output 3
    $quotient = $product / $difference;
    echo "Division operator: $quotient<br/>";
```

Listing 5.1: arithmetic_operators.php

```
    // the increment operator. This will output 4
    $quotient++;
    echo "Increment operator: $quotient<br/>";

    // the decrement operator. This will output 3
    $quotient--;
    echo "Decrement operator: $quotient<br/>";

?>
```

Assignment Operators

Assignment operators are used to change the value of the current variable with the value on the right of the operator. The following are Assignment operators used in PHP:

Table 5.2: Assignment Operators

Operator	Description	Example
=	Assigns the value of the variable on the right to the variable on the left.	C = A + B will assign value of A + B into C
+=	Adds the value on the left to the value on the right and assigns the result to the variable on the left.	C += A is equivalent to C = C + A
-=	Subtracts the value on the left to the value on the right and assigns the result to the variable on the left.	C -= A is equivalent to C = C - A
*=	Multiplies the value on the left to the value on the right and assigns the result to the variable on the left.	C *= A is equivalent to C = C * A
/=	Divides the value on the left by the value on the right and assigns the result to the variable on the left.	C /= A is equivalent to C = C / A

Table 5.2: Assignment Operators

Operator	Description	Example
%=	Divides the value on the left by the value on the right and assigns the remainder (modulus) to the variable on the left.	C %= A is equivalent to C = C % A
.=	The value on the left is concatenated (added on to) the value on the right and is assigned to the variable on the left.	C .= A is equivalent to C = C . A

The following example illustrates the understanding of the assignment operators.

Listing 5.2: assignment_operators.php

```
<?php

    // declare and assign value to variables
    $a = 42;
    $b = 20;

    // c value was 42 + 20 = 62
    $c = $a + $b;
    echo "Assignment Operation: $c <br/>";

    // c value was 42 + 20 + 42 = 104
    $c += $a;
    echo "Addition Operation: $c <br/>";

    // c value was 104 - 42 = 62
    $c -= $a;
    echo "Subtract Operation: $c <br/>";

    // c value was 62 * 42 = 2604
    $c *= $a;
    echo "Multiply Operation: $c <br/>";

    // c value was 2604/42 = 62
    $c /= $a;
    echo "Division Operation: $c <br/>";

    // c value was 62 mod 42 = 20
    $c %= $a;
    echo "Modulus Operation: $c <br/>";
?>
```

Figure 5.1
The use of Assignment Operators yielding various results.

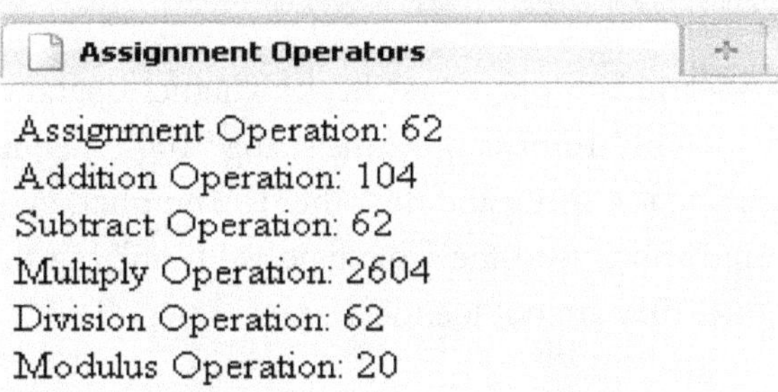
Assignment Operators
Assignment Operation: 62
Addition Operation: 104
Subtract Operation: 62
Multiply Operation: 2604
Division Operation: 62
Modulus Operation: 20

Comparison Operators

Comparison operators are used to check the relationship between variables and/or values. Comparison operators are used inside conditional statements and evaluate to either **true** or **false**. The following are Comparison operators used in PHP. In order to illustrate their usage assume that A holds a value of 5 and B holds 10.

Table 5.3a: Comparison Operators (in terms of the value of operands)

Operator	Description	Example
==	Checks if the value of two operands is equal or not, if yes then the condition becomes true.	(A == B) is not true.
!=	Checks if the values of two operands are equal or not, if values are not equal then condition becomes true.	(A != B) is true.
>	Checks if the value of left operand is greater than the value of right operand, if yes then condition becomes true.	(A > B) is not true.
<	Checks if the value of left operand is less than the value of right operand, if yes then condition becomes true.	(A < B) is true.
>=	Checks if the value of left operand is greater than or equal to the value of right operand, if yes then condition becomes true.	(A >= B) is not true.
<=	Checks if the value of left operand is less than or equal to the value of right operand, if yes then condition becomes true.	(A <= B) is true.

Identity Operators

The === and !== operators checks whether operands are both of the same value and of the same data type. For example, the string "100" is equal to number 100, but not identical because one is a string and the other is a number, even though their values are equal. Also, the string "john" is of the same type as "John" but they are not of the same value. Therefore, they are not identical.

Table 5.3b: Comparison Operators (in terms of the value and type of operands)

Operator	Description	Example
===	Checks if the value of two operands is equal both in terms of type and value.	"100" === 100 is not true.
!==	Checks if the value of two operands is not equal both in terms of type and value.	"john" !== "John" is true.

The following example further provides understanding of comparison operators.

Listing 5.3: comparison_operators.php

```
<?php

    $a = 114;
    $b = 126;
    // Equal operator
    if($a == $b ){
        echo "a is equal to b<br/>";
    }
    else{
        echo "a is not equal to b<br/>";
    }

    // Greater than operator
    if( $a > $b ){
        echo "a is greater than  b<br/>";
    }
    else{
        echo "a is not greater than b<br/>";
    }
```

Continuation of Listing 5.3: comparison_operators.php

```
    // Less than operator
    if( $a < $b ){
       echo "a is less than  b<br/>";
    }
    else{
       echo "a is not less than b<br/>";
    }

    // Not equal to operator
    if( $a != $b ){
       echo "a is not equal to b<br/>";
    }
    else{
       echo "a is equal to b<br/>";
    }

    // Greater than or equal to operator
    if( $a >= $b ){
       echo "a is either greater than or equal to b<br/>";
    }
    else{
       echo "a is neither greater than nor equal to b<br/>";
    }

    // Less than or equal to operator
    if($a <= $b ){
       echo "a is either less than or equal to b<br/>";
    }
    else{
       echo "a is neither less than nor equal to b<br/>";
    }
?>
```

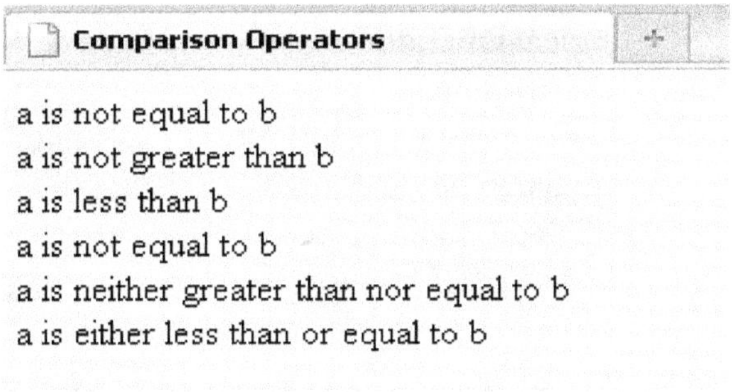

Figure 5.2
The use of Comparison Operators yielding various results.

Comparison Operators
a is not equal to b
a is not greater than b
a is less than b
a is not equal to b
a is neither greater than nor equal to b
a is either less than or equal to b

Combining Arithmetic and Relational Operators

In this example we combined the use of both arithmetic and relational operators. Assuming the value of $x is 1, the value of $y=4, and the value of $z is 14, the following table gives the values of various expressions.

Note that in expressions involving arithmetic and relational operators, the arithmetic operators are performed first.

Table 5.4: Arithmetic and Relational Operators

Expression	Value	Interpretation
$x < $y + $z	1	True
$y = = 2 * $x + 3	0	False
$z < = $x + $y	0	False
$z > $x	1	True
$x != $y	1	True

Logical Operators

Logical Operators allow you to determine the status of conditions. Depending on the condition of a variable different script actions can occur. Logical operators are used extensively with PHP decision structures. The following are the Logical Operators used in PHP. Assume variable **A** holds 5 and variable **B** holds 10 then:

Table 5.5: Logical Operators

Operator	Description	Example
And	Logical AND operator. If both operands are true then the condition becomes true.	(A and B) is true.
Or	Logical OR Operator. If any of the two operands is non zero then the condition becomes true.	(A or B) is true.

Table 5.5: Logical Operators

Operator	Description	Example
&&	Logical AND operator. If both the operands are non zero then the condition becomes true.	(A && B) is true.
||	Logical OR Operator. If any of the two operands is non zero then the condition becomes true.	(A || B) is true.
!	Logical NOT Operator. Use to reverse the logical state of its operand. If a condition is true then Logical NOT operator will make it false.	!(A && B) is false.

The following example shows the understanding of some of the Logical Operators.

Listing 5.4: logical_operators.php

```
<?php

    // Declare and assign values to your variables
    $a = 42;
    $b = 0;

    // Logical AND operator
    if( $a && $b ){
       echo "Both a and b are true<br/>";
    }else{
       echo "Either a or b is false<br/>";
    }

    // Logical AND operator
    if( $a and $b ){
       echo "Both a and b are true<br/>";
    }else{
       echo "Either a or b is false<br/>";
    }
```

Cotinuation of Listing 5.4: logical_operators.php

```
    // Logical OR Operator.
    if( $a || $b ){
       echo "Either a or b is true<br/>";
    }else{
       echo "Both a and b are false<br/>";
    }

    // Logical OR Operator.
    if( $a or $b ){
       echo "Either a or b is true<br/>";
    }else{
       echo "Both a and b are false<br/>";
    }
?>
```

Figure 5.3
The use of Logical Operators yielding various results.

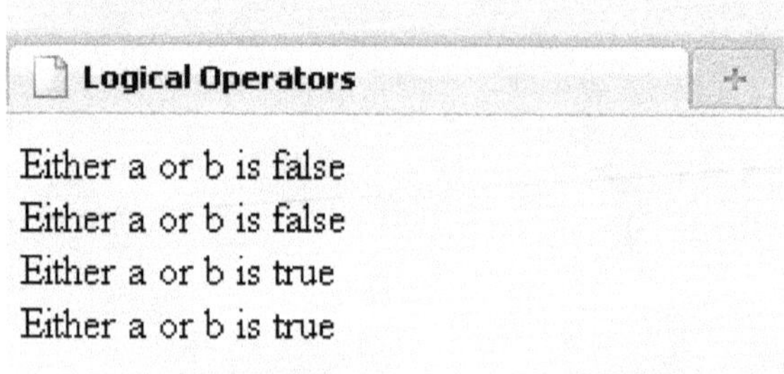

Conditional Operator

There is one more operator called conditional operator. It first evaluates an expression for a **true** or **false** value and then executes one of the two given statements depending upon the result of the evaluation. The conditional operator has this syntax:

Table 5.6: Conditional Operators

Operator	Description	Example
? :	Conditional Expression	If Condition is true ? Then value A : Otherwise value B

The following example gives the understanding of the conditional operator.

Listing 5.5: conditional_operators.php

```
<?php

    // Declare and assign value to variables
    $a = 10;
    $b = 20;

    /* If condition is true then assign $a to $result
    otherwise assign $b */
    $result = ($a > $b)? $a : $b;
    echo "Value of result is $result<br/>";


    /* If condition is true then assign $a to $result
    otherwise assign $b */
    $result = ($a < $b) ? $a:$b;
    echo "Value of result is $result<br/>";

?>
```

The following examples illustrate the use of logical and relational operators.

1. **Example on logical operators.**

PHP provides the logical operators **and**, **or**, and **not**. The logical **and** is also denoted **&&**, the logical **or** is also denoted | |, and the logical not is denoted **!**. The results of using these operators are given in the following table.

Table 5.7: Example of Logical Operators

$x	**$y**	**$x && $y**	**$x | | $y**	**! $x**
T	T	T	T	F
T	F	F	T	F
F	T	F	T	T
F	F	F	F	T

Example on logical and relational operators.

Assuming that the value of $x is 1, the value of $y is 4, and the value of $z is 14, the following table gives the values of various logical expressions:

Table 5.8: Example of **logical and relational operators**

<table>
<tr><th>Number</th><th>Expression</th><th>Value</th></tr>
<tr><td>1</td><td>$x <= 1 && $y == 3</td><td>0</td></tr>
<tr><td>2</td><td>$x <= 1 || $y == 3</td><td>1</td></tr>
<tr><td>3</td><td>!($x >1)</td><td>1</td></tr>
<tr><td>4</td><td>! $x >1</td><td>0</td></tr>
<tr><td>5</td><td>! ($x <= 1 || $y == 3)</td><td>0</td></tr>
<tr><td>6</td><td>$x >= 1 && $y == 3 || $z < 14</td><td>0</td></tr>
</table>

Explanation:

1. In number 1, the expression $x <= 1 && $y == 3, we first evaluate $x <= 1 (which is true) and then $y == 3 (which is false). Because the logical **and** of a true expression and a false expression is false, the expression in number (1) is false, that is 0.
2. In the expression x <= 1 && y == 3, we first evaluate x <= 1, which is true; thus, the expression y == 3 is not evaluated. The value of the expression x <= 1 || y == 3 is true (1).
3. In the expression !($x >1), the parentheses force us to evaluate the expression x > 1 first, which is false. Negating the false expression gives the value true (1).
4. In the express ! $x >1, ! is the unary not operator and is evaluated first. Because x is 1 (true), !x is false (0). Because the expression 0 > 1 is false, the expression !x > 1 is false (0).
5. We have already observed that the expression $x <= 1 || $y == 3 is true. Negating a true expression gives the value false (0). Because && is evaluated before ||, the expression $x >= 1 && $y == 3 || $z < 14 has the same value as ($x >= 1 && $y == 3) || $z < 14.

6. To determine the value of the expression $x <= 1 && $y == 3, we first evaluate x >= 1, which is true. We then evaluate y == 3, which is false. Thus the expression $x >= 1 && $y == 3 is false. Finally, we evaluate z < 14, which is false. Thus the expression $x <= 1 && $y == 3|| $z < 14 is false (0).

Precedence of PHP Operators

When an expression is evaluated, there is a given order in which the operations are carried out. This order is called operator precedence. Operator precedence affects how an expression is evaluated. Certain operators have higher precedence than others; for example, the multiplication operator has higher precedence than the addition operator:

For example A = 2 + 3 * 4; Here A is assigned 14, not 20 because operator * has higher precedence than + so it first gets multiplied with 3*4 and then adds 2 to it.

Here, operators with the highest precedence appear at the top of the table, those with the lowest appear at the bottom. Within an expression, higher precedence operators will be evaluated first.

Table 5.9: PHP Operation Precedence

Category	**Operator**	**Associativity**
Unary	! ++ --	Right to left
Multiplicative	* / %	Left to right
Additive	+ -	Left to right
Relational	< <= > >=	Left to right
Equality	== !=	Left to right
Logical AND	&&	Left to right
Logical OR	||	Left to right
Conditional	?:	Right to left
Assignment	= += -= *= /= %=	Right to left

PHP 7 Null Coalescing Operator

A new feature, known as null coalescing operator (??), has been introduced in PHP 7. It is used to replace the ternary operation in conjunction with **isset()** function. The Null coalescing operator returns its first operand if it exists and is not NULL; otherwise it returns its second operand.

Let us look at the following code.

```
<?php
// get the value of $_GET['amount']

// assume that the amount is not passed
$amount = $_GET['amount'] ?? 'Amount is not Passed';
print($amount);
print("<br/>");

// assume that the amount is passed and has a value of 65
$amount = $_GET['amount'] ?? 'Amount is not Passed';
print($amount);
print("<br/>");

// using ternary operator, assuming amount is not passed
$amount = isset($_GET['amount']) ? $_GET['amount'] : 'Amount is
          not Passed';
print($amount);
print("<br/>");

// using ternary operator, amount is passed and has a value of 65
$amount = isset($_GET['amount']) ? $_GET['amount'] : 'Amount is
          not Passed';
print($amount);
print("<br/>");

?>
```

In the fisrt instance, the value of **$_GET['amount']** will be null, and therefore the second operand (**'Amount is not Passed'**) will be printed.

As a whole, the script will produce the following results:

Amount is not Passed
65
Amount is not Passed
65

PHP 7 Spaceship Operator

A new feature, spaceship operator, has been introduced in PHP 7. The spaceship operator (<=>) is also known as combined comparison operator. It is used to compare two expressions. It returns:

- -1 (when the first expression is less than the second expression)
- 0 (when the first expression is equal to the second expression)
- 1 (when the first expression is greater than the second expression)

Let us look at the following example.

```
<?php

   // integer comparison
   print( 10 <=> 10); // this print 0
   echo "<br/>";
   print( 10 <=> 20); // this print -1
   echo "<br/>";
   print( 20 <=> 10); // this print 1
   echo "<br/>";

   // float comparison
   print( 1.5 <=> 1.5);   // this print 0
   echo "<br/>";
   print( 1.5 <=> 2.5);   // this print -1
   echo "<br/>";
   print( 2.5 <=> 1.5);   // this print 1
   echo "<br/>";
```

Continuation

```
    // string comparison
    print( "a" <=> "a");   // this print 0
    echo "<br/>";
    print( "a" <=> "b");   // this print -1
    echo "<br/>";
    print( "b" <=> "a");   // this print 1

?>
```

Increment (++) and Decrement (- -) Operators

The increment operator ++ adds 1, and the decrement operator -- subtracts 1. Like the assignment operator, the increment and decrement operators also have a value. We describe these in more detail.

When we execute $i++ ($i=$i + 1); two things happen:

- The value of the variable $i is increased by 1.
- The value of the expression $i++ is equal to the original value of $i.

For example:

If the value of $i is 3, after we execute $y = $i++;

The value of $i will be 4 (because ++ causes $i to be incremented), and the value of $y will be 3 (the value of the expression $i++). That is to say that when the unary operator comes after the variable, $i++ or $i- -, the original value of the variable is assigned to the variable at the left (e.g. $y = $i++) before the increment or decrement is performed on the value of $i.

Detailed Examples

Q1. Centigrade to Fahrenheit

Write a script that converts centigrade to Fahrenheit. The formula is

$$F = \frac{9}{5}C + 32$$

where F is the Fahrenheit temperature and C is the centigrade temperature. Use the following set of test data to determine whether the application is calculating properly:

Centigrade	Fahrenheit
100	212
0	32
56	132.8

Suggested Solution:

The form design and the program listing are presented below. You may review Chapter 11 on form design tags and processing.

Converting From Centigrade To Fahrenheit

Convert To Fahrenheit

Enter Value for Centigrade: 5

Value for Fahrenheit: 41

Convert Reset Exit

Listing 5.6: fahrenheit_calculation.php

```
<html>
<head>
</head>
<body bgcolor="f3f3f3">
<h3>Converting From Centigrade To Fahrenheit</h3>
```

Continuation of Listing 5.6: fahrenheit_calculation.php

```
<?php

//declare variables
$centigradeValue='';
$fahrenheitvalue ='';

/* check whether the user clicks on the Convert button */
if(isset($_POST['calculateFahrenheit'])){

        // assign form values to variables
        $centigradeValue=$_POST['centigradeValue'];

        //calculate fahrenheit temperature
        $fahrenheitvalue = (9 / 5 * $centigradeValue) + 32;
}
?>
<!-- Start HTML form -->
<form action="fahrenheit_calculation.php" method="post">
<fieldset style="width:25%;"><legend>Convert To
Fahrenheit</legend><br>
  <table width="99%" border="0">
    <tr>
      <td width="15%" nowrap>Enter Value for Centigrade:</td>
      <td width="85%" colspan="2"> <input type="text"
       name="centigradeValue" value="<?php echo $centigradeValue ?>"
       size="10"> </td>
    </tr>
    <tr>
      <td nowrap>Value for Fahrenheit:</td>
      <td colspan="2"><input type="text" readonly="readonly"
       name="fahrenheitvalue" value="<?php echo $fahrenheitvalue ?>"
       size="10"></td>
    </tr>
    <tr>
      <td>  </td>
      <td><input type="submit" name="calculateFahrenheit"
       value="Convert" align="right"></td>
    </tr>
```

Continuation of Listing 5.6: fahrenheit_calculation.php

```
</table>
</fieldset>
</form>
</body>
</html>
```

Q2. Average Inventory and Turnover

In retail sales, management needs to know the average inventory figure and the turnover of merchandise. Create a form that allows the user to enter the beginning inventory, the ending inventory, and the cost of goods sold. Include Calculate and Clear buttons on the form. You script should calculate and display the average inventory and the turnover. The formulae for average inventory and the turnover are as follows.

$$\text{Average inventory} = \frac{\textit{Beginning inventory} + \textit{Ending inventory}}{2}$$

$$\text{Turnover} = \frac{\textit{Cost of goods sold}}{\textit{Average inventory}}$$

Note: The average inventory is expressed in dollars: the turnover is the number of times the inventory turns over.

You may use the following test data to check your answers.

Test Data

Beginning	Ending	Cost of Goods Sold
58500	47000	400000
75300	13600	515400
3000	1960	48000

Results

Average Inventory	Turnover
$52,750.00	7.6
44,450.00	11.6
2,480.00	19.4

Suggested Solution:

The form design and the program listing are presented below. You may review chapter 99 on form design design tags and processing.

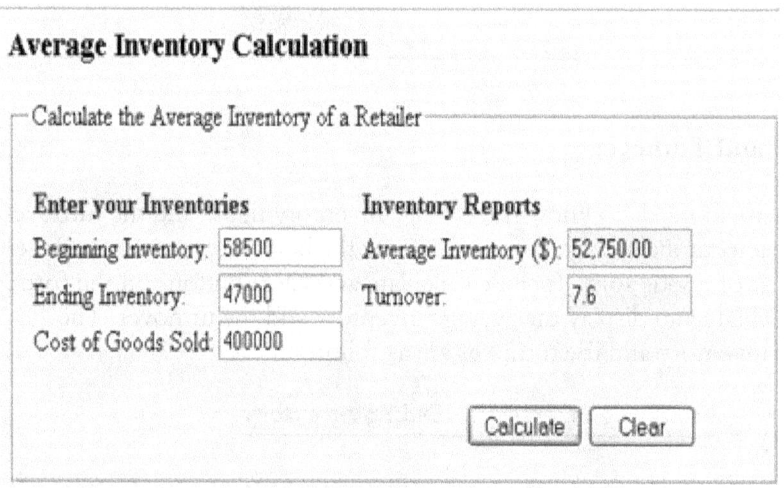

Listing 5.7: average_inventory.php

```
<html>
<body bgcolor="f3f3f3">
<h3>Average Inventory Calculation</h3>
<?php

//declare variables
$beginningInventory='';
$averageInventory='';
$endingInventory='';
$turnover='';
$goodsSold='';

// if the Calculate button is clicked
if(isset($_POST['calculate'])){

        // assign form values to variables
        $beginningInventory = $_POST['beginningInventory'];
        $endingInventory = $_POST['endingInventory'];
        $goodsSold = $_POST['goodsSold'];
```

Continuation of Listing 5.7: average_inventory.php

```
     // calculate average inventory
      $averageInventory = ($beginningInventory +
      $endingInventory)/2;

     // calculate turnover
     $turnover = $goodsSold / $averageInventory;
}

//the Clear control button
if(isset($_POST['clear'])){
     // assign empty values to variables
     $beginningInventory = '';
     $endingInventory = '';
     $goodsSold = '';
}
?>
<form action="average_inventory.php" method="post">
<fieldset style="width: 40%; ">
<legend>Calculate the Average Inventory of a Retailer </legend>
<br>
<table width="95%" border="0">
<tr>
  <td height="21" colspan="2"><font color="#660000" size="3">
      <strong>Enter your Inventories </strong></font></td>
  <td width="7%" nowrap> </td>
  <td width="11%" nowrap><font color="#660000" size="3">
      <strong>Inventory Reports</strong></font></td>
  <td width="65%"> </td>
</tr>
<tr>
  <td width="11%" nowrap><div align="left">Beginning Inventory:
      </div></td>
  <td width="6%" nowrap><input type="text" size="10"
      name="beginningInventory" value="<?php echo
      $beginningInventory ?>"></td>
  <td width="7%" nowrap> </td>
  <td width="11%" nowrap><div align="left">Average Inventory
      ($):</div></td>
```

Continuation of Listing 5.7: average_inventory.php

```
<td><input type="text" size="10" readonly="readonly"
        name="averageInventory" value="<?php echo
        number_format($averageInventory,2) ?>" ></td>
</tr>
<tr>
   <td nowrap><div align="left">Ending Inventory:</div></td>
   <td nowrap><input type="text" size="10" name="endingInventory"
       value="<?php echo $endingInventory ?>"></td>
   <td width="7%" nowrap> </td>
   <td nowrap><div align="left">Turnover:</div></td>
   <td><input type="text" size="10" readonly="readonly"
     name="turnover" value="<?php echo
     number_format($turnover,1)?>"> </td>
</tr>
<tr>
      <td nowrap><div align="left">Cost of Goods Sold:</div></td>
      <td nowrap><input type="text" size="10" name="goodsSold"
          value="<?php echo $goodsSold ?>"></td>
      <td width="7%" nowrap> </td>
      <td nowrap><div align="right"></div></td>
      <td> </td>
</tr>
<tr>
      <td colspan="5">  </td>
</tr>
<tr>
      <td>  </td>
      <td colspan="4">
          <input type="submit" name="calculate"
          value="Calculate">
          <input type="submit" name="clear" value="Clear"></td>
</tr>
</table>
</form>
</body>
</html>
```

Programming Challenge

1. Assuming that the value of $x is 21, the value of $y is 4, the value of $z is 8, fill in the missing entries in the following table.

Expression		Value
1	$x + $y >= $z	1
2	$y == $x – 2 * $z – 1	
3	6 * $x != $x	
4	$x = $y == 4	
5	($x = $y) == 4	
6	($x = 1) == 1	

Note that in boolen expressions, 0 represents **False** and 1 represents **True**.

2. Create a form and write a script that determines the future value of an investment at a given interest rate for a given number of years. The formula for the calculation is

   Future value = Investment amount * (1 + Interest rate) ^ Years

   Your script should calculate and display the future value when the user clicks on the *Calculate button.* You may use the test data below to cross-check your answers.

Test Data

Amount	Rate	Years
2000.00	.15	5
1234.56	.075	3

Results

Future Value
$4,022.71
$1,533.69

3. Assuming that the value of $x is 11, the value of $y is 6, the value of $z is 1, fill in the missing entries in the following table. Note that 0 represents False and 1 represents True.

<table>
<tr><th></th><th>Expression</th><th>Value</th></tr>
<tr><td>1</td><td>$x > 9 && $y != 3</td><td>1</td></tr>
<tr><td>2</td><td>$x == 5|| $y != 3</td><td></td></tr>
<tr><td>3</td><td>! ($x > 14)</td><td></td></tr>
<tr><td>4</td><td>! ($x > 9 && $y != 23)</td><td></td></tr>
<tr><td>5</td><td>$x <= 1 && $y == 6 || $z < 4</td><td></td></tr>
<tr><td>6</td><td>5 && $y != 8 || 0</td><td></td></tr>
</table>

6

Decision Structures

Choices in life are just 'if' statements. Based on that, your whole life may crash or run to completion.
- Assaad Chalhoub

Learning Objectives

After studying this chapter, you should be able to:

- Understand how to use **if, if … else**, and **if … elseif ….else** decision constructs.
- Know how to use **switch … case** construct.
- Apply the use of **break** keyword in decision constructs.
- Code and execute scripts relating to decision constructs.

Introduction

Decision structures consist of making choices between (two) or among (more than two) options based on testing of condition(s). In the two-alternative case, either a particular block (sequence of one or more statements) will be executed if the condition is **true**, or an alternative block will be executed if the condition is **false**. The condition may consist of relational operators (==, >, >=, <, <=, !=) and logical operators (&&, | |, !).

In this chapter we will learn how to use the following decision structures in PHP.

1. **if** Statement (simple **if** statement)
2. **if ... else** Statement (**if** with two alternatives)
3. **if ... elseif ... else** Statement (**if** with multiple alternatives)
4. **switch ... case** Statement

The `if` Statement

The **If Construct** is a way to make decisions based upon the result of a condition. For example, you might have a script that checks if a condition is **true** or **false;** if a variable contains a number or string value; if an object is empty or populated; etc. Once the condition is met, the block statements within the curly braces { } following the condition will be executed.

We can classify the **if** construct into four:

1. Simple **if**.
2. **If** with exactly two alternatives.
3. **If** with more than two alternatives.
4. Nested **if**

The simple `if` statement

In this construct only one side of the decision is tested. Nothing is done with the other side of the decision. The syntax is as follows:

```
if (condition)
{
        statements
        .....
}
```

The **if** statement is a way to make decisions based upon the result of a condition. In the syntax above, if the condition evaluates to **true**, the statements within the curly brackets will be executed. On the other hand, the statements within the curly bracket will not be executed when the condition is **false**. The program, therefore, jumps to the statement just below the closing bracket.

We shall now take a look at the following examples. In the example below, the condition will evaluate to **true.** As such, Sunday will be displayed on the screen. Notice that there is no option for any other alternative.

Example 1:

```
$day = 1;
if ($day == 1)
{
   $description = 'Sunday';
   echo $description;
}
```

The if ... else Statement

We use this when there are two options. We use the **if .. else** statement to execute a block of statements if a logical condition is **true**. Once the condition is **not true**, the block within the **else** braces will be executed. This means that the condition is **false**. The syntax for **if ..else** statement is as follows on the next page.

The condition can be any expression that evaluates to **true** or **false**. If the condition evaluates to **true**, **statements1** is executed; otherwise, **statements2** is executed.

```
if (condition)
{
        statements1
}
else
{
        statements2
}
```

Example 2:

The following example determines whether a student has passed an exam or not with a pass mark of 50.

In the example, the student has scored 49, which is stored in $mark variable. The conditional statement checks whether the student scores more than or equal to 50. If so, the **echo** command prints **Passed**, otherwise it prints **Failed**.

Listing 6.1: if.php

```
<?php

    // mark scored by the student
    $mark = 49;

    // check whether student scores more than or equal to 50
    if ($mark >= 50)
    {
        echo "Passed <br />";
    }
    // if student scores less than 50, print Failed
    else
    {
        echo "Failed <br />";
    }
?>
```

The `if .. elseif .. else` Statement

You may also compound the statements using **elseif** to have multiple conditions tested in sequence. You should use this construction if you want to select one of many sets of conditions to execute.

The syntax is as follows.

```
if (condition1)
{
        statement1
}
[elseif (condition2)
{
        Statement2
}]
...
...
...
[elseif (condition n-1)
{
        Statement n-1
}]
[else {
        Statement n
}]
```

Note that items in the square bracket [ ] are optional.

Example 3:

This example uses the **`elseif`** variant of the **`if`** statement. This allows us to test for other conditions if the first one is not **true**. The program will test each condition in sequence until:

- It finds one that is **true**. In this case it executes the code for that condition.
- It reaches an **else** statement. In which case it executes the code in the **else**

statement.

- It reaches the end of the **if ... elseif ... else** structure. In this case it moves to the next statement after the conditional structure.

Listing 6.2: elseif.php

```
<?php

  // mark scored by the student
  $mark = 49;

  // check whether student scores more than or equal to 80
  if($mark >= 80)
  {
        echo "Passed: Grade A <br />";
  }
  // check whether student scores more than or equal to 70
  elseif($mark >= 70)
  {
        echo "Passed: Grade B <br />";
  }
  // check whether student scores more than or equal to 60
  elseif($mark >= 60)
  {
        echo "Passed: Grade C <br />";
  }
  // if student scores less than 60, print Failed
  else
  {
        echo "Failed <br />";
  }

?>
```

Combining if ... elseif ... else with Logical Operators

The multiple **if** statement can be combined with the logical operators as in the following example.

Listing 6.3: if_elseif_else.php

```
<?php

   // declare variable
   $mark  = 55 ;

   // determine whether $mark is outside the range 0-100
   if($mark >=100 || $mark < 0)
   {
        print "Mark out off range. Mark must be from 0-100";
   }
   elseif($mark >= 70 && $mark <= 100)
   {
        print "Grade is A";
   }
   elseif($mark  >=60 && $mark <= 69)
   {
        print "Grade is B";
   }
   elseif($mark  >=50 && $mark <= 59)
   {
        print "Grade is C";
   }
   else
   {
        print "Grade is F";
   }
?>
```

The Nested `if` Statement

When an **if** statement is inside another **if** statement, it is known as **nested if** statement. The syntax for nested if statement is as follows:

```
if(condition)
{
        if (condition) {
                statements
        }
        else
        {
                statements
        }
else
{
    statements
}
```

Let us look at the following example.

Listing 6.4: nested_if.php

```
<?php

$age = 55;

// determine whether age is in the range 10-50
if (age >= 10 && age <= 50)
{
    // determine whether age is in the range 10-18
    if(age >= 10 && age <= 18)
    {
        print "You are a Teenage";
    }
    // means age is outside the range 10-18 but within 10-50
    else
    {
        print "You are not a Teenager";
    }
}
else
{
    // means age is outside the range 10-50
    print "You are more than 50 years";
}

?>
```

The `switch...case` Statement

In addition to the **if statements** discussed in the previous section, PHP includes another type of conditional construct called the **switch** statement. The **switch** statement is very similar or an alternative to the **if...elseif...else** commands. The **switch** statement will test a condition. The outcome of that test will decide which option to execute. The **switch** is normally used when you are testing for an exact (equal) value instead of testing for a greater or less than value. When testing a range of values, the **if** statement should be used. However, **switch** statement can also handle range of values in the test condition.

A **switch** statement allows a program to evaluate an expression and attempt to match the expression's value to a **case label**. If a match is found, the program executes the associated statement(s). As in the syntax below, the program first looks for a **case** clause with a label matching the value of expression and then transfers control to that clause; executing the associated statements. If no matching label is found, the program looks for the optional **default** clause, and if found, transfers control to that clause; executing the associated statements. If no default clause is found, the program continues execution at the statement following the end of **switch**. Use **break** to prevent the code from running into the next **case** block automatically.

The syntax for the switch statement is as follows:

```
switch (expression)
{
    case label1:
            statements1
            [break;]

    case label2:
            statements2
            [break;]
            .....
            .....
    default:
            statements_n
            [break;]
}
```

Next a series of **case** statements are called to compare the expression to other values. These values are placed immediately after the **case** statement (NOTE: if the values being tested are strings, they should be enclosed in quotation marks). The value being compared to the expression is followed by a colon (:). **Case** statements are similar to the **if** and **elseif** constructs. If a **case** statement is **true**, any code associated with the statement is executed and the **break** statement is executed. The **break** statement forces the **switch** statement to terminate. In this case, no remaining cases will be evaluated. Finally, the **switch** statement includes a **default** case. This is similar to the **else** statement. If none of the **case** statements evaluate to **true**, the **default** statement is executed.

Like the **if** statement, lines of code within the **switch** statement are enclosed within curly braces. The braces define the beginning and end of the **switch** statement. Listing 6.5 and Listing 6.6 demonstrate the use of the **switch** statement.

Listing 6.5: switch_case1.php

```
<?php

// declare variable with initial value
$taxRate = 0.25;

// assign the initial value to the switch
switch ($taxRate) {

    // case 1
    case 0.17:
            echo "The tax rate is $taxRate ";
            break;

    // case 2
    case 0.25:
            echo "The tax rate is $taxRate ";
            break;

    // case n
    default:
            echo "The tax rate is not 0.17 or 0.25";
}
?>
```

A **switch** statement can include many cases. In Listing 6.5, two cases are shown. A variable **$taxrate** is created and assigned the value 0.25. The **switch** statement is used to compare the value of **$taxrate** against other values (0.17, 0.25). The expression to be tested or compared (in this case **$taxrate**) is placed inside of parenthesis immediately following the **switch** statement. Because the value of the **$taxrate** is equal to the case 0.25, "The tax rate is 0.25" will be printed, as shown below.

Figure 6.1

This is the output from the above script.

The tax rate is 0.25

In addition to simple equality you can also test the expression for other conditions, such as greater than and less than relationships. The expression you are testing against must be stated in the **case** statement. Let us take a look at the Listing 6.6. If an expression successfully evaluates to the values specified in more than one case statement, only the first one encountered will be executed. Once a match is made, PHP stops looking for more matches. This is accomplished through the **break** statement. Because none of the cases satisfies the expression ($initValue), the **default** block will be executed, producing the result below.

Listing 6.6: switch_case2.php

```
<?php

// set the initial value
$initValue = 3;

// initial value as expression in the switch statement
switch ($initValue)
{
    case 0:
        echo "Zero is unacceptable as the initial
        value.";
        break;
```

Continuation of Listing 6.6: switch_case2.php

```
    // test whether $initValue is less than 0
    case $initValue < 0:
        echo "Negative values are not allowed.";
        break;

    // test whether $initValue is less than 3
    case $initValue < 3:
        echo "These values are not allowed.";
        break;

    // test whether $initValue is greater than 3
    case $initValue > 3:
        echo "These values are not allowed.";
        break;

    /* if all the above conditions failed, then execute
        the default option */
    default:
        echo "These values are acceptable.";
        break;
}
?>
```

Figure 6.2
The output from the above script.

```
These values are acceptable.
```

Now, let us look at an example where you can execute a specific code block if the variable is one of multiple specific values. Here is an example.

Listing 6.7: switch_case3.php

```
<?php

// set the initial value
$day = 3;
switch($day)
{
```

Continuation of Listing 6.7: switch_case3.php

```
    // day 1 (Sunday) and day 7 (Saturday)
    case 1:
    case 7:
         echo "Non-working days.";
         break;
    case 2:
    case 3:
    case 4:
    case 5:
    case 6:
           echo "Official working days.";
    break;

    default:
    echo "Invalid.";
    break;
}
?>
```

We can rewrite **Listing 6.3** as follows. Notice that the opening braces are replaced with a colon and the final closing brace is replaced by **endif**.

Listing 6.8: end_if.php

```
<?php

// declare variable with initial value
$mark = 55;
if($mark >=  100 || $mark < 0 ):
    print "Mark out off range. Mark must be from 0 to
         100";
elseif($mark >= 70 && $mark <= 100):
    print "Grade is A";
elseif($mark >= 60 && $mark <= 69):
    print "Grade is B";
elseif($mark >= 50 && $mark <= 59):
    print "Grade is C";
else:
    print "Grade is F";
endif;
?>
```

The syntax for **switch** and **endswitch** is shown below.

```
switch (expression):

  case label1:
            statements1;
            [break;]

  case label2:
            statements2;
            [break;]

  default:
            statements_n;
            [break;]

endswitch;
```

Our previous example (**Listing 6.5**) can be re-coded as follows. Once again, notice that the opening braces are replaced with a colon and the final closing brace is replaced by **endswitch**.

Listing 6.9: end_switch.php

```php
<?php

$taxRate = 0.25;

switch ($taxRate):
  case 0.17:
         echo "The tax rate is $taxRate ";
         break;

  case 0.25:
         echo "The tax rate is $taxRate ";
         break;

  default:
         echo "The tax rate is not 0.17 or 0.25";

endswitch;

?>
```

Detailed Examples

Q1. Bank Charges

A bank charges $10 per month, plus the following cheque fees for a commercial checking account:

$0.10 each for less than 20 cheques
$0.08 each for 20 through 39 cheques
$0.06 each for 40 through 59 cheques
$0.04 each for 60 or more cheques

Create a form that allows the user to enter the number of cheques written. Your script should compute and display the bank's service fees for the month.

Input validation: Do not accept a negative value for the number of cheques written. Use the following set of test data to determine whether your script is calculating properly:

Number of Checks	Total Fees
15	$11.50
25	$12.00
45	$12.70
75	$13.00

Suggested Solution:

Figure 6.3 shows the form created by HTML tags. In this example two buttons are used to illustrate the use of both switch and if constructs.

Figure 6.3
The form and test output from the script. The PHP and HTML are listed below in Listing 6.10.

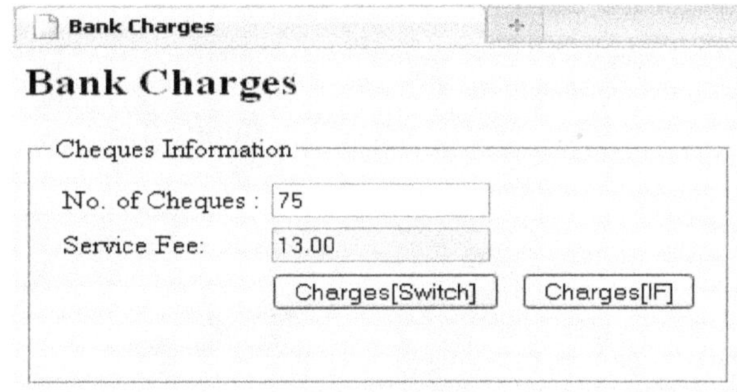

Listing 6.10: bank_charges.php

```
<html>
<head>
</head>
<body bgcolor="f3f3f3">
<h2>Bank Bank Charges </h2>

<?php

// declare variables
$noofCheques='';
$serviceFee='';
$checkingFee='';

// 1. Using Switch
// check whether the user clicks on the Switch button.
if(isset($_POST['calculateChargesSwitch'])){
 // assign form values to variables
 $noofCheques = $_POST['noofCheques'];

 // assign the fixed monthly amount to a variables
 $fixedChargePerMonth = 10;

 // compute bank charges using the switch statement
 switch ($noofCheques){
    //cheques less than 0
    case $noofCheques < 0:
       echo "Cheques written cannot be negative";
       break;

    //cheques less or equal to 20
    case $noofCheques >= 0 && $noofCheques < 20:
       $checkingFee = $noofCheques * 0.10;
        // calculate the monthly service fees
       $serviceFee = $checkingFee + $fixedChargePerMonth;
       break;

    //cheques between 20 & 39
    case $noofCheques >= 20 && $noofCheques <= 39:
       $checkingFee = $noofCheques * 0.08;
```

Continuation of Listing 6.10: bank_charges.php

```
        // calculate the monthly service fees
        $serviceFee = $checkingFee + $fixedChargePerMonth;
        break;

    //cheques between 40 & 59
    case $noofCheques >= 40 && $noofCheques <= 59:
        $checkingFee = $noofCheques * 0.06;
        // calculate the monthly service fees
        $serviceFee = $checkingFee + $fixedChargePerMonth;
        break;

    //cheques more than 60
    case $noofCheques >= 60:
        $checkingFee = $noofCheques * 0.04;
        // calculate the monthly service fees
        $serviceFee = $checkingFee + $fixedChargePerMonth;
        break;

    // if none of the conditions is satisfied
    default:
        echo "Invalid!";
  }
}
// 2. Using IF. Check whether the user clicks on the IF
button.
if(isset($_POST['calculateChargesIF'])){
    // assign form values to variables
    $noofCheques = $_POST['noofCheques'];
    // assign the fixed monthly amount to a variables
    $fixedChargePerMonth = 10;
        //cheques entered is negative
        if($noofCheques < 0)
        {
            echo "Cheques written cannot be negative";
        }
```

Continuation of Listing 6.10: bank_charges.php

```
        //cheques between 0 & 19
        elseif($noofCheques >= 0 && $noofCheques < 20)
        {
            $checkingFee = $noofCheques * 0.10;
            $serviceFee = $checkingFee + $fixedChargePerMonth;
        }
        //cheques between 20 & 39
        elseif($noofCheques >= 20 && $noofCheques <= 39)
        {
            $checkingFee = $noofCheques * 0.08;
            // calculate the monthly service fees
            $serviceFee = $checkingFee + $fixedChargePerMonth;
        }
        //cheques between 40 & 59
        elseif($noofCheques >= 40 && $noofCheques <= 59)
        {
            $checkingFee = $noofCheques * 0.06;
            // calculate the monthly service fees
            $serviceFee = $checkingFee + $fixedChargePerMonth;
        }
        //cheques more than 60
        elseif($noofCheques >= 60)
        {
            $checkingFee = $noofCheques * 0.04;
            // calculate the monthly service fees
            $serviceFee = $checkingFee + $fixedChargePerMonth;
        }
        // if none of the conditions is satisfied
        else
        {
            echo "Invalid!";
        }
}
?>
```

Continuation of Listing 6.10: bank_charges.php

```
<!-- the form starts here. The form action calls itself
'bank_charges.php' -->
<form action="bank_charges.php" method="post">
<fieldset style="width: 30%; "><legend>Cheques
Information</legend>
<table width="60%" border="0" cellspacing="5">
<tr>
      <td width="26%" nowrap>No. of Cheques :</td>
      <td width="74%"> <input name="noofCheques" type="text"
      value="<?php echo $noofCheques ?>" size="15"></td>
</tr>
<tr>
      <td nowrap>Service Fee:</td>
      <td><input type="text" name="serviceFee"
      readonly="readonly"
      value="<?php echo $serviceFee ?>" size="15"></td>
</tr>
<tr>
      <td nowrap> </td>
      <td><input type="submit" name="calculateChargesSwitch"
      value="Charges[Switch]">  
      <input type="submit" name="calculateChargesIF"
      value="Charges[IF]"></td>
</tr>
</table>
</fieldset>
</form>
</body>
</html>
```

Q2. Students' Assessment

A student is assigned a grade A, B, C, D, F according to the following rule:

test score $\geq$ 90 grade is A
80$\leq$ test score $<$ 90 grade is B
70$\leq$ test score $<$ 80 grade is C

$60 \leq$ test score $<$ 70 grade is D
test score $<$ 60 grade is F

Write a script that prints students' names and grades based on the test score.

Suggested Solution:

Figure 6.4
The form and test output from the script. The PHP script and HTML tags are listed below in Listing 6.11.

Students Grade Calculation

Enter Student's Record

Enter Student's Name: Akua Ansaba
Enter Score: 67

Student's Name: Akua Ansaba
Grade: D
Display Grade

Listing 6.11: students_grade.php

```
<html>
<head>
<title>Grade Calculation</title>
</head>
<body bgcolor="f3f3f3">
<h3>Students Grade Calculation</h3>

<?php

   // declare variables
   $studentName='';
   $Score='';
   $studentNameDisplay='';
   $Grade='';
```

Continuation of Listing 6.11: students_grade.php

```
// if the Display Grade control button is clicked
if(isset($_POST['displayGrade'])){

    // assign form values to variables
    $studentName=$_POST['studentName'];
    $Score=$_POST['Score'];

    //check the student's score and compute the grade
    if($Score >= 90 && $Score <= 100)
    {
        $Grade = 'A';
    }
    elseif($Score >= 80 && $Score < 90)
    {
        $Grade = 'B';
    }
    else if($Score >= 70 && $Score < 80)
    {
        $Grade = 'C';
    }
   else if($Score >= 60 && $Score < 70)
    {
        $Grade = 'D';
    }
    else if($Score < 60 )
    {
        $Grade = 'F';
    }
    else
    {
        // error message for invalid score
        echo "Error! Invalied Score Entered";
    }

    //assign student's name to the Display text field
    $studentNameDisplay = $studentName;
}?>
```

Continuation of Listing 6.11: students_grade.php

```
<form action="students_grade.php" method="post">
<fieldset style="width: 30%; "><legend>Enter Student's
Record</legend>
<table width="95%" border="0">
<tr>
      <td width="21%" height="21" nowrap>Enter Student's
       Name:</td>
      <td width="79%" nowrap><input type="text"
       name="studentName" value="<?php echo $studentName ?>"
       size="30"></td>
</tr>
<tr>
      <td height="21">Enter Score:</td>
      <td height="21"><input type="text" name="Score"
       value="<?php echo $Score ?>"
      size="10"></td>
</tr>
<tr>
      <td height="21"> </td>
      <td height="21"> </td>
</tr>
<tr>
      <td width="21%" height="21">Student's Name:</td>
      <td width="79%"><input type="text"
       name="studentNameDisplay"
       value="<?php echo $studentNameDisplay ?>"
       size="30"readonly= "readonly"></td>
</tr>
<tr>
      <td height="21">Grade:</td>
      <td height="21"><input type="text" name="Grade"
       value="<?php echo $Grade ?>"
       size="10" readonly="readonly"></td>
</tr>
```

Continuation of Listing 6.11: students_grade.php

```
<tr>
        <td height="21"> </td>
        <td height="21"><input type="submit" name="displayGrade"
        value=" Display Grade " size="10"></td>
</tr>
</table>
</fieldset>
</form>
</body>
</html>
```

Programming Challenge

1. Use both the **if...elseif...else** and the **switch...case** constructs to write a script to perform the following task. The script should test the student's score and assign a letter grade based on the following grading system:

Test score	Letter Grade
90 or greater	A
80 through 89	B
70 through 79	C
60 through 69	D
below 60	F

2. Using the **switch case** construct, write a script that implements the conditions set in the following table.

Age	Risk Factor
≤ 2	.03
> 2 and < 10	.07
≥ 10 and ≤ 30	.15
> 30	.12

3. An automobile insurance company uses a customer's risk factors to compute the premium for the customer's policy. As an intermediate step, it computes a "risk rate" based on the customer's age and sex.

	Risk Rate	
Age	Male	Female
<= 18	0.34	0.26
>18 and < 21	0.28	0.22
>= 21	0.22	0.18

By using the **nested if** construct, write a script that determines and displays the risk rate for the customer, given the customer's sex and age (use your own values for sex and age. eg $sex="Female" and $age=20).

4. A university uses the following tuition table to determine a student's semester tuition.

	Nationality Status	
	Residence (GHc)	Foreign (GHc)
Undergraduate	1000	1500
Graduate	1700	2275
Professional	1800	2100

Assume that a variable called $*resStatus* holds the value 1 for residence students and the value 2 for foreign students. Also, assume that you have a variable $*classStanding* that holds 1 for undergraduates, 2 for graduates, and 3 for professional students. Given this information, write scripts to assign (pick your own values) the student's class standing ($*classStanding*) and residential status ($*resStatus*). Determine and output the appropriate tuition of the student based on the current $*classStanding and $resStatus.*

5. Write a script that allows the user to provide the price of an item and the quantity. The script should compute and display the gross sales amount (price * quantity), the discount, and the net sales amount. The discount should be computed using the table shown below.

Quantity	Discount
0 – 100	0%
101 – 250	4%
251 – 1000	7%
1001 +	10%

6. A long-distance telephone operator charges the following rates for telephone calls:

Rate Category	**Rate per Minute**
Daytime	$0.06
Evening	$0.11
Night	$0.04

Write a script that allows the user to select a rate category (from a set of radio buttons), and enter the number of minutes of the call, then displays the charges.

7

Performing Repetitive Tasks

while(true) and keep programming - Assaad Chalhoub

Learning Objectives

After studying this chapter, you should be able to:

- Understand how to write scripts to perform repetitive tasks.
- Learn how to use **while … loop, do … while, for. ..loop,** and **foreach … loop**.
- Apply the use of **break** and **continue** keywords in looping statements.
- Code and execute scripts relating to repetitive tasks.

Introduction

In programming, we often want to repeat the same block of code a given number of times, or until a certain condition is met. This can be accomplished using looping statements. There are two major groups of looping statements. These are the **for** and the **while** statements. The **for** statement is best used when you want to perform a loop a specific number of times. The **while** statement is best used to perform a task for an undetermined number of times. In addition, you can use the **break** and **continue** statements within looping statements. In this chapter we shall look at the following looping constructs:

- The **while** Loop
- The **do … while** Loop
- The **for** Loop
- The **foreach** Loop

The While Loop

The **while** statement executes a block of code if and as long as a specified condition evaluates to **true**. If the condition becomes **false**, the statements within the loop stop executing and control passes to the statement following the loop.

While Loop Syntax

The **while** loop syntax is as follows:

```
while (condition)
{
   code block to be run inside loop
   .......
}
```

The code within a **while** loop will repeatedly execute as long as the condition at the beginning of the loop evaluates to **true**. The code block associated with the while statement is always enclosed within the **{** and **}** closing brace symbols.

The **while** loops are most often used to process or display a list of records from the database table where there is no known limit to the number of records selected from the table. In that case the syntax will look like:

```
while (if there are still rows to read from a table)
{
    process the row fetched;
    move to the next row(record);
}
```

While Loop Examples

We shall now take a look at the following examples.

Example 1: Print numbers in Reverse Order from 5 to 2 Using the While Loop

The following example demonstrates a while loop that continues to execute as long as the variable **$number** is greater than or equal to 2, but less than or equal to 5.

Listing 7.1: while_loop_example1.php

```
<?php

    // declare variable and assig value
    $number = 5;

    // looping
    while ($number >= 2)
    {
        // output values: 5432
        echo $number;
        $number -= 1;
    }

?>
```

In the above example, the variable **$number** is initialized to 5. The while loop executes as long as the condition, **($number >=2)**, or **$number** is greater than or equal to 2. The value of **$number** is printed to the browser window. At the end of each loop block, the value of **$number** is decreased by 1.

The output generated by the **while** loop is: **5432**

During the first run, the value of **$number** is equal to 5. Since 5 is greater than 2, the echo statement is used to display the value 5. Next, the value of **$number** is decreased by 1. During the second iteration, the value of **$number** is equal to 4. Since 4 is greater than 2, the echo statement displays the value 4. This process continues while the value of $number is 3 and 2. When **$number** is equal to 2, the echo statement displays the value 2 and the value of **$number** is then decreased to 1. Since 1 is not greater than or equal to 2, the condition is no longer true and the while loop ends.

Example 2: Print Numbers from 0 to 5 in Ascending Order Using the While Loop

This example defines a loop that starts with **$i=0**. The loop will continue to run as long as the variable **$i** is less than, or equal to 5. It will increase by 1 each time the loop runs:

Listing 7.2: while_loop_example2.php

```
<?php

    // initialize the variable
    $i=0;

    // start the looping
    while ($i <= 5)
    {
            // output values from 0 to 5
            echo "The number is ".$i."<br />";
            $i++;
    }

?>
```

In the above example, you can see that the loop is run until the value of **$i** is less than or equal to 5 according to the condition in the loop. The **$i ++** statement increments the value of **$i** by 1 on each iteration of the while loop.

Figure 7.1
Print numbers from 0 to 5 in ascending order using the **while … loop**

The number is 0
The number is 1
The number is 2
The number is 3
The number is 4
The number is 5

Example 3: Print Decimal Numbers from 0.5 to 5.5 Using the While Loop

Here is an example with decimal numbers. This prints decimal numbers from 0.5 to 5.5 in steps of 1.0

Listing 7.3: while_loop_example3.php

```
<?php

 // declare a variable 'i' and assign an initial value to 'i'
 $i = 0.5;

 while ($i <= 5.5)
 {
    // output values from 0.5 to 5.5 in steps of 1.0
    printf("%.1f<br>", $i);
    $i = $i + 1.0;
 }

?>
```

Figure 7.2
Printing of decimal numbers from 0.5 to 5.5 in steps of 1.0

0.5
1.5
2.5
3.5
4.5
5.5

Example 4: Populate Drop-Down Lists of Day, Month and Year Using the While Loop

We shall now consider a more useful example which creates drop-down lists of days, months and years using array. Arrays will be discussed in the subsequent chapters.

Listing 7.4: while_loop_example4.php

```
<html>
<body bgcolor="#F5F5F5">

<?php

// create array $month and assign months of the year
$month = array( "January", "February", "March", "April",
"May","June","July", "August", "September", "October",
"November", "December");

// create a drop-down list and display the days of the month
echo "<Select Day=\"day\">";
$i = 1;
while ($i <= 31) {
   echo "<option value=".$i.">".$i."</option>";
   $i++;
}
echo "</select>";

/* create a drop-down list and display the months using
numeric array index */
echo "<Select Month=\"month\">";
$i = 0;
while ($i <= 11) {
   echo "<option value=".$i.">".$month[$i]."</option>";
   $i++;
}
echo "</select>";

/* create a drop-down list and display the years from 1960 to
date */
echo "<Select Year=\"year\">";
$fromYear = 1960;
$currentYear =date('Y');
```

Continuation of Listing 7.4: while_loop_example4.php

```
while ($fromYear <= $currentYear) {
    echo "<option value=".$fromYear.">".$fromYear."</option>";
    $fromYear++;
}
echo "</select>";
?>

</body>
</html>
```

Make sure the condition in a loop eventually becomes **false;** otherwise, the loop will never terminate, resulting in what is referred to as an indefinite loop..

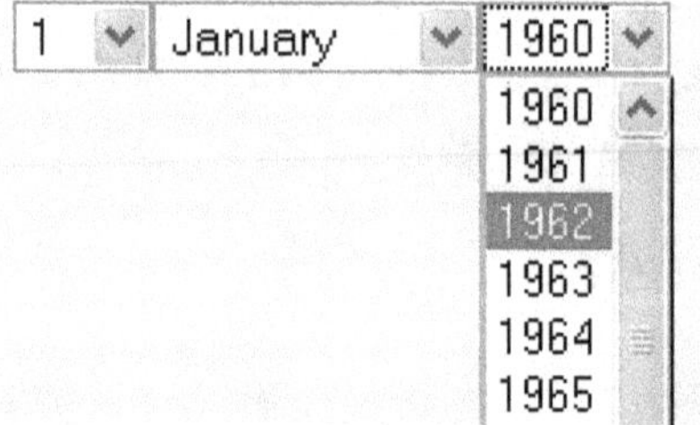

Figure 7.3
Populating drop-down lists of Day, Month and Year using the **while … loop**

The `while` Loop with `break` Statement

We can use the **break** statement to stop the loop from executing. Sometimes when we are working with loops, we want to break the loop when a certain condition is true. For example, we might want to break our loop when $i reaches 3. Let us look at the example in Listing 7.5.

Listing 7.5: while_loop_example5.php

```
<?php

 $i=0;
 while($i <= 50)
 {
   if($i == 3)
   {
       // come out from the loop
       break;
   }

   // output values from 0 to 2
   echo "The number is $i<br />";
   $i++;
 }
?>
```

Figure 7.4
In this example, we break the loop when **$i** reaches 3.

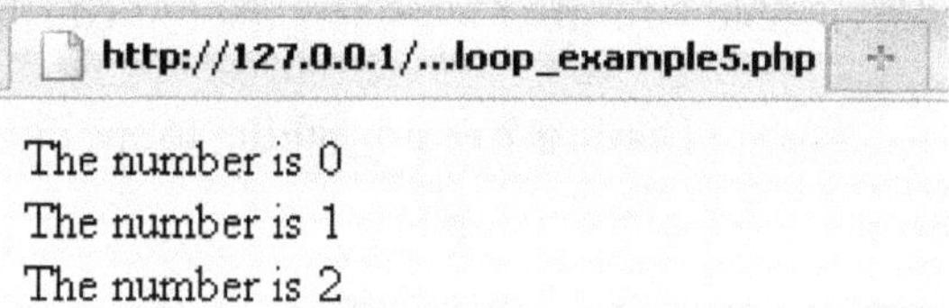
http://127.0.0.1/...loop_example5.php
The number is 0
The number is 1
The number is 2

The do...while Loop

The **do...while** loop is similar in nature to the **do** loop discussed in the previous section. The key difference is that the body of the **do...while** loop is guaranteed to run at least once. This is possible because the conditional statement is evaluated at the end of the loop statement after the loop body is performed.

The do...while Loop Syntax

The **do...while** loop syntax is as follows:

```
do
{
   code to be executed;
}
while(condition);
```

The do…while Loop Examples

Let us take a look at the following examples.

Example 1: Print numbers in Reverse Order from 5 to 1 Using the Do...While Loop

The following example demonstrates a **Do…While** loop that continues to execute as long as the variable **$number** is greater than or equal to 1 but less than or equal to 5

Listing 7.6: do_while_loop_example1.php

```
<?php

$number = 5;
 do
 {
      // output values from 5 to 1
      echo $number . "<br/>";
      // decrease the value of $number by 1
      $number -= 1;

 }while($number >= 1);

?>
```

Figure 7.5
Printing of numbers in reverse order from 5 to 1 using the do…while loop.

5
4
3
2
1

During the first run, the value of **$number** is equal to 5. Since the condition for a **do** loop is not checked until after the loop has run once, the value of **$number**, 5 is displayed. Next, the value of **$number** is decremented by 1, becoming 4. Since 4 is greater than 1, the loop runs again and during the second iteration the **echo** statement is used to display the value 4. A <br/> is concatenated to the display to create a carriage return each time the loop is processed. This process continues while the value of **$number** is greater than 1. When **$number** is equal to 1, the **echo** statement displays the value 1 and the value of **$number** is then decremented by 1. Since 0 is not greater than or equal to 1, the condition is no longer true and the **while** loop ends.

Example 2: **Print Numbers from 0 to 10 in Ascending Order Using the `Do...While` Loop**

The example below will increment the value of **$i** at least once, and it will continue incrementing the variable **$i** as long as it has a value of less than or equal to 10:

Listing 7.7: do_while_loop_example2.php
```
<?php

    $i = 0;

    do
    {
        // output values from 0 to 10
        echo "The number is $i<br/>";
        $i++;

    }while($i <= 10);

?>
```

Figure 7.6
Printing of numbers from 0 to 10 in ascending order using the do…while loop.

```
The number is 0
The number is 1
The number is 2
The number is 3
The number is 4
The number is 5
The number is 6
The number is 7
The number is 8
The number is 9
The number is 10
```

The `for` Loop

In this section we are going to cover the use of **for** loop in PHP. The **for** loop statement is used when you know how many times you want to execute a statement or a list of statements. For this reason, the **for** loop is also known as a definite loop.

The `for` Loop Syntax

The syntax of the **for loop** is a bit more complex, though **for** loop is often more convenient than **while** loop. The **for** loop syntax is as follows:

```
for (initialization; condition; increment/decrement)
{

      code to be executed;

}
```

The **for** loop has three statements in the parenthesis:

initialization	- This initializes a counter variable to a number value.
condition	- This sets a condition (a maximum or minimum number value) until the counter is reached.
increment/decrement	- This sets a value by how much we want the counter variable to be increased/decreased.

The `for` Loop Examples

Let us look at some examples to see how to use the **for** loop in PHP.

Example 1: Print Numbers from 0 to 10 Using the `for` Loop

Listing 7.8: for_loop_example1.php

```
<html>
<body bgcolor="#F5F5F5">

<?php

for($i=0; $i<=10; $i=$i+1)
{
      // output values from 0 to 10
      echo $i." ";
}

?>

</body>
</html>
```

Figure 7.7
Printing of numbers from 0 to 10 using the **for … loop**.

0 1 2 3 4 5 6 7 8 9 10

In the above example, we set a counter variable $i to 0. In the second statement of the **for loop**, we set the conditional value to the counter variable $i to 10, i.e. the loop will execute until $i reaches 10. In the third statement, we set $i to increase by 1.

Note: The third increment statement can be set to increase by any number. In our above example, we can set $i to increase by 2, i.e., $i=$i+2. In that case the code will produce 0 2 4 6 8 10.

Example 2: Print Numbers from 10 to 0 Using the `for` Loop

What if we want to go backwards, that is, print numbers from 0 to 10 in reverse order? We simple initialize the counter variable $i to 10, set its condition to 0 and decrease $i by 1.

Listing 7.9: for_loop_example2.php

```
<html>
<body bgcolor="#F5F5F5">

<?php

    /* declare and initialize variable,
    set the ending and decrement value */
    for($i=10; $i>=0; $i=$i-1)
    {
        // output values from 10 to 0
        echo $i." ";
    }

?>

</body>
</html>
```

Figure 7.8
The above code will output numbers from 10 to 0 as shown.

10 9 8 7 6 5 4 3 2 1 0

Example 3: Print Table with Alternate Colors

Let us have a look at an interesting example of a **for** loop. You have often seen tables cell with alternate colors on different websites. So, let us say we want to print the numbers in a table with alternate background colors. This is how we would do it.

Listing 7.10: for_loop_example3.php

```
<html>
<body bgcolor="#F5F5F5">

<?php

echo "<table width=100>";

for($i=0; $i<=5; $i=$i+1)
{
    if($i % 2 == 0)
    {
        /* if $i is even, print the value with pink  color
        background */
         echo "<tr>";
         echo "<td bgcolor=pink>";
         echo $i;
         echo "</td>";
         echo "</tr>";
    }
    else
    {
        /* if $i is odd, print the value with green color
        background */
         echo "<tr>";
         echo "<td bgcolor=green>";
         echo $i;
         echo "</td>";
         echo "</tr>";
    }
}
echo "</table>";

?>

</body>
</html>
```

The above code sets different background colors to the table cells depending on the value of **$i**. If **$i** is divisible by 2, which means it is even then pink color is displayed, otherwise green color is displayed.

Figure 7.9
Printing table with alternate colors using PHP for … loop.

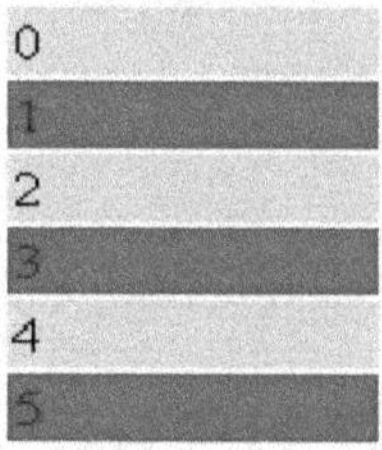

Example 4: Print Multiplication Table from 2 through 12 With the Nested Loop

The following example generates a multiplication table 2 through 12.

Listing 7.11: for_loop_example4.php

```
<html>
<body bgcolor="#F5F5F5">
<?php

echo "<h3>Multiplication table</h3>";
echo "<table border=1 width=50%";

        // this is the outer loop
        for ($i = 1; $i <= 12; $i++)
        {
                echo "<tr>";
                echo "<td>".$i."</td>";

                // inner loop
                for($j = 2; $j <= 12; $j++)
                {
                    echo "<td>".$i * $j."</td>";
                }
                echo "</tr>";
        }

echo "</table>";
?>
</body>
</html>
```

Figure 7.10 Multiplication Table from 2 through 12 with Inner loop.

http://127.0.0.1/...loop_example4.php

Multiplication Table

1	2	3	4	5	6	7	8	9	10	11	12
2	4	6	8	10	12	14	16	18	20	22	24
3	6	9	12	15	18	21	24	27	30	33	36
4	8	12	16	20	24	28	32	36	40	44	48
5	10	15	20	25	30	35	40	45	50	55	60
6	12	18	24	30	36	42	48	54	60	66	72
7	14	21	28	35	42	49	56	63	70	77	84
8	16	24	32	40	48	56	64	72	80	88	96
9	18	27	36	45	54	63	72	81	90	99	108
10	20	30	40	50	60	70	80	90	100	110	120
11	22	33	44	55	66	77	88	99	110	121	132
12	24	36	48	60	72	84	96	108	120	132	144

Example 5: Print the Sum of Numbers, Even Numbers, and Odd Numbers

In this last example, we shall consider the uses of 3 variables in the **for loop**. One variable to add all the numbers from 1 to 10 and the others to add only the even numbers and odd numbers.

Listing 7.12: for_loop_example5.php

```
<?php

// assign zero to variables
$total = 0; $even = 0; $odd =0;

for($y = 1; $y <= 10; $y++)
{
        // check if the number is odd or even
        if(($y % 2) == 0)
        {
            // number is even, sum even numbers from 1 to 10
            $even = $even + $y;
        }
        else
        {
            // number is odd, sum odd numbers from 1 to 10
            $odd = $odd + $y;
        }
    // sum all numbers from 1 to 10
        $total = $total + $y;
}
```

Continuation of Listing 7.12: for_loop_example5.php

```
// print the values
echo "The Total Sum From 1 to 10: ".$total."<br />";
echo "The Sum of Even Numbers From 1 to 10: ".$even."<br/>";
echo "The Sum of Odd  Numbers From 1 to 10: ".$odd;

?>
```

Figure 7.11
Printing the sum of all numbers, even and odd numbers.

The Total Sum From 1 to 10: 55
The Sum of Even Numbers From 1 to 10: 30
The Sum of Odd Numbers From 1 to 10: 25

The `foreach` Loop

The **foreach** loop is a variation of the **for** loop and allows you to iterate over elements in an array. You will see extensive usage of **foreach** in the later chapters.

There are two different versions of the **foreach** loop. These are

Syntax 1:

```
foreach(array as $value)
{
    code to be executed;
}
```

Syntax 2:

```
foreach(array as key => $value)
{
    code to be executed;
}
```

The first type of **foreach** loop is used to loop over an array denoted by **array**. During each iteration through the loop, the current value of the array is assigned to the variable - $value and the loop counter is incremented by a value of one. Looping continues until the **foreach** loop reaches the last element or upper bound of the given array. During each loop, the value of the variable - $value can be manipulated but the original value of the array remains the same. To change the actual value of the array, it is necessary to replace the "$" symbol with the "&" symbol (refer to chapter 9 on arrays for further explanations on this). Any changes made to &value, can be assigned to the array element at the current index. The examples below will explain this into details.

The `foreach` Loop Examples

The examples below demonstrate the use of **foreach** loop with a given array.

Example 1: Print Values in an Array

The following demonstrates how the **foreach** loop is used to iterate over the values of an array:

Listing 7.13: foreach_loop_example1.php

```
<html>
<body>

<?php

// define the array with its values
$my_array = array('red','green','blue','pink' ,'violet');

// the $value is the individual contents of the array
foreach($my_array as $value)
{
    // this prints:  red green blue pink violet
    $colors  = $value . " ";
    echo $colors;
}

?>
</body>
</html>
```

During each loop, the color name associated with the current array element is assigned to a variable - **$colors**. A single space " " is also added between each of the color names for display purposes.

Figure 7.12
Printing values in an array.

red green blue pink violet

Example 2: Print Continents in a Drop-Down List using foreach Loop

In this example we want to use a drop down list to display continents. We shall use an array to store the names of the continents and use **foreach** loop in conjunction with HTML to make the drop down box. Let us have a look at the code example to see how this is done.

Listing 7.14: foreach_loop_example2.php

```
<?php

// declare an array $continents
$continents = array("Africa", "Asia", "Australia", "America",
"Europe");

// the select tag to begin dropdown list
echo "<select>";

// display the array here
foreach($continents as $value)
{
     // print the continents in drop-down list
     echo "<option name='$value'>$value</option>";
}
echo "</select>";

?>
```

Figure 7.13
Print continents in a drop-down list using **foreach** loop.

Example 3: Print the Key and Value in an Array

An alternative form of **foreach** loop gives you access to the current key:

Listing 7.15: foreach_loop_example3.php

```
<html>
<body>

<?php

// declare the array with values
$student = array('name' => 'John Baba', 'age' => 18,
'address' => 'P.O. Box 99, Accra.');

foreach($student as $key => $value)
{
    // print the current key and value pair
    echo $key." is ".$value."<br />";
}
?>

</body>
</html>
```

In this case, the key for each element is placed in **$key** and the corresponding value is placed in **$value**. The **foreach** construct does not operate on the array itself, but rather on a copy of it. During each loop, the value of the variable, **$value**, can be manipulated but the original value of the array remains the same.

Figure 7.14
Print the Key and Value in an array.

name is John Baba
age is 18
address is P.O. Box 99, Accra.

The `Break` and `Continue` Statements

The `break` Statement

The **break** statement terminates the current **while** or **for** loop and continues executing the code(if any) that follows after the loop. Optionally, you can put a number after the **break** keyword to indicate how many levels of loop structures to **break** out of. In this way, a statement buried deep in nested loops can break out of the outermost loop.

Listing 7.16 shows how to use the **break** statement:

The `continue` Statement

The **continue** statement terminates execution of the block of statements in a **while** or **for** loop and continues execution of the loop with the next iteration.

Listing 7.17 shows how to use the **continue** statement:

Listing 7.16: break.php

```
<html>
<body bgcolor="#F5F5F5">
<?php

for ($i=0; $i<=10; $i++)
{
   // break from the loop when $i is 5
   if ($i==5)
   {
      break;
   }
   // prints: 0 1 2 3 4
   echo "The number is ".$i."<br /> ";
}
// creating outer and inner loops
$i = 0;
$j = 0;
while ($i <= 10)
{
   while ($j <= 10)
   {
      // breaks out of the two while loops when $j is 5
      if ($j == 5)
      {
          break 2;
      }
         $j++;
   }
   $i++;
}
echo "The First Number is ".$i."<br />";
echo "The Second Number is ".$j."<br />";
?>
</body>
</html>
```

Figure 7.15
Use of break statement

The number is 0 The number is 1 The number is 2 The number is 3 The number is 4 The First Number is 0
The Second Number is 5

Listing 7.17: continue.php

```
<html>
<body bgcolor="#F5F5F5">

<?php

// note that 5 Will Not Print
for ($i=0; $i<=10; $i++)
{
      // if $i is 5, continue to execute the next iteration
      if($i==5)
      {
         continue;
      }

      /* this will output values: 0 1 2 3 4 6 7 8 9 10.
         the value 5 will not be printed */
      echo $i .' ' ;
}

?>

</body>
</html>
```

Figure 7.16
Use of **continue** statement.

Note that 5 Will Not Print:
0 1 2 3 4 6 7 8 9 10

Detailed Examples

Q1. Sum of Integers

Write a script that uses the **for** loop to display the sum of the integers in the interval 11 … 29.

Suggested Solution:

Listing 7.18: sum_of_integers.php

```
<html>
<body bgcolor="#F5F5F5">
<?php

// declare a variable total and assign initial value
$total = 0;

// the heading with an underline
echo "<u>Number</u>".' '."<u>Cumulating Total </u><br />";

/*
   1. $number = 11; sets the beginning value for the loop
      (initialization)
   2. $number <= 29; sets the end value of the loop
   3. $number++ sets the increment for the loop */

for($number = 11; $number <= 29; $number++ )
{
   // compute total
   $total = $total + $number;
   // display value on the screen
   echo $number."        ". $total."<br />";
}
?>
</body>
</html>
```

Figure 7.17
Sum of integers from 11 to 29.

Number	Cumulating Total
11	11
12	23
13	36
14	50
15	65
16	81
17	98
18	116
19	135
20	155
21	176
22	198
23	221
24	245
25	270
26	296
27	323
28	351
29	380

Q2. Sum of Even Numbers

Using a **for** loop, write a script that computes and prints the values of the sum 2 + 4 +...+ 100.

Suggested Solution:

Listing 7.19: sum_even_numbers.php

```
<html>
<body bgcolor="#F5F5F5">
<?php

// initialize the variable $total
$total = 0;
// create a table
echo "<table width='20'>";

/* Start the loop
   1. $i=2; sets the beginning value for the loop (initialization)
   2. $i<=100; sets the end value of the loop
   3. $i=$i+1 sets the increment for the loop */
```

Continuation of Listing 7.19: sum_even_numbers.php

```
for($i=2; $i<=100; $i=$i+1)
{
   // check even numbers
   if($i % 2 == 0)
   {
        // compute the total
        $total = $total + $i;
        // table data 1(column 1)
        echo "<tr>";
        echo "<td >";
        echo $i;
        echo "</td>";

        // table data 2(column 2)
        echo "<td>";
        echo $total;
        echo "</td>";

        echo "</tr>";
    }
}
echo "</table>";

//display the total on the screen
echo "The Total Sum of Even Numbers From 2 to 100:".$total."<br
/>";
?>

</body>
</html>
```

Figure 7.18
Sum of even numbers from 2 to 100.

```
84  1806
86  1892
88  1980
90  2070
92  2162
94  2256
96  2352
98  2450
100 2550
The Total Sum of Even Numbers From 2 to 100: 2550
```

Programming Challenge

Utility Bill

Write a script to compute customers' monthly electricity and water bills. The bill is computed as follows:

- The first 1500 gallons of water cost $0.011 per gallon.
- Each gallon over 1500 costs 0.015 per gallon.

- The first 500 kwh of electricity cost $0.044 per kwh
- 501 to 1000 kwh cost $0.065 per kwh
- More than 1000 kwh cost $0.097 kwh.

The user should enter the gallons of water and the number of kwh of electricity used along with his/her customer number. Your script should be able to compute bills for 100 users.

8

Functions

It should be noted that no ethically-trained software engineer would ever consent to write a "DestroyBaghdad" procedure. Basic professional ethics would instead require him to write a "DestroyCity" procedure, to which "Baghdad" could be given as a parameter.
- Nathaniel S. Borenstein

Learning Objectives

After studying this chapter, you should be able to:

- Understand the concepts of functions and why they are important in PHP.
- Distinguish between pre-defined and user-defined functions.
- Learn how to call a function, pass parameters to functions, and return values from functions.
- Familiarize yourself with a host of pre-defined functions such as mathematical, error, email, file, ODBC functions and how they can be used.
- Code and execute scripts relating to functions.

Introduction

A complete PHP application might contain dozens of individual script files with hundreds of lines of code in each. Within all of these, there will be many instances where the same piece of code is reused: something as simple as outputting a string to the browser or as complex as making sure users are logged in across multiple pages and prompting them for login information if they are not. As you might imagine, copying the same code to every location you need it is neither practical nor efficient. In this chapter, we will be covering functions. We will also be taking a careful look at PHP's user-defined functions before focusing on pre-defined functions.

What is a Function

In technical terms, a function is a group of instructions that perform a task. In a simpler term, a function is a block of code with a name which can be used in our code whenever we need it. In most cases, they accept input from the main script (calling program) as arguments, and return a result. They can help modularise a script by allowing the programmer to break the script down by task. They make your script portable, so if you write a useful function for one script, you can easily reuse it in another.

Types of Functions

Two types of functions have been identified: User-defined functions and Pre-defined functions (Built-in functions).

User-Defined Functions

User-defined functions are functions that you create to be used in your applications, as opposed to functions in built-in classes that perform predefined tasks. PHP allows you to write your own functions. The primary advantage of custom functions (user-defined) is reusability. If you do not write functions, you may have to write the same piece of code numerous times in your application, whether it is within the same PHP file or in another.

Built-in (Pre-Defined) Functions

One thing that makes PHP so easy to use is the wealth of built-in functions. These functions provide the tools to easily complete many of the everyday tasks you need to perform in the course of writing a full-fledged application. There are functions for working with just about everything in PHP: strings, arrays, databases, dates and times, email, numbers, even functions for working with other functions. PHP functions are numerous, as such it would be impossible to cover all of them in this chapter. However, as the chapters unfold, you will be introduced to many more commonly used ones. You can also find the complete list of PHP's built-in functions at the **www.php.net** website.

User-Defined Functions

Function Syntax

The syntax for creating a function is given below. First, we must tell PHP that we want to create a function. We do this by typing the keyword function, followed by the function name and some optional arguments (parameters) within parenthesis.

```
function function_name(parameters)
{
    block of codes
    ........
}
```

A typical function has three components to it:

- Starts with the word **`function`**.
- Has a function name followed by parentheses **( )**. A function name can only start with a letter or an underscore.
- The code block in the function normally goes inside curly brackets **{ }.**

Creating and Calling a Function

Now, let's look at how we can create a function, Listing 8.1.

In the script, we create our own function named **myfirst_function()** and we call that function by just typing its name. The script outputs **" You are becoming a PHP guru, bravo!"**.

Listing 8.1: myfirst_function.php

```
<?php

    // create a function named myfirst_function.
    function myfirst_function()
    {
            echo "You are becoming a PHP guru, bravo!";
    }

    // call the function by its name.
    myfirst_function();

?>
```

Figure 8.1
A simple example of creating and calling a PHP function without passing a parameter.

You are becoming a PHP guru, bravo!

Functions with Parameters

A function can receive values or information from the main program through the parameters. This is useful when we want to add more functionality to our functions. For example, we can modify the above function to pass a person's name and a message into it and display that information.

Listing 8.2: parameter_function.php

```
<?php

// Create a function named parameter_function.
function parameter_function($firstname, $lastname, $message)
{
        echo "$firstname $lastname, $message";
}

/* Call the function by its name and pass the value for the
parameters. */
parameter_function("John", "Baba", "You are becoming a PHP
guru, bravo!.");

?>
```

Parameters appear within the parentheses "()". They are just like the normal PHP variables.

In the above example we created a function with three parameters, **$firstname, $lastname** and **$message**. We used these parameters to send our custom arguments (values) to our function. The above example will output: **John Baba, You are becoming a PHP guru, bravo!.**

Figure 8.2
A simple example of creating and calling a PHP function by passing parameters.

John Baba, You are becoming a PHP guru, bravo!.

In our function, we can put as many parameters as we want. Parameters appear within the parentheses "()". They are like normal PHP variables.

We can have functions to return a value. So, instead of echoing or printing the value inside the function, we can have the function return that value. The value can be a string, an integer, a float value, an array or an object. We use the term **return** to return a value in a function.

We shall see an example here. In this example, you can see that a function called **calcVol** is defined, and that it receives three parameters, **$x, $y,** and **$z**. These are being used to specify the lengths of the three axes of a solid object, which the function multiplies together to determine the volume of the object. The function then returns the volume to the calling code.

Listing 8.3: volumecompute_function.php

```
<?php

 // create a function named calcVol.
 function calcVol($x, $y, $z)
 {
         $vol = $x * $y * $z;
         return $vol;
 }

 /* assign values to parameters, pass the values for the
 function and print the result */
 $length = 4;
 $width = 5;
 $height = 6;
 echo  "The volume of this object is " . calcVol($length,
 $width, $height) . "litres units.";

?>
```

The function is called from the middle of a print statement, which passes the three values contained in the variables **$length, $width** and **$height**. Thus, the **print** statement displays the result of the calculation: **The volume of this objects is 120 litres units**.

Note that a functions can only return a value once. That means you can only use the return statement once in your function.

PHP Functions Returning String Value

The following function returns a string value.

Listing 8.4: string_value_function.php

```
<?php

    // create a function name string_value_function.
    function string_value_function($name)
    {
        return "You are a guru, $name!";
    }

    /* call the function by its name and pass the value for
    the parameter */
    echo string_value_function("John Baba");

?>
```

PHP Functions Returning an Integer Value

Let us create a function to return an integer value.

Listing 8.5: integer_value_function.php

```
<?php

 // create a function name integer_value_function.
 function integer_value_function($price, $tax)
 {
        $total_price = $price + $tax;
        return $total_price;
 }

 /* call the function by its name and pass the values of the
parameters */
 echo "Total Cost is " . integer_value_function(120, 10);

?>
```

Figure 8.3
A simple PHP function returning an integer value.

Total Cost is 130

In the above function we calculate the total price and return it. The code outputs **Total Cost is: 130**.

When the function is called and finished executing, the value returned to the main program would be held in the name of the function. To capture this value, you can set a variable and assign the function name to it. Something like:

$variable = function_name();

We can demonstrate this by using a simple function that returns the product of two integers.

Listing 8.6: number_product.php

```
<?php

// create a function name number_product.
function number_product($number1, $number2){
        $total = $number1 * $number2;
        return $total;
}

/* store the result of number_product function in
$number_product. */
$number_product = number_product(7,3);
echo "The result is = " . $number_product . "<br />";

?>
```

We set the variable **$number_product** equal to the function **number_product()**. In this case, the result was 7 * 3 = 21, which was successfully stored in **$number_product** and displayed to the screen. The output would be: **The result is = 21**.

PHP 7 Return Type Declarations

A new feature, known as Return Type Declaration, has been introduced in PHP 7. Return type declaration specifies the type of value that a function should return. The following return types can be declared.

- int
- float
- bool
- string
- interfaces
- array
- callable

Let us consider the following example.

```
<?php

   // declaring the variables as strict
   declare(strict_types = 1);

   // the function declared to return int value
   function returnIntValue(int $value): int {
      return $value;
   }

   // call the function to print the result
   print(returnIntValue(35));

?>
```

In this example, the function specified the return type as **int**. Therefore, the script will output: **35**

However, in the following example, the function will produce an error message. Obviously, an error will occur. This is because a float value (25.0) is being added to the integer value to be returned. This will produce the following browser output:

> Fatal error: Uncaught TypeError: Return value of returnIntValue() must be of the type integer, float returned...

```
<?php

   // declaring the variables as strict
   declare(strict_types = 1);

   // the function declared to return int value
   function returnIntValue(int $value): int {
      return $value + 25.0;
   }

   // call the function to print the result
   print(returnIntValue(35));

?>
```

The Scope of a Variable

Variable scope determines where within a script a variable can be accessed. In PHP, variables are available (accessible) for use within the main script and any included or required files, but *not* within functions. In contrast, a variable created or altered within the function would not automatically be available to the entire script, because it was created within the local scope of the script (which is within a function).

Obviously, you need to be able to move variables from the scope of the main script to the scope of the function in order to work with them. You also must be able to take those variables back from the function into the scope of the main script. To do this, we pass variables to, and return them from the function. Since we have already taken a brief look at returning variables from functions, let us look at several of the more common ways to move a variable from the global scope of the script (main script) to the local scope of a function.

Pass the Variable as an Argument to the Function

This is the easiest and most common method. To illustrate this, let us look at a simple script. Rather than passing the name directly to the script as an argument, it will be defined as a variable first:

Listing 8.7: pass_variable1.php

```
<?php

$name = "John Baba";

// create a function name pass_variable.
function pass_variable($name) {
        return "Welcome, $name!";
}

// pass the value of $name (John Baba) as the parameter.
echo pass_variable($name);

?>
```

The output of the script would be: **Welcome, John Baba!**. It is important to keep in mind that when you pass a variable like this, you are actually copying the value of the original variable to a new variable within the local scope of the function. This means that even if you use the same name, changes to the variable within the function will not affect the variable outside the function. Take a look at this example to see this rule in action:

Listing 8.8: pass_variable2.php

```
<?php

 $x = 1;
 // create a function name add.

 function add($x)
 {
        // the value of $x is being changed.
        $x++;
        echo $x;
 }

// call the function.  This will output a value of 2.
 add($x);

 // the value of $x will still be 1.
 echo $x;

?>
```

Pass the Variable as a Reference

We will take a quick look at how references can be used with functions. This method is very similar to the above; however, instead of copying the value of a variable to a new one within a function, you are pointing the new variable name to the same value. Technically, two different variable names, one within the global scope of the script, and the other within the local scope of the function will both point to the same value. If this seems confusing, try the following example and compare the results of this script to the previous one. Notice the "**&**" before the variable name in the function definition, which marks it as a reference.

Listing 8.9: reference_add.php

```
<?php

$x = 1;
// create a function name reference_add.

function reference_add(&$x)
{
    // the value of $x is being changed.
    $x++;
}

// call the function.  This will output 2.
echo reference_add($x);

// the value of $x here will also be 2.
echo $x;

?>
```

Since we are altering the actual value of **$x** from within the function, there is no need to even return anything from the function. When **$x** is printed out, both values will have increased by one.

Figure 8.4
Example of passing a variable as a reference.

```
2
```

Declare the Variable As Global within the Function

Declaring a variable as global has much the same effect as using a reference, but the reasoning behind it is a little different. Rather than creating a new variable name that references the same value as another, we are telling the script to use the same variable and value inside the function. You can make more than one variable global just by separating them by commas. Take a look at Listing 8.10 and Listing 8.11 to understand this concept.

Listing 8.10: global_variable.php

```
<?php

  $x = 1;

  // create a function name global_add.
  function global_add()
  {
       global $x;
       $x++;
  }

  // call the function.  This will output 2.
  global_add();
  echo $x;

?>
```

Listing 8.11: global_variable2.php

```
<?php

  global $x;
  $x = 1;

  // create a function name global_add.
  function global_add()
  {
       $x++;
  }

  // call the function.  This will output 2.
  global_add();
  echo $x;

?>
```

Accessing the Variable via the GLOBALS Array

You can also access variables from the global scope of the script by using PHP's GLOBALS Array. This is an Associative Array which allows you to access each variable in the form of **$GLOBALS["varname"]:**

Listing 8.12: global_array_add.php

```
<?php

    $x = 1;

    // create a function name global_array_add.
    function global_array_add()
    {
            $GLOBALS["x"]++;
    }

    // call the function.  This will output a value of 2.
    global_array_add();
    echo $x;

?>
```

Built-in (Pre-Defined) Functions

Just like any other programming language, PHP offers several built-in functions for day-to-day use in your coding. Most of these functions are very helpful in achieving your programming goals and are well documented. One thing that makes PHP so easy to use is the wealth of built-in functions. These functions provide the tools to easily complete many of the everyday tasks you need to perform in the course of writing a full-fledged application. There are functions for working with just about everything in PHP: strings, arrays, databases, dates and times, email, numbers, even functions for working with other functions.

With so many functions out there, it would be impossible to cover all of PHP's functions in this section. You can find the complete list of PHP's built-in functions at **www.php.net**. Now, let us take a look at a couple of these functions, just to explore how they can be used.

Some uses of built-in functions are as mentioned below:

- Converting a string of letters to uppercase and lowercase
- Displaying and using the date and time
- Initializing and closing a database connection
- Declaring and using an array
- Handling files anf folders
- Accessing data on forms
- Function to open FTP (File Transfer Protocol) connections
- Email related functions
- Mathematical Functions
- MySQL specific functions
- URL Functions

Let us take a look at some important built-in functions.

Basic Mathematical Functions

This function group provides a basic set of functions for performing mathematical computations (see Table 8.1a and Table 8.1b). It also offers a set of named constants providing useful values. These functions are part of the standard function set built into PHP and can only be disabled by either modifying the source code or by using the **disable_functions** directive in **php.ini**.

Some Examples of Mathematical functions

Both **ceil()** and **floor()** take just one parameter - the number to round. **Ceil()** takes the number and rounds it to the nearest integer above its current value, whereas **floor()** rounds it to the nearest integer below its current value. Here sre some examples of mathematical functions (see Listing 8.13).

Table 8.1a: Basic Mathematical Functions

Function	Description
ceil(fraction)	Rounds a fraction up to the next highest integer.
floor(fraction)	Rounds a fraction down to the next lowest integer.
number_format("number", "decimals", "decimal point", "thousands_sep")	Returns formatted version of a specified number.
pow(number, exponent)	Returns the value of a given number, raised to the power of a given exponent.
rand(min, max)	Generates a random value from a specific range of numbers.
round(fraction)	Rounds a fraction up to the next higher or next lower integer.
sqrt(number)	Returns the square root of a given number.

Listing 8.13: mathematical_functions.php

```
<html>
<body>
<?php

  // declare variables with initial values
   $value = 99.9;
  $number=7;
  $square=100;

  // use the ceil function
  $ceiled = ceil($value);
  echo $ceiled;
  echo "<br>";
```

Continuation of Listing 8.13: mathematical_functions.php

```
// use the floor function
$floored = floor($value);
echo $floored;
echo "<br>";

// use the round function
$a = round(49.9);
echo $a;
echo "<br>";

// use the round function
$b = round(49.5);
echo $b;
echo "<br>";

// use the round function
$c = round(49.4999);
echo $c;
echo "<br>";

// use the round function
$d = round(49.123456, 3);
echo $d;
echo "<br>";

// use the round function
$e = round(49.12345, 4);
echo $e;

// use the round function
$f = round(1000 / 160);
echo $f;
echo "<br>";

// use the exponential function
$power=pow($number, 2);
echo $power;
echo "<br>";
```

Continuation of Listing 8.13: mathematical_functions.php

```
 // use the square root function
 $sqrroot=sqrt($square);
 echo $sqrroot;
 echo "<br>";
?>
</body>
</html>
```

Figure 8.5
Example of the use of some mathematical functions.

```
100
99
50
50
49
49.123
49.12356
49
10
```

The following are the list of some additional Maths functions.

Table 8.1b: Additional Mathematical Functions

Function	Description	Example
abs ()	Absolute value	echo abs(-7); echo abs (7.2); prints 7
bindec ()	Binary to Decimal	echo bindec('1010'); prints 10 echo bindec ('110010'); prints 50
decbin()	Decimal to Binary	echo decbin(5); prints 101 echo decbin (20); prints 10100
dechex()	Decimal to hexadecimal	echo dechex(15); prints f echo dechex(12); prints c
decoct()	Decimal to octal	echo decoct (8); prints 10 echo decoct (20); prints 24
getrandmax()	Shows largest possible random value	echo getrandmax (); prints 32767

Function	Description	Example
hexdec()	Convverts hexadecimal to decimal	echo hexdec ("ff"); returns 255 echo hexdec ("a"); returns 10
is_nan()	Finds whether a value is not a number	echo is_nan (5.2); returns false
max()	Finds the highest number	echo max(12,3,15,40,8); prints 40
min()	Finds the lowest value	echo min(12,3,15,40,8); prints 3
octdec()	Converts octal to decimal	echo octdec(10); prints 8
pi()	Gets the value of pi	echo pi(); prints 3.1415926535898

PHP 7 Integer Division

PHP 7 introduces a new function intdiv(), which performs integer division of its operands and return the division as **int**. Let us look at the following example.

```
<?php

// do the integer division
$value = intdiv(67,3);

// to display the type and value of the variable
var_dump($value); echo "<br/>";

// display the value of the variable
print($value);

?>
```

It produces the following browser output.

```
int(22)
22
```

String Functions

Here is the list of some commonly used string functions.

Table 8.2: String Functions

Function	Description
strlen(string)	Determines the length of a string.
ltrim(string)	Strips whitespace from the beginning of a string.
rtrim(string)	Strips whitespace from the end of a string.
trim(string)	Strips whitespace from the beginning and the end of a string.
strpbrk(string, char)	Searches the string for the character (char). Returns **false** or a string beginning with the character (char) when found.
strtoupper(string)	Converts string to uppercase.
strtolower(string)	Converts string to lowercase.
unfirst (string)	Converts the first letter in a string to uppercase.
ucwords (string)	Converts the first letter in each word of a string to uppercase.
strrev(string)	Reverses a string.
eregi(string pattern, string subject)	Performs a case insensitive expression match. Searches subject for a match to the regular expression given in pattern.
substr($string, $start, $end)	Get a chunk of $string
str_repeat($string, $n)	Repeat $string $n times

Function	Description
addslashes($string)	Adding backslashes before characters that need to be quoted in $string
print()	Accepts a string as an argument and outputs it. It's a little unique because it works with or without parentheses.
include()	Allows you to include one file inside of another,

The following block of code demonstrates how to use some PHP string functions.

Listing 8.14: string_functions.php

```
<?php

$string = "Hello World";
$another_string = "Welcome to PHP";

echo strlen($string);           // Output would be 11
echo strtoupper($another_string); // Output: WELCOME TO PHP
echo strrev($another_string);  // Output: PHP ot emocleW
echo strpbrk($string, "W");    // Output: World

echo substr('123456789', 0, 2); // prints '12'
echo substr('123456789', 4);   // prints '56789'
echo substr('123456789', -2);  // prints '89'

echo str_repeat('A', 10);      // Outputs AAAAAAAAAA
echo trim('  abc def      ');  // print 'abc def'

// extract information from comma separated values
$csv = 'Really, John Baba,  you are  a PHP guru';
$info = explode(',', $csv);
```

Continuation of Listing 8.14: string_functions.php

```
/*
Output of  $info would be in an array form which can be
extracted
Array
 (
[0] => Really
[1] => John Baba
[2] => you are a PHP guru
)
*/

// print ordered list of names in array
$names = array('Amos Tutuwola', 'Jesse Mensah', 'Joe Moru',
'Daniel Momalla');
echo '<ol><li>' . implode('</li><li>', $names) .
'</li></ol>';

/*
The result of the above code is like an ordered list just as
shown below
        1.  Amos Tutuwola
        2.  Jesse Mensah
        3.  Joe Moru
        4.  Daniel Momalla
*/
?>
```

Figure 8.6
Results of the use of string functions.

11WELCOME TO PHPPHP ot emocleWWorld125678989AAAAAAAAAAabc def

1. Amos Tutuwola
2. Jesse Mensah
3. Joe Moru
4. Daniel Momalla

Error Functions

Take a look at two error functions

exit("message") - displays error message and terminates current script.

die("message") - displays error message and terminates current script.

Email Function

mail("recipient","subject", "message", "mail headers") - sends mail to a recipient.

HTTP/Session Functions

Table 8.3: HTTP/Session Functions

Function	**Description**
header()	Allows you to send a raw HTTP header. One of the most common uses is something relatively simple: redirecting the user. This has the same effect as the META redirection tag in HTML.
setcookie("name", "value", "expire", "path", "domain", "secure")	Sends a cookie to the user.
session_start("name", "value", "expire", "path", "domain", "secure")	Initialises session data. This function is called prior to creating a new session variable using $_SESSION.
session_destroy()	Destroys all data registered to a script's current session.

File Functions

Table 8.4: File Functions

Function	Description
fopen(filename, mode)	Used to open a file. The function requires a filename and mode. It returns a file pointer which provides information about the file and is used as a reference.
fread(resource handler, length)	Used to read the contents of a file. Reads up to length bytes from the file pointer referenced by handler. Reading stops when length bytes have been read, EOF (end of file) is reached.
fgetcsv(resource handle, length, delimiter)	Used to read the contents of a file and parses the data to create an array. Data is parsed on the delimiter parameter supplied to the function.
filesize(filename)	Returns the size of a file. If an error occurs the function returns a false value.
fclose(resource handle)	Used to close a file. The function requires the file pointer created when the file was opened using the fopen() function. Returns TRUE on success or FALSE on failure.
fwrite(resource handle,string)	Writes the contents of string to the file stream pointed to by handle. If the length argument is given, writing will stop after length bytes have been written or the end of string is reached, whichever comes first.
copy(original filename, new filename)	Copies the contents of an original file defined by the first parameter to a new file defined by the second function parameter. The function returns a true or false value.

Function	Description
unlink(filename)	Deletes the file defined by the first parameter. The function returns a **true** or **false** value.
rename($orig_filename, $new_filename)	Renames the file defined by the first parameter to the name defined as the second parameter. The function returns a **true** or **false** value.

ODBC Functions

ODBC functions are listed below:

Table 8.5: ODBC Functions

Function	Description
odbc_connect(dsn/dsn-less connection string, username,password)	Used to connect to an ODBC datasource. The function takes four parameters: the data source name or a dsn-less connection string, username, password, and an optional cursor type. In cases where a username, password, and cursor type are not required, the parameters can be replaced with a null string - ''. The connection id returned by this functions is needed by other ODBC functions. You can have multiple connections open at once as long as they either use different database or different credentials.
odbc_exec(connection_id, SQL query_string)	Used to execute an SQL statement. The function takes two parameters: a connection object created using the **odbc_connect()** function and a SQL statement. Returns FALSE on error. Returns a record set if the SQL command was executed successfully.

Function	Description
odbc_fetch_array(recordset name)	Used to retrieve records or rows from a record set as an associative array. The recordset name is created when the **odbc_exec()** function is called. This function returns TRUE if it is able to return rows, otherwise it returns FALSE.
odbc_num_rows(recordset name)	Returns the number of rows in an ODBC result set. The function will return -1 if an error occurs. For INSERT, UPDATE and DELETE statements odbc_num_rows() returns the number of rows affected. For a SELECT clause this can be the number of rows available. **Note**: Using **odbc_num_rows()** to determine the number of rows available after a SELECT will return -1 with MS Access drivers.
odbc_close(connection_id)	Will close down the connection to the database server associated with the given connection identifier.

MySQL Functions

Table 8.6: MySQL Functions

Function	Description
mysql_connect(MySQL server name, username,password)	Opens a connection to MySQL server.
mysql_select_db(database name,connection identifier)	Selects a database residing on the MySQL server. The database name parameter refers to an active database on the MySQL server that was opened with the **mysql_connect** function. The connection identifier is a reference to the current MySQL connection.

Function	Description
mysql_query(sql query)	Sends a query to the currently active database.
mysql_fetch_array(resource result)	Returns an array that corresponds to the fetched row and moves the internal data pointer ahead.
mysql_affected_rows(resource result)	Determines the number of rows affected by the previous SQL operation.
mysql_close(link_identifier)	Closes MySQL connection.

Detailed Examples

Q1. Retail Price Calculation

Write an application that accepts from the user the wholesale cost of an item and its markup percentage. (For example, if an item's wholesale cost is $5 and its retail price is $10, then the markup is 100%). The program should contain a function, named '*CalculateRetail*' that receives the wholesale cost and markup percentage as arguments, and returns the retail price of the item. When the user clicks the **Retail Price** button, the program should do the following:

a) Verify that the values entered by the user for the wholesale cost and the markup percent are numeric and not negative.

b) Call the *CalculateRetail* function. Display the retail price as returned from the function.

Suggested Solution

The form with text data are shown in Figure 8.7. The program Listing 8.15 shows both the HTML form tags that create the form and the PHP scripts that perform the retail price computation. The **Clear** button is provided to clear the contents of the textboxes.

Figure 8.7
Retail Price Form.

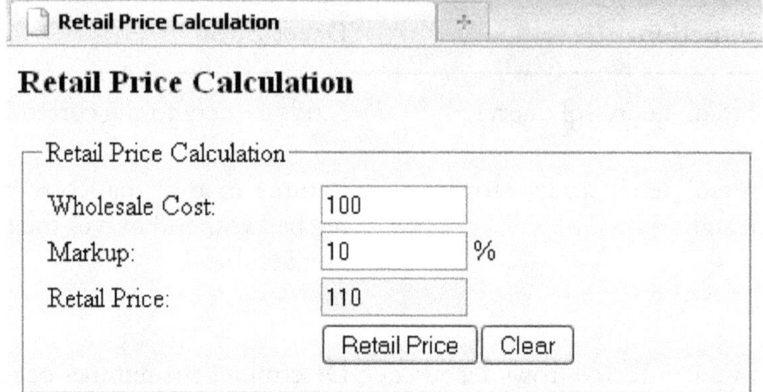

Listing 8.15: retail_price_calculation.php

```
<html>
<head>
<title>Retail Price Calculation</title>
</head>
<body bgcolor="f3f3f3">
<h3>Retail Price Calculation</h3>

<?php

// declare variables
$wholesaleCost='';
$markup='';
$retailPrice='';

// the function to calculate the retail price is defined here
function CalculateRetail($wholesaleCost,$markup){
     $retailPrice = $wholesaleCost +
                    ($wholesaleCost * $markup/100);
     return $retailPrice;
}

// when the user clicks on the Calculate Price button
if(isset($_POST['calculatePrice'])){

     // assign form values to variables
     $wholesaleCost = $_POST['wholesaleCost'];
     $markup = $_POST['markup'];
```

Continuation of Listing 8.15: retail_price_calculation.php

```
    // validate to ensure numeric fields
    if(is_numeric($wholesaleCost) && is_numeric($markup)){

      /* call calculateRetail function and assign the returned
         value to $retailPrice */
      $retailPrice = CalculateRetail($wholesaleCost,$markup);
      }
      else
      {
         echo "Fields should be numeric!";
      }
}

// when the user clicks on the clear button
if(isset($_POST['clear'])){

    // assign form values to variables
    $_POST['wholesaleCost'] = ' ';
    $_POST['markup']= ' ';
    $_POST['retailPrice'] = ' ';
}

?>

<!-- the form starts here. The form action calls itself
'retailpricecalculation.php' -->
<form action="retail_price_calculation.php" method="post">
<fieldset style="width: 30%; "><legend> Retail Price
Calculation</legend>
<table width="90%" border="0">
<tr>
    <td width="156" nowrap>Wholesale Cost:</td>
    <td width="737" > <input type="text" name="wholesaleCost"
    value="<?php echo $wholesaleCost ?>" size="10"></td>
</tr>
<tr>
   <td nowrap>Markup: </td>
   <td><input type="text" name="markup" value="<?php echo
   $markup ?>"
   size="10"> %</td>
</tr>
```

Continuation of Listing 8.15: retail_price_calculation.php

```
<tr>
   <td nowrap>Retail Price:</td>
   <td><input type="text" name="retailPrice"  value="<?php echo
   $retailPrice ?>" size="10" readonly="readonly"></td>
</tr>
<tr>
   <td>  </td>
   <td><input type="submit" name="calculatePrice" value="Retail
   Price"> </td>
</tr>
</table>
</fieldset>
</form>
</body>
</html>
```

Q2. Hospital Bill

Design a form and write PHP scripts to calculate the total cost of a stay in the hospital. The script should accept the following input:

a. The number of days spent in the hospital
b. The amount of medication charges
c. The amount of surgical charges
d. The amount of lab fees
e. The amount of physical rehabilitation charges

The hospital charges $50 per day. Write scripts for the following functions.

Function Name	Description
CalcStayCharges	Calculates and returns the base charges for the hospital stay. This is computed as $350 times the number of days in the hospital.
CalcMiscCharges	Calculates and returns the total of the medication, surgical, lab and physical rehabilitation charges.
CalcTotalCharges	Calculates and returns the total charges

Input Validation:

Do not accept a negative value for length of stay, medication charges, surgical charges, lab fees or physical rehabilitation charges.

Suggested Solution

The form with text data are shown in Figure 8.8. The program Listing 8.16 shows both the HTML form tags that create the form and the PHP scripts that perform the computation of the total hospital charges. The **Clear** button is provided to clear the contents of the textboxes.

Figure 8.8
Computation of Hospital Bill

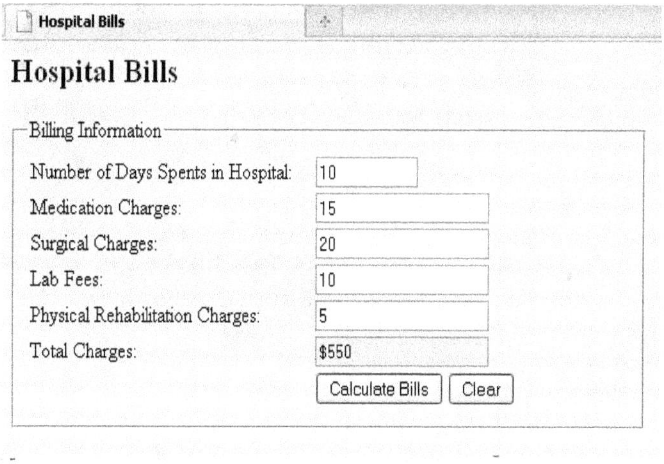

Hospital Bills

Hospital Bills

Billing Information

Number of Days Spents in Hospital: 10

Medication Charges: 15

Surgical Charges: 20

Lab Fees: 10

Physical Rehabilitation Charges: 5

Total Charges: $550

Calculate Bills | Clear

Listing 8.16: hospital_charges.php

```
<html>
<head>
<title> Hospital Bills</title>
</head>
<body bgcolor="f3f3f3">
<h2>Hospital Bills </h2>
<?php

  // declare variables
  $noofDays='';
  $medicationCharges='';
  $surgicalCharges='';
```

Continuation of Listing 8.16: hospital_charges.php

```
   $labFee='';
   $PRhCharges='';
   $totalCharges='';

// 1. function to calculate stay charges
function calculateStayCharges($noofDays){
      $stayCharges=$noofDays * 50;
      return $stayCharges;
}
// 2. function to compute miscellaneous charges
function calculateMiscCharges($labFee, $PRhCharges,
$surgicalCharges, $medicationCharges){
      $miscCharges = $labFee + $PRhCharges + $surgicalCharges +
      $medicationCharges;
      return $miscCharges;
}

// 3. function to compute total charges
function calculateTotalCharges($stayCharges,$miscCharges){
      $totalCharges=$stayCharges +  $miscCharges;
      return $totalCharges;
}

// when the user clicks on calculate bill button
if(isset($_POST['calculateBills'])){

      // assign form values to variables
      $noofDays = $_POST['noofDays'];
      $labFee = $_POST['labFee'];
      $PRhCharges = $_POST['PRhCharges'];
      $surgicalCharges = $_POST['surgicalCharges'];
      $medicationCharges = $_POST['medicationCharges'];

      // validate against negetive values
      If($noofDays >=0 && $labFee >=0 && $PRhCharges >=0 &&
         $surgicalCharges >=0 && $medicationCharges >=0){
```

Continuation of Listing 8.16: hospital_charges.php

```
        // call Stay Charges function
        $stayCharges = calculateStayCharges($noofDays);

        // call Miscellaneous Charges function
        $miscCharges =
        calculateMiscCharges($labFee,$PRhCharges,
        $surgicalCharges, $medicationCharges);

        // call Total Charges function
        $totalCharges = calculateTotalCharges ($stayCharges,
        $miscCharges);
    }
    else
    {
        echo "Please check empty fields!";
    }
}
?>

<! -- the form starts from here -- >
<form action=" hospital_charges.php" method="post">
<fieldset style="width: 40%; "><legend>Billing
Information</legend>
<table width="100%" border="0">
<tr>
    <td width="47%" nowrap>No. of Days in Hospital:</td>
    <td width="53%"> <input type="text" name="noofDays"
     value="<?php echo $noofDays ?>" size="10"> </td>
</tr>
<tr>
    <td nowrap>Medication Charges:</td>
    <td> <input type="text" name="medicationCharges"
    value="<?php echo $medicationCharges ?>" size="20"> </td>
</tr>
```

Continuation of Listing 8.16: hospital_charges.php

```
<tr>
    <td nowrap>Surgical Charges:</td>
    <td> <input type="text" name="surgicalCharges"
    value="<?php echo $surgicalCharges ?>" size="20"></td>
</tr>
<tr>
    <td nowrap>Lab Fees:</td>
    <td> <input type="text" name="labFee" value="<?php echo
     $labFee ?>"
     size="20"></td>
</tr>
<tr>
    <td nowrap>Physical Rehabilitation Charges:</td>
    <td> <input type="text" name="PRhCharges"
     value="<?php echo $PRhCharges ?>" size="20"></td>
</tr>
<tr>
    <td nowrap>Total Charges:</td>
    <td> <input type="text" name="totalCharges"
    readonly="readonly" value="<?php echo '$'.$totalCharges
    ?>" size="20"></td>
</tr>
<tr>
    <td> </td>
    <td nowrap><input type="submit" name="calculateBills"
     value="Calculate Bills">
     <input type="submit" name="clear" value="Clear"></td>
</tr>
</table>
</fieldset>
</form>
</body>
</html>
```

Programming Challenge

Q1. Software Sales

A software company sells three packages, Package A, Package B, and Package C, which retail for $99, $199, and $299, respectively. Quantity discounts are given according to the following table:

Quantity	Discount
10 through 19	10%
20 through 49	20%
50 through 99	30%
100 or more	40%

Design a form that allows the user to enter the number of units sold for each package. Write a script to calculate and display the total cost of software ordered.

Input validation: Make sure the number of units for each package is not negative.

Q2. Economic Order Quantity (EOQ)

Write a user-defined function PHP script that computes the *economic order quantity* (EOQ) using the *fixed order quantity lot size* decision rule. This rule helps retailers, manufacturing managers, etc., determine the number of units to order each time a particular item must be ordered because of low stock. The equation for computing the economic order quantity is

$$EOQ = \frac{2*R*S}{k*C}$$

where S is the cost to prepare an order.
R is the annual demand.
C is the cost per unit.
k is the cost rate of carrying one of the inventory per year.

Your function name should be **EOQCalculation** which will accept four parameters, namely **S, R, C and *k***.

Q3. Working with String Functions

Given the following string:

$string = "nothing matters, everything matters. It is a key of entrance into suffering. He who knows only one-half of the paradox can never enter that door of mystery and survive".
By Thomas Kelly.

Write a script to do the following:

a. Find the number of characters in the string.

b. Capitalize all the letters in the string.

c. Make all the characters lowercase.

d. Use the **substr**() function to print 'It is a key of entrance into suffering'. The first letter in each word should be in uppercase.

e. Trim out the whitespace at the beginning of the string.

f. Find the index position of the word 'paradox'.

g. Replace 'everything matters' with 'all things matter' (case insensitive).

h. Find the number of words in the string.

9

Arrays

The workers and professionals of the world will soon be divided into two distinct groups.
Those who will control computers and those who will be controlled by computers.
It would be best for you to be in the former group.
- Lewis D. Eigen

Learning Objectives

After studying this chapter, you should be able to:

- Understand the concepts of arrays and how they are defined in PHP.
- Distinguish between Numeric and Associative arrays.
- Understand the use of one and multi-dimensional arrays.
- Code and execute scripts relating to single and complex array structures.

Introduction

The concept of Arrays are said to be "difficult to understand at first, easy to use once you do, and impossible to live without." In this chapter, we will be taking a look at why arrays are so important to program development and explore how to work with them. We will distinguish between numeric and associative arrays and learn how to program using both one-dimensional and multi-dimensional arrays .

What are Arrays

An array is a data type which allows groups (pieces) of related data to be stored in adjoining (contiguous) memory locations. An array, which is a series of related data, is assigned to a single variable. This single variable can hold dozens of individual pieces of data. Each individual bit of the data in the array is referred to as an **array element**. Within every array element there are two parts: the **value,** which contains the actual data you want to store, and a unique **key**(**index**), which identifies the location of the value. You will learn later how keys play an important role in the process of accessing and manipulating array elements. Keys can either be non-negative integers (0,1,2,3,...) or strings.

If you visualize an array, it will look something like the following.

Table 9.1: Arrays

$names	
0	John Baba
1	Amos Momalla
2	Jesse Mensah
3	Alhasan Abubakari
4	Jones Jude

This array is called **$names** (variable name that holds the data) . It has 5 values, and is considered a Numeric Array because the keys are integers. The array elements are the individual rows such as (0. John Baba; 1. Amos Momalla). The array element consists of two parts: the key (0,1,2,3,4) and the value (John Baba, Amos Momalla, Jesse Mensah, Alhasan Abubakari, Jones Jude)

Arrays are also classified as a One-Dimensional Array, because it holds only a single layer (row or column) of information. PHP includes supports for Two-Dimensional Arrays as well, which allow you to have multiple layers of information (row and column).

Types of Arrays

There are two different types of arrays and each array value is accessed using a key which is called array index. They are **Numeric arrays** and **Associative arrays.**

Numeric Arrays

This is an array with a numeric index (0,1,2,3,4,5,….). Values are stored and accessed in linear fashion. These arrays can store numbers, strings and any object but their index will be represented by numbers. By default, array index starts from zero. The first value in an array has an index of 0, the second value has an index of 1, the next has an index of 2, and so on.

Example 1

The following is the example showing how to create and access numeric arrays.

We use **array()** function to create an array.

```
$my_array = array('John', 'Amos', 'Jesse')
```

This code creates a numerically indexed array called **$my_array**. The array is assigned three elements – John, Amos, and Jesse. Each element is identified by a numeric index.

```
$my_array[0] = 'John'      // index 0 corresponds to element John
$my_array[1] = 'Amos'      // index 1 corresponds to element Amos
$my_array[2] = 'Jesse'     // index 2 corresponds to element Jesse
```

To access the contents of an array, use the array name and the index, such as **$my_array[1]**. The following code is used to display the values of the **$my_array** variable.

Listing 9.1: name_numeric_array.php

```
<?php

  // create an array with 3 elements.
  $my_array = array('John', 'Amos', 'Jesse');

  // output the array elementts.
  echo  $my_array[0];  // this would print John
  echo  $my_array[1];  // this would print Amos
  echo  $my_array[2];  // this would print Jesse

?>
```

Figure 9.1
Display the values of the numeric array.

JohnAmosJesse

Example 2

The following is another example to show you how to create and access numeric arrays. Here again we have used **array()** function to create the array.

Listing 9.2: numbers_numeric_arrays.php

```
<html>
<body>

<?php

   // create an array with 5 elements.
   $numbers = array( 1, 2, 3, 4, 5);

   // output the array elements.
   foreach($numbers as $value)
   {
      echo $value . ' ' ;
   }

   // create array.
   $numbers[0] = "One";
   $numbers[1] = "Two";
```

Continuation of Listing 9.2: numbers_numeric_arrays.php

```
    $numbers[2] = "Three";
    $numbers[3] = "Four";
    $numbers[4] = "Five";

    // output the array elements
    foreach($numbers as $value)
    {
        echo $value . ' ' ;
    }

?>

</body>
</html>
```

Figure 9.2
Display the values of the numeric array.

1 2 3 4 5 One Two Three Four Five

Associative Arrays

This is an array with strings as index. Associate arrays store element values in association with key values rather than using ordered numeric index. Associative arrays allow you to specify index values. With numerically indexed arrays, index values are created automatically, beginning with 0. However, associative arrays permit numeric and string index values. The symbol between the index and values is an equal sign immediately followed by a greater than symbol (=>).

$members = array('fname' => John, 'lname' => Baba, 'age' => 25)

Example 3

In this example, the array **$members** contain three elements, however the string indices - fname, lname, and age are used.

```
$members['fname'] = 'John'   // index fname corresponds to element John
$members['lname'] = 'Baba'   // index lname corresponds to element Baba
$members['age'] = '25'       // index age corresponds to element 25
```

To access the contents of an array, we use the array name and the index. The following code is used to display the values of the **$members** variable.

Listing 9.3: members_associative.php

```
<?php

    // create an associative array, $members.
    $members = array('fname' => 'John', 'lname' => 'Baba',
    'age' => 25);

    // output the array elements.
    echo $members['fname'] ." ";
    echo $members['lname'] ." ";
    echo $members['age'];

?>
```

Figure 9.3
Display the values of the associative array.

John Baba 25

It is important to note that associative arrays are very similar to numeric arrays in terms of functionality but they are different in terms of their index. Associative arrays will have their index as string so that you can establish a strong association between key and values.

It is important to note that associative arrays are very similar to numeric arrays in terms of functionality but they are different in terms of their index. Associative arrays will have their index as string so that you can establish a strong association between key and values.

Example 4

In the following example we shall store the salaries of employees in an array. We would use the employees names as the keys in our associative array, and the value would be their respective salaries.

Listing 9.4: salary_associative.php

```
<?php

// first method to create an associate array.
$salaries = array("John" => 2000,"Amos" => 1000,
 "Jesse" => 500);

// output the array elements.
echo "Salary of John is ". $salaries['John'] . "<br />";
echo "Salary of Amos is ".  $salaries['Amos']. "<br />";
echo "Salary of Jesse is ".  $salaries['Jesse']. "<br />";

// second method to create an associate array.
$salaries['John'] = "high";
$salaries['Amos'] = "medium";
$salaries['Jesse'] = "low";

// output the array elements.
echo "Salary of John is ". $salaries['John'] . "<br />";
echo "Salary of Amos is ".  $salaries['Amos']. "<br />";
echo "Salary of Jesse is ".  $salaries['Jesse']. "<br />";

?>
```

Do not keep associative arrays inside double quote while printing otherwise it would not return any value. You can say **echo $salaries['John'],** but nothing will be printed if you write **echo "$salaries['John']"**.

The above code will produce the following result:

Figure 9.4
Display the values of the associative array.

```
Salary of John is 2000
Salary of Amos is 1000
Salary of Jesse is 500
Salary of John is high
Salary of Amos is medium
Salary of Jesse is low
```

PHP 7 Constant Arrays

Array constants can now be defined using the **define()** function in PHP 7. In PHP 5.6, they could only be defined using **const** keyword.

Let us look at the following example:

```
<?php

//define a array using define function
define('names', ['Baba','John','Brown','Yoofi','Rebecca']);
print(names[2]);

?>
```

This script will output: **Brown**

Multi-dimensional Arrays

Multidimensional arrays contain two or more arrays and values and are accessed using multiple indices. In a multi-dimensional array, each element in the main array can also be an array. And each element in the sub-array can be an array, and so on. Values in the multi-dimensional array are accessed using multiple index.

Two Dimensional Arrays

Example 5

In this example we create a two dimensional array to store marks of three students in three subjects:

Listing 9.5: multi_dimensional_arrays.php

```
<html>
<body>

<?php

    // create the two-dimensional array.
    $marks = array(
            "John" => array(
                "English" => 55,
                "Maths" => 39,
                "Science" => 32
            ),
            "Amos" => array(
                 "English" => 67,
                 "Maths" => 39,
                 "Science" => 91
             ),
             "Jesse" => array(
                  "English" => 88,
                  "Maths" => 29,
                  "Science" => 44
             )
     );

    // accessing multi-dimensional array values
    echo "Marks for John in English : " ;
    echo $marks['John']['English'] . "<br />";

    echo "Marks for Amos in Maths : ";
    echo $marks['Amos']['Maths'] . "<br />";

    echo "Marks for Jesse in Science: " ;
    echo $marks['Jesse']['Science'] . "<br />";

?>

</body>
</html>
```

This will produce the following result:

Figure 9.5
Display the values from two-dimensional array.

Marks for John in English : 55
Marks for Amos in Maths : 39
Marks for Jesse in Science: 44

The above example is an associative array, you can create a numeric array in the same fashion.

Example 6:

The table below represents two-dimensional array of items in a shop. Each row represents a type of item and each column – a certain attribute.

Table 9.2: Two Dimensional Arrays

Title	Price	Quantity
Candy	0.25	10
Cake	0.25	20
Biscuit	0.15	15

This example shows that the **$shop** array contains three arrays. As you might remember, to access data in one-dimensional array you have to point to array name and index. The same is true with regards to a two-dimensional array, with one exception: each element has two indexes – row and column. To display elements of this array we could have organized manual access to each element or make it by putting "**for loop**" inside another "**for loop**":

Listing 9.6: two_dimensional_arrays.php

```
<?php

// create the array and store the values
$shop = array( array("Candy", 0.25 , 10),
               array("Cake", 0.25 , 20),
               array("Biscuit", 0.15 , 15)
             );
```

Continuation of Listing 9.6: two_dimensional_arrays.php

```
// output the items
echo "<h2>Manual Access of Items</h2>";

echo $shop[0][0]." costs ".$shop[0][1]." and you get
".$shop[0][2]."<br />";
echo $shop[1][0]." costs ".$shop[1][1]." and you get
".$shop[1][2]."<br />";
echo $shop[2][0]." costs ".$shop[2][1]." and you get
".$shop[2][2]."<br />";

// output the items
echo "<h1>Using loops to display array elements</h1>";
echo "<ol>";

// outer loop
for ($row = 0; $row < 3; $row++)
{
    echo "<li><b>The row number $row</b>";
    echo "<ul>";
    // inner loop
    for ($col = 0; $col < 3; $col++)
    {
          echo "<li>".$shop[$row][$col]."</li>";
    }
   echo "</ul>";
   echo "</li>";
 }
 echo "</ol>";

?>
```

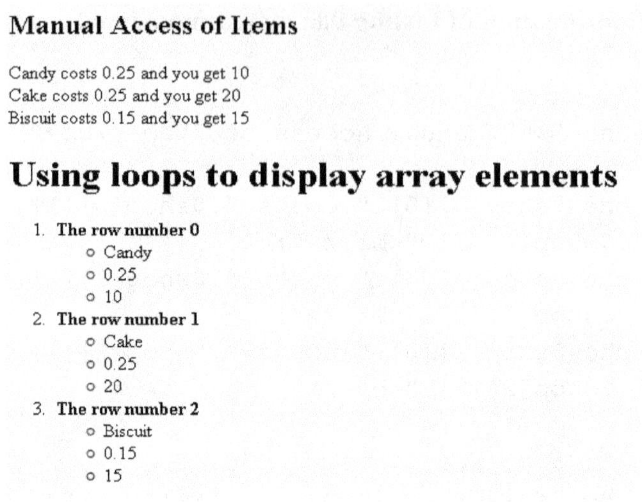

Figure 9.6
Display the values from two-dimensional array.

Manual Access of Items

Candy costs 0.25 and you get 10
Cake costs 0.25 and you get 20
Biscuit costs 0.15 and you get 15

Using loops to display array elements

1. **The row number 0**
    - Candy
    - 0.25
    - 10
2. **The row number 1**
    - Cake
    - 0.25
    - 20
3. **The row number 2**
    - Biscuit
    - 0.15
    - 15

Three-dimensional Arrays

The same way as array elements can contain other arrays, three -dimensional arrays, in turn, can contain new arrays. Three-dimensional array is characterized by height, width, and depth. Each element can be referenced by its layer, row, and column. From the previous example, we can classify items in our shop into categories; we can keep data on them using three-dimensional array. We can see from the code below, that three-dimensional array is an array containing array of arrays. As this array has only numeric indexes, we can use nested "**for loop**" to display its values:

Listing 9.7: three_dimensional_arrays.php

```
<?php

// create the array
$shop = array(array(array("Candy", 0.25 , 10),
                    array("Cake", 0.25 , 20),
                    array("Biscuit", 1.15, 7)
                   ),
              array(array("Candy", 0.25 , 10),
                    array("Cake", 0.25 , 20),
                    array("Biscuit", 1.15, 7)
                   ),
```

Continuation of Listing 9.7: three_dimensional_arrays.php

```
                array(array("Candy", 0.25 , 10),
                        array("Cake", 0.25 , 20),
                        array("Biscuit", 1.15, 7)
                      )
              );
    echo "<ul>";
    // output the result
    // outer loop
    for ($layer = 0; $layer < 3; $layer++ )
    {
            echo "<li>The layer number $layer";
            echo "<ul>";

            // inner loop
            for ( $row = 0; $row < 3; $row++ )
            {
                    echo "<li>The row number $row";
                    echo "<ul>";

                        // inner loop
                        for ( $col = 0; $col < 3; $col++ )
                        {
                            echo
                            "<li>".$shop[$layer][$row][$col].
                            "</li>";
                        }
                        echo "</ul>";
                    echo "</li>";
            }
            echo "</ul>";
            echo "</li>";
    }
    echo "</ul>";
?>
```

This way of creating multi-dimensional arrays allows you to create four- and five-dimensional arrays. Syntax rules do not limit the number of dimensions, but the majority of practical tasks logically correspond to the constructions of three or less dimensions.

Figure 9.7
Display the values from three-dimensional array.

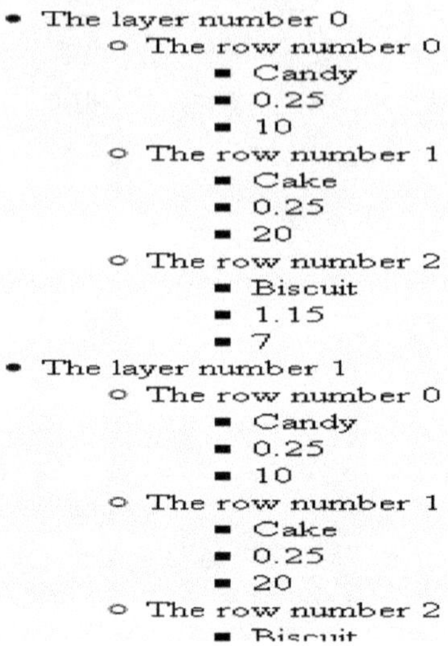

- The layer number 0
  - The row number 0
    - Candy
    - 0.25
    - 10
  - The row number 1
    - Cake
    - 0.25
    - 20
  - The row number 2
    - Biscuit
    - 1.15
    - 7
- The layer number 1
  - The row number 0
    - Candy
    - 0.25
    - 10
  - The row number 1
    - Cake
    - 0.25
    - 20
  - The row number 2
    - Biscuit

Array Functions

Besides the **array()** function, PHP includes numerous other functions for use with arrays. The following section describes some of the most common functions (see Table 9.3). A more extensive list is available at the PHP web site (**www.php.net**).

The following code shows how the array functions are used.

Listing 9.8: array_function.php

```
<?php

// two arrays are created
$numbers = array(50,20,18,30,10,7);
$colors = array('red', 'blue', 'green');

// determines the size of the array $numbers - returns 6
$array_size = sizeof($numbers);

/* sorts the elements of $numbers - returns
array(7,10,18,20,30,50) */
sort($numbers);
```

Continuation of Listing 9.8: array_function.php

```
// randomizes the elements= of the $numbers.
shuffle($numbers);

/* $merged_array returns
array(7,10,18,20,30,50,'red','blue','green') */
$merged_array = array_merge($numbers,$colors);

/* slice the numbers 18 and 20 from the sorted $numbers
array. */
$slice = array_slice($numbers, 2, 2);

$Array = array("http://www.yahoo.com",
"http://www.internet.com", "http://www.google.com",
"http://www.cnn.com", "http://www.php.net");

// print the array
/*
Output of $Array would be ([0] => http://www.yahoo.com [1] =>
http://www.internet.com [2] => http://www.google.com [3] =>
http://www.cnn.com [4] => http://www.php.net)
*/

print_r($Array);

?>
```

Table 9.3: Array Functions

Function	Description
count()	The **count** function is used to count the number of elements in an array.
sort()	The **sort** function is used to sort the elements of an existing array.
asort()	Sorts associative array by the values.
ksort()	Sorts an associative array according to the key.
rsort()	Sorts one-dimensional numerically indexed array by the values in reverse order.
arsort()	Sorts one-dimensional associative array by the values in reverse order.
krsort()	Sorts one-dimensional associative array by the keys in reverse order.
shuffle()	The **shuffle** function is used to randomize the elements of a given array.
sizeof()	The **sizeof** function is an alias of the **count()** function.
array_slice ($array_name, offset, length)	The **array_slice** function is used to extract a chuck of an existing array. **$array_name** is the name of the array to slice, offset denotes the position where the slice will begin, length indicates the number of elements that will be sliced from the array.
array_merge ($array_name, $array_name)	The **array_merge** function is used to combine or merge two or more existing arrays. The names of the arrays are separated by commas.
print_r()	Prints the values in a format that shows keys and elements.

Combining Associative and Numeric Arrays

A single PHP array can have numeric key, associative key or both. The value of an array can be of any type. This can be seen in this example.

Listing 9.9: mixed_arrays.php

```
<html>
<head>
<title>Mixed Arrays</title>
</head>
<body>

<?php

    // numeric Array
    $numbers = array(1, 2, 3, 4, 5, 6);

    // associative Array
    $age = array("mom" => 45, "pop" => 50, "bro" => 25);

    // mixed
    $mixed = array("hello" => "World", 2 => "It's two");

    // output results
    echo "numbers[4] = {$numbers[4]} <br>";
    echo "My mom's age is {$age['mom']} <br>";
    echo "mixed['hello'] = {$mixed['hello']} <br>";
    echo "mixed[2] = {$mixed[2]}";

?>

</body>
</html>
```

Figure 9.8

Combining both numeric and associative arrays.

```
numbers[4] = 5
My mom's age is 45
mixed['hello'] = World
mixed[2] = It's two
```

Sorting an Array

It is often necessary to arrange the elements in an array in numerical order from highest to lowest values (descending order) or vice versa (ascending order). If the array contains string values, alphabetical order may be needed. Sorting one-dimensional array is quite easy. Let us take a look at the following.

Sorting numerically indexed arrays

- Sorting associative arrays
- Sorting arrays in the reverse order
- Sorting numerically indexed arrays

At first we will consider an array which contains string values. The code below sorts array elements in ascending alphabetical order:

Listing 9.10: sort_alphabetic_order.php

```
<?php

// create an array $names
$names = array("John", "Amos" , "Momalla", "Roseline",
"Alhassan");

// sort numeric array elements in ascending order
sort($names);

// prints the array elements in ascending order
for($i=0; $i <= 4; $i++){
    echo $names[$i]."<br>";
}

?>
```

Figure 9.9
Sorting array elements in ascending alphabetical order.

Alhassan
Amos
John
Momalla
Roseline

The sort function is case sensitive, i.e. all capital letters come before all lowercase letters. So "A" is less than "Z", but "Z" is less than "a".

We can sort values in numerical order too. If we have an array containing prices of items, we can sort it into ascending numeric order. Have a look at the example:

Listing 9.11: sort_numeric_order.php

```
<html>
<body>

<?php

// create an array $prices
$prices = array(1.25, 0.75 , 1.15, 1.00, 0.50);

// sort numeric array elements in ascending order
sort($prices);

// prints the array elements in ascending order
for($i=0; $i <= 4; $i++){
    echo $prices[$i]."<br>";
}

?>
</body>
</html>
```

Figure 9.10
Sorting array elements in numerical order.

```
0.5
0.75
1
1.15
1.25
```

Sorting Associative Arrays

If we are using an associative array we cannot sort an array by using the **sort()** function. If we apply the **sort()** function on an associative array, it will be sorted by the numeric value of the index. To sort an associative array, we need to use the **asort()** function to keep keys and values together as they are sorted.

The following code creates an associative array containing the three items and their associated prices, and then sorts the array into ascending price order:

Listing 9.12: sorting_associative_arrays.php

```
<?php

// create an array $shop
$shop = array("Candy" => "2.00",
              "Cake" => "4.30",
              "Buscuit" => "1.50",
              );
// sort associative array elements in ascending order
asort($shop);

// prints the array elements in ascending order
foreach($shop as $key => $value)
       echo $key." Costs ".$value." Dollars <br/>";

?>
```

The **asort()** function orders the array according to the value of each element. In this array, the values are the prices and the keys are the names of the items.

Figure 9.11
The **asort()** function used on an associative array.

Buscuit costs 1.50 dollars
Candy costs 2.00 dollars
Cake costs 4.30 dollars

If instead of sorting by price (value) we want to sort by item name (key), we use **ksort()** function to sort an associative array according to the key.

The following code will result in the keys of the array being ordered alphabetically:

Listing 9.13: sort_key.php

```
<?php

   // create an array $shop
   $shop = array("Candy" => "2.00",
                       "Cake" => "4.30",
                    "Buscuit" => "1.50",
                    );
   // sort associative array elements in ascending order
   ksort($shop);

   // prints the array elements in ascending order
   foreach($shop as $key => $value){
      echo $key." costs ".$value." dollars<br />";
   }
?>
```

Figure 9.12
The ksort() function used on an associative array.

Buscuit costs 1.50 dollars
Cake costs 4.30 dollars
Candy costs 2.00 dollars

Sorting Arrays in the Reverse Order

In the previous sections, we have discussed **sort(), asort(),** and **ksort()** functions. All these functions sort arrays in the ascending order. Each of them has corresponding function that sorts an array in the descending order. These reverse functions are called **rsort(), arsort()** and **krsort()** respectively.

Detailed Example

Working with Various Array Functions

Create a string of names consisting of "John, Jerry, Ann, Sanji, Wen, Paul, Louise, Peter"

1. Create an array out of the string.
2. Sort the array in ascending order.
3. Reverse the array.
4. Remove the first element from the array.
5. Add "Willie" and "Daniel" to the end of the array.
6. Replace "Paul" with "Andre".
7. Add "Alisha" to the beginning of the array.
8. Create another array of names.
9. Merge both arrays together and display them in sorted order.

Suggested Solution

Listing 9.14: arrays.php

```
<?php

    //1. Create an array $names
    $names = array("John", "Jerry", "Ann", "Sanji", "Wen",
    "Paul", "Louise", "Peter");

    //2.  Sort an array elements in ascending order
    sort($names);

    //3.  Sort an array elements in reverse order
    rsort($names);
```

Continuation of Listing 9.14: arrays.php

```
    //4. delete an array elements
    $deleted = array_splice($names, 0, 1);

    //5. add an elements into an existing array
    $names[ ] = 'Willie';
    $names[ ] = 'Daniel';

    //6. replace the value of an existing element in array
    $new = array('Andre');
    array_splice($names, 2, 1, $new);

    //7. add new element to the beginning of the array
    $add_new = array_unshift($names, "Alisha");

    //8. create another array
    $new_names = array("Rosely", "Becky", "Benji", "Suzzy",
    "Mande");

    //9. merge the two separate array
    $merge_array = array_merge((array)$names,
    (array)$new_names);

    sort($merge_array);

    // prints the array elements in ascending order
    for($i=0; $i<=sizeof($merge_array); $i++){
        echo $merge_array[$i]."<br>";
    }

?>
```

Programming Challenge

Working with Associative Array

Create a PHP associative array called "student" of key-value pairs. The keys are "Name", "ID", "Address", "Major", "Email", and "Phone". The values will be entered by the user in an HTML form. Check that each field was filled out. Assign the values extracted from the form to correspond to the keys in the $student array.

- Sort the array by keys.
- Print the array as an HTML table.
- Print just the values.
- Print the student's name, e-mail address, and phone number.

10

Fundamentals of Object-Oriented Programming

Life is just a class, override it. Assaad Chalhoub

Learning Objectives

After studying this chapter, you should be able to:

- Understand what it means by object-oriented programming, why it is useful, and its fundamental principles.
- Understand the concepts of classes, objects, properties and methods.
- Define and use classes, objects and properties.
- Work with public, private, and protected properties and methods.
- Use constructors and destructors.
- Write scripts involving const, static, final classes, methods, and properties.

Introduction

Object-oriented programming revolves around a construct called a **class**. Classes are the templates that are used to define objects. We can think of the universe as having made up of different objects like sun, earth, moon, stars, etc. Similarly we can imagine a car as consisting of many different objects such as engine, wheel, steering, gear, brake, etc. In the same way. an object oriented programming concepts assume everything as an object and implement software around the objects. Each object is regarded as containing two main parts; properties and behaviors. In this chapter you shall explore various ideas and concepts involving object-oriented programming (OOP) and discuss how you will write scripts to handle basic OOP concepts including classes, objects, methods, properties, constructors, and inheritance.

Why use Object-Oriented Programming

Here are some reasons why you may prefer to use object-oriented concepts in writing your PHP scripts.

1. Organization - Codes written in OOP (object-oriented programming) are much more organized. There is a hierarchy of classes and interfaces that take what could be potentially thousands of new functions and breaks them down into logical groups.

2. Security - Usage of static classes is safe. Private and protected properties can hide sensitive information. Also, **type** safety can be enforced using PHP's type hinting instead of using if/then statements.

3. Reusability - Instead of coding logic for the same data in multiple places in the script, OOP centralizes the codes into one place, making it reusable. A simple script written in OOP can be accessed and re-used several times.

4. Modular Design and Extensibility – With OOP, a single object can be updated instead of many files containing functions that do not all need to be updated. Likewise, a single object can be replaced to completely change functionality instead of introducing new functions or replacing old ones.

Principles in Object-Oriented Programming

Object-oriented programming is based on three main concepts (paradigms or beliefs). These are Encapsulation, Inheritance, and Polymorphism. In this section we shall define and discuss the key principles underlying these concepts.

Encapsulation

Encapsulation is one of three fundamental principles in object-oriented programming. Encapsulation is the ability of an **object** to be a container (or capsule) for related properties (ie. data variables) and methods (ie. functions) that it contains. Older languages did not enforce any property/method relationships. This often resulted in side effects where variables had their contents changed or reused in unexpected ways that were difficult to discover. Data hiding is the ability of objects to hide variables from external access. Those variables or properties declared as **private** can only be seen or modified through the use of public accessor (getter) and mutator (setter) methods. This permits validity checking at run time. Access to other variables can be allowed but with tight control on how it is done. Methods can also be completely hidden from external use. Depending on the level of data hiding required, the keywords use in encapsulation will include **private**, **protected**, and **public**.

Inheritance

Inheritance is the capability of a **class** to use the **properties** and **methods** of another class while adding its own functionality. An example of where this could be useful is with an employee records system. You could create a generic employee class with properties (characteristics or features) and methods (actions) that are common to all employees. Then more specific classes could be defined for salaried, commissioned and hourly employees. The generic class is known as the parent (superclass or base class) and the specific classes as children (or subclasses or derived classes). The concept of inheritance greatly enhances the ability to reuse code as well as making design a much simpler and cleaner process.

Polymorphism

This is the third basic principle of object-oriented programming. Polymorphism is the capability of an action or **method** to do different things based on the object that it is acting upon. Overloading, overriding, and dynamic method binding are three types of polymorphism. *Overloaded methods* are methods with the same name signature but either a different number of parameters or different data types in the parameter list. *Overridden methods* are methods that are redefined within an inherited or subclass. They have the same signature and the subclass definition is used. *Dynamic (or late) method binding* is the ability of a program to resolve references to subclass methods at runtime. As an example, assume that three subclasses (Cow, Dog and Snake) have been created based on the Animal abstract class, each having their own **speak()** method. Although each method reference is to an Animal, the program will resolve the correct method reference at runtime.

Definition of a Class

A **class** is a user defined data type that contains **properties (**also known as attributes, variables, or data members**)** and **methods (**i.e functions**)** which work on the data members. To create a **class**, you need to use the keyword **class** followed by the name of the **class**. The name of the class should be meaningful and should describe the purpose of the class. The body of the class is placed between two curly brackets { } within which you declare class data members or variables and class methods. Now, it is time to get to know how to create classes and objects using PHP code. First, let us look at creating a class. The basic structure for creating a class is as stated in the following syntax.

You can see from the general syntax above that to define a class a keyword "**class**" is used followed by the **className.** The class name is the programmer's own defined word. A class, as already mentioned, is a template that contains objects (properties and functions); all enclosed in braces { }. Note that the **properties are of the object's variables** and the **functions are the methods**. The name properties or variables and methods or functions can respectively be used interchangeably.

Syntax:

```
<?php

class className
{

	// properties or data members go here
	public $property1;
	public $property2;

	// methods or functions go here
	function functionName1([$arg1, $arg2])
	{
		…
		…
	}

	function functionName2([$arg3, $arg4])
	{
		…
		…
	}

	// you may add more methods or functions here
	…
	…
}

// this segment is outside the body of the class

// you may create objects here

…

// you put other php statements here

…

?>
```

Note that the **properties** are of the object's **variables** and the **behaviors/functions** are the **methods**. The name properties or variables and methods or functions can respectively be used interchangeably.

Function (method) definition looks much like PHP ordinary functions discussed in the earlier chapters, but are local to the class and will be used to set and access object data. In the above structure, the two function definitions have two parameters (arguments) each: **functionName1** has **$arg1** and **$arg2**.and **functionName2** has **$arg3** and **$arg4.** The parameters are optional and may be used depending on what you are doing. We will illustrate how the parameters will be used in the later sections.

Now, let's use Listing 10.1 as an example to illustrate the above structure.

Listing 10.1: class.php

```
<?php
class Person{

    // the data members
    private $first_name, $last_name;

   // class method
   public function setData($first_name, $last_name)
   {
          $this->first_name = $first_name;
          $this->last_name = $last_name;
   }

   // class method
   public function printData()
   {
          echo $this->first_name . " : " . $this->last_name;
   }
}
?>
```

In the above script, **Person** is the name of the class and **$first_name** and **$last_name** are attributes or data members. The **setData()** and **printData()** are methods of the class. Keyword such **private, public** and **protected** would be discussed in the following sections.

Naming Conventions

Though naming of **classes**, **objects**, **properties**, and **methods** are programmer defined, it is important to follow the naming convention (generally accepted standard) when naming them.

As a general **Object-Oriented Programming** practice, it is better to name the class as the name of the real world entity rather than giving it a fictitious name.

The same rule applies for class methods. The name of the method should tell you what action or functionality it will perform. For example **getData()** tells you that it will accept some data as input and **printData()** tells you that it will print data. So ask yourself what you would name a method which retrieves data from a database. If you said **getDataFromDb()** you would be right. Moreover, when naming methods, follow the principle of capitalization. The first character of the first word of the method name is a lowercase. The other words in the method name should have thier first characters uppercase. Therefore, it becomes **getDataFromDb().**

Attributes or properties of a class should be named on the basis of the data that they hold. You should always give meaningful names to your attributes. For attributes, you should split the words with an underscore (_) i.e. **$first_name**, **$last_name**, etc.

Definition of an Object

An object is an instance (a special type of variable) that is created from a class (template or blueprint). This means that an object is created from the definition of the class and is loaded into memory. A good analogy to understand this is to compare objects with vehicles. Cars and buses can all be regarded as objects. If car designer wants to design cars, what is easier for him to do? Create and define properties and attributes of each car separately or create a one-time template (that contains properties and behaviours of vehicles) and generate objects out if it? I think having one-time template (class) and create cars, buses, etc from it would be easier. Therefore, this one-time template is a **class** and all of various cars, buses, etc are the various instances of the class (objects of the vehicle class).

Objects contain actual data and functions (methods) from the class (from which it has been created). The object can call the methods within the class to manipulate its data (properties).

Several objects can be created from a single class; such as from Listing 10.2 where several individuals can be created from **Person** class. Though many objects are created from the same class, each object may function independently of the other objects. For instance, we can define a class known as **Person**. We can create objects such as **Student** or **Lecturer** from the same class **Person** and certain behaviors (actions or methods) of a **student** may be the same (as in Figure 10.1) or may even differ from that of **lecturer**.

Each object may have its own properties (attributes) and behavior (methods) or share similar properties contained within the class from which the object is created. Because an object is created from a class, it is often said to be an instance of a class, and the process of creating an object from a class is called **instantiation**. So we can instantiate (create) the **Student** or **Lecturer** object.

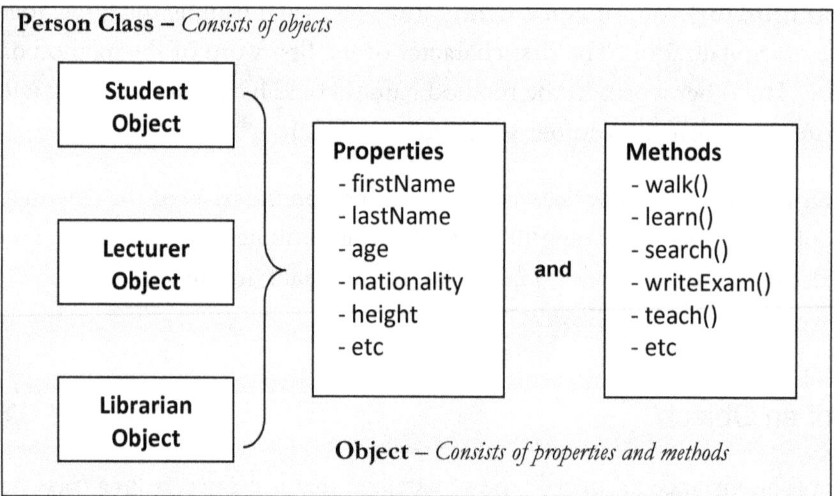

Figure 10.1: Relationship among Class, Objects, Methods, and Properties

Creating (Instantiating) an Object

You create an object of a class by using the **new** keyword, as follows:

$objectName = new className()

This creates an object of the class **className**. The object created is stored in a variable known as **$objectName**.

To create an object known as **student** from the **Person's** class for instance, we will use the following code:

$student = new Person()

We can also create another (say **lecturer**) object from the same **Person** class:

$lecturer = new Person()

Also, if we want to create an object called **staffMember** from the **Person** class, we will use:

$staffMember = new Person()

We shall use the following example to illustrate how to create objects as shown in Listing 10.2.

Listing 10.2: object_creation.php

```
<?php

class Person{

   // data members
   private $first_name, $last_name;

   // define getData function
   public function getData($first_name, $last_name)
   {
           $this->first_name = $first_name;
           $this->last_name = $last_name;
   }

   // define printData function
   public function printData()
   {
      echo $this->first_name . " : " . $this->last_name;
   }
}

// create three objects
$student = new Person();
$lecturer = new Person();
$staffMember = new Person();

?>
```

In the above example, **$student**, **$lecturer,** and **$staffMember** are three objects of the **Person** class. These objects are allocated different blocks in the memory. This is to say that each object has its own memory space that can hold independent data values.

Defining Data Members

The data values that an object holds are stored in special variables known as properties or data members. An object's properties are closely tied to the object. Although all objects created from a given class have the same properties, one object's properties can have different values from another object's properties.

The **Person** class may have name, age, and nationality properties. Hence, we can declare the properties as

```
<?php

class Person{

    // data members
    private $name;
    public $age;
    private $nationality
}

?>
```

Definition Class Method

A class method (function) is the functionality (the behavior) of a class i.e. it provides the necessary code for the class in which it is defined. Examples could be the **getData()** and **printData()** methods defined in the **Person** class. Methods act (perform operations) on the data members (properties) of the class. A class method is exactly similar to PHP functions (as discussed in an earlier chapter). The only difference is that the class functions are declared inside classes and accessed using the **->** (arrow operator / dereferencing operator) as shown in Listing 10.3. Methods can also be declared as either **public, protected** or **private**. The following example provides understanding of class methods.

In the following example, **setName()** is the class method of the **Person** class. The **setName()** class method is responsible for accepting the name of the **student** and storing it in the internal data member known as **$name**.

Listing 10.3: method.php

```
<?php

class Person{

   // data members
   private $name;
   private $age;
   private $nationality

   // method or function
   public function setName($name)
   {
         $this->name = $name;
   }
}
// create or instantiate student object
$student = new Person();
$student->setName("John Baba");
?>
```

The `$this` Variable

We have used **$this** variable in our earlier examples and we have to explain its function. The **$this** is a pointer to the object making the function call (refers to the object currently accessing the function). The **$this** variable is, however, not available in **static** methods. We will learn more about static methods in the later section. Listing 10.4 explains the use of **$this** variable.

In the example, **$lecturer** and **$student** are two separate objects in the **Person** class. Each object has its own memory to store names. But you will notice that the function setName() is common. During run time, how can it make a difference as to which memory location to use to store the function values? Therefore, it uses the **$this** variable. As mentioned earlier, **$this** variable is a pointer to the object making a function call.

Listing 10.4: this.php

```
<?php

class Person{

  private $name;

   // the $this variable
   public setName($name)
   {
      $this->name = $name;
   }
}

// create lecturer and student objects
$lecturer = new Person();
$student = new Person();

// calling the methods
$lecturer->setName("Dan Emeka");
$student->setName("Vida Idan");

?>
```

That is, when we execute **$lecturer->setName("Dan Emeka")**, **$this** in the **setName()** function is a pointer or a reference to the **$lecturer** object. Hence, **$this** represents **$lecturer** object. Similarly, when we execute **$student->setName("Vida Idan")**, **$this** in the **setName()** function is a pointer or a reference to the **$student** object. Therefore, **$this** represents **$student** object.

Class Access Specifiers (`public, private` and `protected`)

In the earlier sections we have seen keywords like **public**, **private** and **protected**. These are known as **access specifiers**. We shall look at what access specifiers are and how we can use them in our scripts. Access specifiers specify the level of access that the outside world (i.e. other class objects, external functions and global level code) have on the class methods and class data members. In other words, how visible (accessible) are data members and methods by other methods that want to use them. Access specifiers can either be **public, private** or **protected.** Access specifiers are key components of encapsulation and data hiding. By using either of the access specifiers i.e. **public, private** or **protected** you can hide or show the internals of your class to the outside world (other classes and methods).

By using either of the access specifiers i.e. **public, private** or **protected** you can hide or show the internals of your class to the outside world (other classes and methods).

Private

A private access specifier is used to hide the data member or member function (method) to the outside world. This means that only the class that defines such data members and member functions have access to them. Look at the example shown in Listing 10.5.

Listing 10.5: private_class.php

```
<?php

class Person{

   // declare a data member as private
   private $name;

   public function setName($name)
   {
        $this->name = $name;
   }

   public function getName()
   {
        return $this->name;
   }
}
```

Continuation of Listing 10.5: private_class.php

```
// create student object
$student = new Person();
$student->setName("John Baba");

/* this gives error as $name cannot be accessed from outside
the class $name can only be accessed from within the class */
echo $student->name;

/* this works, as the methods of the class have access
to the private data members or methods */
echo $student->getName();

?>
```

In Listing 10.5, **echo $student->name** will give you an error as **$name** in class **Person** has been declared **private** and hence can only be accessed by its member functions internally. Therefore, the following line **echo $student->getName()** will display the name.

Public

A public access specifier provides the least protection to the internal data members and member functions. A public access specifier allows the outside world to access or modify the data members directly unlike the private access specifier. Example of public class coding is shown in Listing 10.6:

In the example, **echo $student->name** will work as it has been declared as **public** and hence can be accessed by class member functions and the rest of the script.

Listing 10.6: public_class.php

```
<?php

class Person{

   // declare data member as public
   public $name;

   public function setName($name)
   {
       $this->name = $name;
   }

   public function getName()
   {
       return $this->name;
   }
}

// create student object
$student = new Person();

// call or invoke setter function
$student->setName("John Baba");

// this will work as it is public
echo $student->name;

// this also does not give an error
$student->name = "Mary Tettey";
echo $student->name;

?>
```

Protected

A protected access specifier is mainly used with inheritance. A data member or member function declared as **protected** will be accessed within the base class and its child classes but not from the outside world (i.e. rest of the script). We can also say that a protected data member is public for the class that declares it and it's child class; but is private for the rest of the program. Listing 10.7 describes how a protected access identifier is called.

Listing 10.7: protected_class.php

```
<?php

// the parent class
class Person{
    protected $name;

    public function setName($name) {
            $this->name = $name;
    }
    public function getName() {
            return $this->name;
    }
}
// the child class
class Female extends Person{
    private $height;

    public function setData($name, $height)
    {
    /* this is storing $name to the Person class $name
    variable. This works as it is a protected variable */
    $this->name = $name;
    $this->height = $height;
    }
}

$student = new Female();
$student->setData("John Baba",5.3);

/* this does not work as $name is protected and hence
only available in Person and Female classes */
echo $student->name;
?>
```

In the above example (Listing 10.7), **echo $student->name** will not work because **$name** has been defined as a protected variable and hence it is only available in **Person** and **Female** classes.

It is important to note that access specifiers are **public** by default. This means that if you don't specify an access specifier for a data member or method then the default **'public'** is automatically applicable.

Getter (Accessor) and Setter (Mutator) Methods

Based on the knowledge gained from the discussions from **Access Specifiers** in the previous section, let's delve into accessor and mutator methods.

Accessor Methods

Accessor methods are also know as getter methods. The reason why we need an accessor method is to be able to read the value of a property or attribute in a class object. In practice, most of the data members that you define would either be private or protected, therefore to access such data members that have been defined as either private or protected will require an implementation of accessor or getter methods. Remember that data members and functions declared as private or protected cannot be accessed directly from outside the class (for private) or outside the class and child classes (for protected). With the use of accessor (getter) method, the data member can be available outside of the class. However, if you want to make a property or data member not accessible to the outside world, you should not provide a getter or accessor method.

Mutator Methods

Mutator methods are sometimes referred to as the setter methods. Mutator methods provide a mechanism to store data in data members that have either been declared as **private** or **protected**. The reason why you should provide a mutator method could be to provide necessary validation on the data that is to be stored in the data member of the class.

To make a property or data member as read only; you should not provide a setter or mutator method.

We shall use Listing 10.8 to illustrate accessor and mutator methods.

Listing 10.8: mutator_methods.php

```
<?php

class Person{
 // private data member
 private $name;

     // mutator or setter method
    public function setName($name){
        if(trim($name) != ""){
            $this->name = $name;
            return true;
        }else{
            return false;
        }
    }

    // accessor or getter method
    public function getName(){
        return $this->name;
    }
}
// create lecturer object
$lecturer = new Person();

// call the setter method
$lecturer->setName("John Baba");

// call the getter method
echo $lecturer->getName();
?>
```

Output: John Baba

In the Listing 10.8, the **setName()** method accepts a persons' name and validates to check if **$name** is blank. If **$name** is blank the **setName()** function returns **false**; otherwise it stores the **$name** in the **$this->name** of the class and returns **true**. The **getName()** returns the name stored in the **$name** data member of the **$lecturer** object.

Constructors [__construct()]

A **constructor** is a special function of a class that is automatically executed whenever an object of a class gets instantiated. Constructor function is special because it is automatically executed or called or invoked when an object of a class is created. Constructors are necessary as they provide an opportunity for doing necessary setup operations like initializing class variables, opening database connections or socket connections, etc. In simple terms, it is needed to setup the object before it is used. Constructors are defined by implementing the **__construct()** method. The constructor method has the following structure:

```
class Person{

      // constructor method
      public function __construct(){

            your code here
            .........

      }

}
```

Listing 10.9 explains how constructors work. In the above example, we create a new object of the **Person** class. The **new** operator is responsible for creating the lecturer object. At this point PHP searches the Person class to see if a constructor has been defined. Therefore, it calls the constructor method i.e. **__construct().** The **__construct()** method sets the **$first_name** and **$last_name** to "John" and "Baba" respectively.

Parameterized Constructor

A parameterized or argument constructor is a constructor which accepts values in the form of arguments in the constructor. Unlike other programming languages such as Java where overloaded argument constructor is possible, in PHP you cannot overload constructors.

Listing 10.10 explains how we can pass parameters to the constructor.

Listing 10.9: constructor.php

```
<?php
class Person{

        // data members
        private $first_name;
        private $last_name;

        // constructor method
        public function __construct() {
                $first_name = "John";
                $last_name = "Baba";
        }

        // setter method
        public function setData($first_name, $last_name) {
                $this->first_name = $first_name;
                $this->last_name = $last_name;
        }

        // print method
        public function printData(){
           echo "Name: ".$first_name." ".$this->last_name.
           "\n";
        }
}

// create an object; the constructor is invoked immediately
$lecturer = new Person();

?>
```

In the Listing 10.10, we create a new object **$student** and pass values "John" and "Baba" to the constructor. The constructor now takes the two arguments and stores them in the internal private variable **$first_name** and **$last_name** respectively. Because the constructor set the initial values automatically, **Name : John Baba** will be printed when we call **echo $student->printData()** function.

Listing 10.10: constructor2.php

```
<?php

class Person {
        private $first_name;
        private $last_name;

        // constructor with parameters
        public function __construct($first_name, $last_name) {
                $this->setData($first_name, $last_name);
        }
        // setter method
        public function setData($first_name, $last_name) {
                $this->first_name = $first_name;
                $this->last_name = $last_name;
        }

        // print method
        public function printData() {
            echo "Name : " . $this->first_name . " " . $this->>
        last_name ."\n";
        }
}
// create an object; pass parameters to the constructor
$student = new Person("John","Baba");
echo $student->printData();

?>
```

Output: Name : John Baba

Destructors [__destruct()]

A destructor is a special function of a class that is automatically executed whenever an object of a class is destroyed. It is special because it is automatically executed or called or invoked when an object of a class is destroyed. An object of a class is destroyed when the following occurs:

1. the object goes out of scope,
2. when the object is specifically set to null,
3. when it is set to **unset** or when the program execution is over.

Destructors are important as they provide opportunity for doing clean-up operations like unsetting internal class objects, closing database connections or socket connections, etc. In simple terms, it is needed to clean-up the object as it is destroyed. Destructors are defined by implementing the **__destruct()** method. Unlike constructors, it is important to note that destructors cannot take any arguments. The destructor method has the following structure:

```
class Person{

        // destructor method
        public function __ destruct(){

            your code here
            ...
        }
}
```

An object of a class is destroyed when the following occurs:

- The object goes out of scope,
- When the object is specifically set to null,
- When it is set to **unset** or when the program execution is over.

Listing 10.11 is an example to explain how destructors work.

Listing 10.11: destructors.php

```
<?php

class Person{

   // declaring data members
   private $first_name;
   private $last_name;

   // constructor method
   public function __construct() {
          $first_name = "";
          $last_name = "";
   }

   // setter method
   public function setData($first_name, $last_name) {
          $this->first_name = $first_name;
          $this->last_name = $last_name;
   }

   // print method
   public function printData() {
      echo "Name : ". $first_name ." ". $last_name .
      "\n";
   }

   // destruct cannot have parameters
   public function __destruct() {
          unset($this->name);
          unset($this->lecturer);
   }
}
$name = "John";
$lecturer = new Person();
$lecturer->setData("John","Baba");

?>
```

In Listing 10.11, we create a new object **$student** of the Female class. The arguments of the constructor of the **Person** class takes two parameters i.e. $name and $lecturer object. After the program completes its execution, the object **($lecturer** object) goes out of scope because the program stops execution and hence the destructor is automatically called.

Defining Class Constants

You can define a class level constant. These constants are specific to the class and hence do not span the global level constant space.

To declare a constant in a class, a keyword **const** is used, as shown in Listing 10.12.

Listing 10.12: class_constants.php

```
<?php

class Person{

    // declare GENDER constant
    const GENDER = "Male";
}

// display result
echo "Gender: " . Person::GENDER;

?>
```

Output: Gender : Male

In Listing 10.12, **const** is a keyword and **GENDER** is the name of the constant. Outside the class definition we **echo** the value of the constant by using the scope resolution operator (::) like this **Person::GENDER**. You would observe that you do not need to create an object of the class to access the value of the constant. This is because a constant belongs to the class definition scope and not to an object.

Listing 10.13 shows how to access the class constant within a function.

Listing 10.13: class_constants2.php

```
<?php

class Person{

   // declare GENDER as constant
   const GENDER = "Male";

   public function displayConstant(){
         // print the the GENDER value
         echo "Gender is: " . Person::GENDER;
   }
}

// create student object
$student = new Person();

// call dispalyConstant function
$student->displayConstant();

?>
```

Output: Gender is : Male

Important observations about Constants:

1. The contents of constants cannot be changed.
2. Only a string or numeric value can be assigned to a constant.
3. Arrays, objects and expressions cannot be assigned to a constant.
4. A class constant can only be accessed via the scope resolution operator (::) executed on the class name.
5. A class constant cannot have access specifiers (private, public, protected) assigned to it.

Static Data Members

A data member that is commonly available to all objects of a class is called a static member. Unlike regular data members, static members share the memory space between all objects of the same class. To define a static member you need to prefix the class member name with the keyword **static**.

Listing 10.14 describes how static data method is called.

Listing 10.14: static_data.php

```
class Person{

   // regular member
   private $first_name;

   //static data member
   static public $last_name;

}
```

In the above example **$last_name** is declared as a static data member

Accessing Static Data Members

A static member data can be accessed using the name of the class along with the scope resolution operator (::). Just like **const**, you do not need to create an instance of that class before accessing the static data member.

A static member data can be accessed using the name of the class along with the scope resolution operator (::).

Listing 10.15 describes how data can be accessed from static data method.

In the example, **$age** is a static data member. Every time a new object is created the constructor is executed and the **$age** variable is decreased by one. To **echo** the value contained in **$age** variable, we use the **::** (scope resolution) operator.

Listing 10.15: accessing_static_data.php

```
<?php

class Person{

   // static data member
   static public $age = 40;

   // constructor method
   public function __construct(){
          Person::$age--;
   }

   // destructor method
   public function __destruct(){
          Person::$age++;
   }

   // getter method
   public function getFirstName(){

          //body of method
   }

   // getter method
   static public function getAge(){

          //body of method
   }
}

$student = new Person();
$lecturer = new Person();

// print static member
echo Person::$age;

?>
```

Output: 38

Static Methods

A static method is a class method that can be called without creating an instance of a class. Such methods are useful when creating utility classes. To define a static data method you need to prefix the class method name with the keyword **static**.

A static method is a class method that can be called without creating an instance of a class.

Let us look at how static methods are declared. In the example **getAgeCounter** is declared as a **static** method

```
class Person{

  // regular method
  public function getFirstName(){

        body of method
  }

  // static method
  static public function getAgeCounter(){

        body of method

  }
}
```

Accessing Static Method

A static method can be accessed using the name of the class along with the scope resolution operator (::). You do not need to create an instance of that class. However, you can also access it with an instance variable.

A static method can be accessed using the name of the class along with the scope resolution operator (::).

Listing 10.16 shows how static method can be accessed.

Listing 10.16: static_method.php

```
<?php

class Person{

   // static data member
   static public $age = 0;

   // constructor method
   public function __construct(){
          Person::$age++;
   }

   // destructor method
   public function __destruct(){
          Person::$age--;
   }

   public function getFirstName(){
          //body of method
   }

   static public function getAgeCounter(){
          return Person::$age;
   }
}

// create two objects
$student = new Person();
$lecturer = new Person();
```

Continuation of Listing 10.16: static_method.php

```
// this is using the scope resolution operator
echo Person::getAgeCounter();
echo '<br>';

// this is using the instance variable
echo $lecturer->getAgeCounter();

?>
```

Output:

2

2

Important observations static methods:

- A static method can only access static data members.
- A static method does not have access to the **$this** variable.

Working with Final Classes

A final class is a class that cannot be extended. To declare a class as final, you need to prefix the **class** keyword with **final** as shown Listing 10.17.

In Listing 10.17, **ParentClass** is declared as **final** and hence cannot be extended (inherited). The **ChildClass** tries to extend from **ParentClass** and hence the compiler will throw a compile error. Consequently, you should declare a class as final when you think that your implementation of that class should not change in the derived (child) class. You should do this mainly for Utility classes where you don't want the behavior or implementation of your class to change.

A class defined as **final** cannot be extended.

Listing 10.17: final_class.php

```
<?php

// define base class as final
final class ParentClass {
   public function myMethod() {
          echo "Parent class method called";
     }
}

/* an error will occur because we cannot extend a base
class with final keyword */
class ChildClass extends ParentClass {

   public function myMethod() {
          echo " Child class method called";
   }
}

// create object from child class
$child = new ChildClass();
$child->myMethod();

?>
```

Working with Final Methods

A final method is a method that cannot be overridden. To declare a method as final, you need to prefix the function name with the 'final' keyword. Listing 10.18 explains how final class can be used.

A method defined as **final** cannot be overridden.

Listing 10.18: final_class2.php

```
<?php

class ParentClass {

   // define method as final
   final public function myMethod() {
         echo "Parent Class method called";
   }
}

// define the child class
class ChildClass extends ParentClass {

    /* an error will occur because we cannot override a
    Method with  final keyword */
    public function myMethod() {
           echo "Child class method called";
   }
}

// create object from the child class
$child = new ChildClass();
$child->myMethod();

?>
```

In the above example, **ChildClass** extends from **ParentClass**. The **ParentClass** has the method **myMethod()** declared as **final** and this cannot be overridden. In this case the compiler causes a compile error.

Detailed Example

Bank Account Class

You are a programmer for the Hightel Software Company. You have been assigned to develop a class that models the basic workings of a bank account.

The class should have the following properties:

Balance: Holds the current account balance.
Amount: Holds amount to withdraw or deposit

The class should have the following methods:

Make Deposit: Takes an argument, which is the amount of the deposit. This argument is added to the Balance property.

Withdraw: Takes an argument that is the amount of the withdrawal. This value is subtracted from the balance property, unless the withdrawal amount is greater than the balance. If this happens, an error message is displayed.

Suggested Solution:

Listing 10.19: bank_account.php

```
<?php

// define the bank account class
class BankAccount
{
   // declare the class properties
   private $balance;
   private $amount;

   // make deposit
   public function deposit($amount)
   {
          $this->balance += $amount;
          return $balance;
   }
```

Continuation of Listing 10.19: bank_account.php

```
    // define the withdrawal method
    public function withdraw($amount)
    {
            // check if bal is greater than amount to withdraw
            if($this->balance > $amount)
            {
                $this->balance -= $amount;
                return $balance;
            }else{
                echo 'You have insufficient amount of money';
            }
    }
    // set the balance
    public function setBalance($balance)
    {
            $this->balance = $balance;
    }
    // get the balance
    public function getBalance()
    {
            return $this->balance;
    }
}

// create customer object
$customer = new BankAccount();

// initial deposit of 1000
$customer->setBalance(1000);
echo "Initial Balance  :".$customer->getBalance()."<br>";

// make a deposit of 550
$customer->deposit(550);
echo "Balance After Deposit:".$customer->getBalance()."<br>";

// make a withdrawal of 100
$amount = $customer->getBalance();
$customer->setBalance($amount);

$customer->withdraw(100);
echo "Balance After Withdrawal:". $customer->getBalance();

?>
```

The output from this program is:

Initial Balance : 1000
Balance After Deposit: 1550
Balance After Withdrawal: 1450

Programming Challenge

Q1. Account Class

You are a programmer for the Home Software Company. You have been assigned to develop a class that models the basic workings of a bank account. The class should have the following properties:

Balance: Holds the current account balance.
IntRate: Holds the interest rate for the period.
Interest: Holds the interest earned for the current period.
Transactions: Holds the number of transactions for the current period.

The class should have the following methods:

Make Deposit: Takes an argument, which is the amount of the deposit. This argument is added to the Balance property.

Withdraw Takes an argument that is the amount of the withdrawal. This value is subtracted from the balance property, unless the withdrawal amount is greater than the balance. If this happens, an error message is displayed.

Q2. Fast Freight Shipping

The Freight Shipping Company charges the following rates:

Shipping Rates	
Weight of Package (in kilograms)	Rate per 600 Miles Shipped
2 Kg or less	$1.70
Over 2 Kg but not more than 6 Kg	$2.40
Over 6 Kg but not more than 10 Kg	$3.60
Over 10 Kg	$4.90

Design and implement the PHP class **shippingCharges** that stores the **weight** of a package and the **miles shipped** and has a method that returns the shipping charges

1. You need **two** private instance variables:
    - one to store the **weight** (double)
    - and the other to store the **miles shipped** (int)

2. The **constructor** method should accept two **parameters**:
    - package weight (double)
    - miles to be shipped (int)

The method **getShippingCharges()** should calculate and return the total shipping charges.

11

Basic Form Processing

The sooner you start to code, the longer the program will take.- Roy Carlson
(From More Programming Pearls: Confessions of a Coder)

Learning Objectives

After studying this chapter, you should be able to:

- Learn how to create forms with HTML form control tags (textbox, radio buttons, checkbox, command buttons, etc).
- Understand the use of **$_POST, $_GET, $_REQUEST** global variables to gather form values.
- Code and run scripts that process form data or values.

Introduction

Form processing is a very important feature of PHP. Through the use of forms the users interact with your Web site. Forms provide for data entry into your data processing systems. Forms are the primary means of capturing the data that your scripts process to generate information, to update files and databases, and to respond to user requests for information output. As you proceed through this chapter you will learn about some basic aspects of forms processing, including the following:

- Text input controls
- Buttons
- Checkboxes
- Radio buttons
- Select or drop-down boxes
- File select boxes
- Hidden controls

Form Syntax

HTML (Hypertext Markup Language) form controls are displayed on a web page by coding them within **<form>...</form>** tags. Form tags surround the form controls. Within the **<form>...</form>** tags, the form controls can be used, even intermixed with other HTML tags or text. The syntax is:

```
<form name="formName" method="POST" or "GET" action="url" enctype="x-www-form-urlencoded">

  ........

  .........

</form>
```

The **<form>** tag contains three important attributes for form processing as described in Table 11.1:

Table 11.1: Form Syntax

Attribute	Description
name	Like other controls, forms should be named. The name can be used in client-side validation of data. Forms are named by coding **name="formName"** within the **<form>** tag. You can give your form any relavant name.
action	The **action="url"** attribute of the **<form>** tag identifies the location and the name of the page to which information from the form is to be sent for processing. If the page that will process the data captured on the form is in the same folder as the page containing the form, then the URL in the **action** parameter is simply the name of that page. Otherwise, it can be a full URL specifying a Web address on a different server or in a different folder on the same server.
method	The **method="GET | POST"** attribute specifies the means used to send the form data to the page where they will be processed. There are two methods from which to choose. • **The GET method.** With this method (**method="get"),** the data from the form are appended to the end of the URL of the page to which the data are being sent (the URL in the **action** attribute). The form data comprise a text string that is concatenated to the URL, following a question mark (?). You probably have seen this happening in your browsing of the Web. This method is no longer preferred for submitting form data since there is a limit to the number of characters that can be sent and there is no privacy as the data from the form can be seen in the browser.

	• **The POST method**. This method (**method="post")** sends the form data to the action page as a separate data stream which does not appear in the browser address bar. It also transmits as many characters as are required to send your entire form for processing. It recommended to always use this method.
enctype	In most cases you will not need to use this attribute at all. The default value (i.e. if you don't specify this attribute) is "application/x-www-form-urlencoded", which is sufficient for almost any kind of form data. The one exception is if you want to do file uploads. In that case you should use enctype = "multipart/form-data".

Form Handling Super Global Variables

PHP includes three types of form handling variables for storing and processing user form input: **$_GET, $_POST**, and **$_REQUEST**. These are actually associative arrays of values. These variables are also referred to as super-globals. This simply means that the variables are accessible (available) in all scopes throughout a script. Table 11.2 defines the global variables in details.

Table 11.2: Global Variables

Global Variable	Description
$_GET[ ]	An associative array containing any values provided to a script through a form's GET method.
$_POST[ ]	An associative array containing any values provided to a script through a form's POST method.
$_REQUEST[ ]	An associative array containing any values provided to a script through a form's POST and GET method.

Differences between the GET and POST methods are discussed in Table 11.3.

Table 11.3: Comparison of global variables

GET Method	POST Method
1. GET method has no security since data can be viewed in address bar (URL). For example, it is not recommended to use this method for user login, since login data can be seen.	POST method has security of data because it hides the data. Therefore, it can be used for user login.
2. We can bookmark link with the GET method.	We cannot bookmark page links with POST method as the URL is hidden.
3. Server can log all actions (all the URLs).	Server does not log all actions as the URL is hidden.
4. Because of server log, we can pass upto 255 characters as query string in the URL.	We can pass unlimited data by this method as query string.

The `Input` Tag

Following is some of the list of attributes for **<input>** tag.

<input type = " " **name** = " " **value** = " " **size** = " " **maxlength** = " "**>**

- **type:** Indicates the type of input control you want to create. This element is also used to create other form controls such as radio buttons and checkboxes.
- **name:** Used to give the name to the textbox. It holds the value entered into the textbox.
- **value:** Provides an initial value for the text input control that the user will see when the form loads.
- **size:** Allows the user to specify the width of the text-input control in terms of

characters.

- **maxlength:** Allows you to specify the maximum number of characters a user can enter into the text box.

Text `Input` Controls

There are three types of text input used on forms:

- **Single-line text input controls:** Used for items that require only one line of user input, such as search boxes or names. They are created using the **<input>** element.
- **Password input controls:** Single-line text input that mask the characters a user enters.
- **Multi-line text input controls:** Used when the user is required to give details that may be longer than a single line. Multi-line input controls are created with the **<textarea>** element.

Single-Line Text `Input` Controls

Single-line text input controls are created using an **<input>** element whose type attributes have a value of text.

Syntax:

```
<input type="text">
```

Listing 11.1 is a basic example of a single-line text input used to enter the first name and the last name:

Listing 11.1: text.php

```
<html>
<body bgcolor="#f7f7f7">

<form action="hello_get.php" method="get">
   First name:   <input type="text" name="first_name"
                 /><br><br>
   Last name:    <input type="text" name="last_name" />
</form>

</body>
</html>
```

Figure 11.1 shows the output of the scripts in Listing 11.1.

Figure 11.1
Displays text input control field

First name:

Last name:

Password `Input` Controls

This is also a form of single-line text input control that is created using an **<input>** tag whose type attribute has a value of password. A password input control usually chnges text characters to unreadable characters as they are being entered in order to prevent the users from wiewing what is been typed. Figure 11.2 is an example showing how text characters are shown in password controls.

Syntax:

```
<input type="password">
```

An example of a single-line password input is shown in Listing 11.2. This is normally used to take user password, PIN, or any confidential information.

Listing 11.2: password_control.php

```
<html>
<body bgcolor="#f7f7f7">

<form name="formName"
method="POST"action="password_control.php">
     Login :    <input type="text" name="login" /><br>
     Password: <input type="password" name="password_control"
/>
</form>

</body>
</html>
```

Figure 11.2 is the result generated from the scripts in Listing 11.2:

Figure 11.2:
Display password input control field.

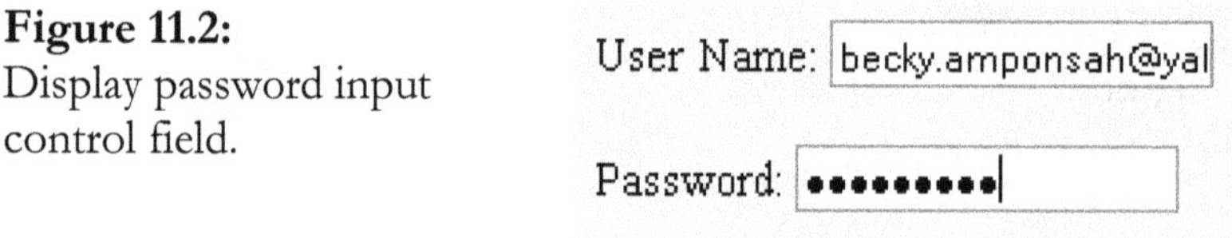

Multiple-Line Text `Input` Controls

If you want to allow a visitor to your site to enter more than one line of text, you should create a multiple-line text input control using the **<textarea>** element.

Syntax:

```
<textarea name=" " rows=" " cols=" " >

    ……

</textarea>
```

Listing 11.3 is an example of a multi-line text input.

Listing 11.3: text_area.php

```
<html>
<body bgcolor="#f7f7f7">

 <form name="formName" method="POST" action="text_area.php">
        Description :<br>
        <textarea rows="3" cols="30" name="description">
              Enter description here...
        </textarea>
</form>

</body>
</html>
```

The above script will produce the result as shown in Figure 11.3:

Figure 11.3:
Display text area or multiple-line text input control

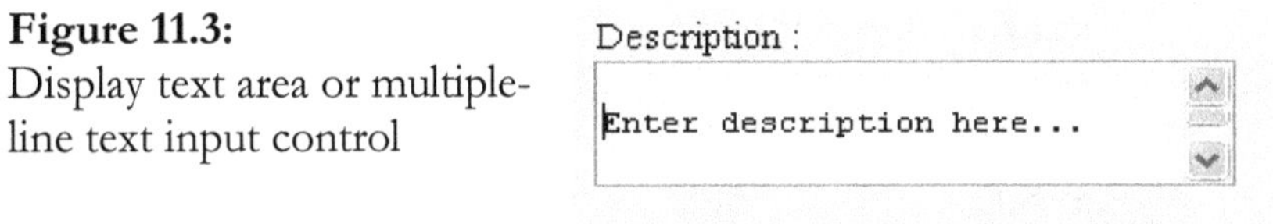

Following are the attributes for <textarea> tag.

- **name:** The name of the control. This is used in the name/value pair that is sent to the server.
- **rows:** Indicates the number of rows of text area box.
- **cols:** Indicates the number of columns of text area box.

Button `Input` Controls

There are various ways in HTML to create clickable buttons. You can create clickable buttons using **<input>** tag. When you use the **<input>** element to create a button, the type of button you create is specified using the **type** attribute. The **type** attribute can take the following values:

- **submit:** This creates a button that automatically submits a form.
- **reset:** This creates a button that automatically clears the values in the input controls.
- **button:** This creates a button that is used to trigger a client-side script when the user clicks that button.

Listing 11.4 is an example of input-type button controls:

Listing 11.4: input_control_button.php

```
<html>
<body bgcolor="#f7f7f7">

<form method="POST" action="input_control_button.php">
    Input control buttons<br>
    <input type="submit" name="submit" value="Submit">
    <input type="reset" name="reset" value="Reset">
    <input type="button" name="button" value="Button">
</form>

</body>
</html>
```

Figure 11.4 displays the control buttons for submit, reset and button.

Figure 11.4: Display input type buttons

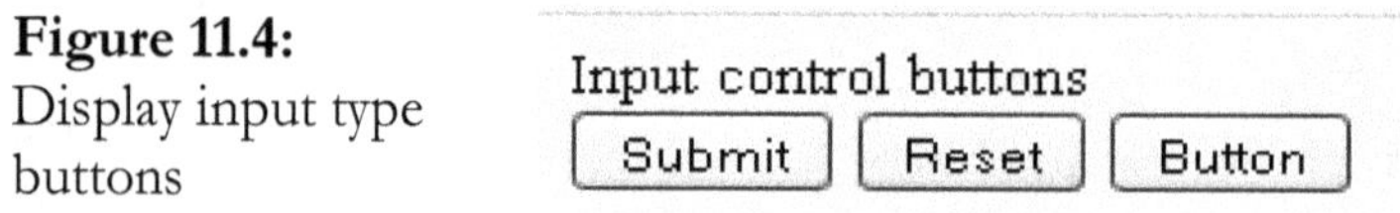

You can use an image to create a button as shown in 11.5 and Figure 11.5 respectively.

Listing 11.5: image_button.php

```
<html>
<body bgcolor="#f7f7f7">

<form name="formName" method="POST" action="image_button.php">
    <input type="image" name="imagebutton"
    src="images/add.bmp"/>
</form>

</body>
</html>
```

Here **src** attribute specifies a location of the image on your web server.

Figure 11.5:
Display an image type button

You can also use **<button>** element to create various buttons as shown in Listing 11.6 and Figure 11.6 respectively. Here is the syntax:

Listing 11.6: buttons.php

```
<html>
<body bgcolor="#f7f7f7">

<form name="formName" method="POST" action="buttons.php">
 <button type="submit">Submit</button>
 <button type="reset">Reset</button>
 <button type="button">Button</button>
</form>

</body>
</html>
```

This will produce the following result:

Figure 11.6:
Display button controls

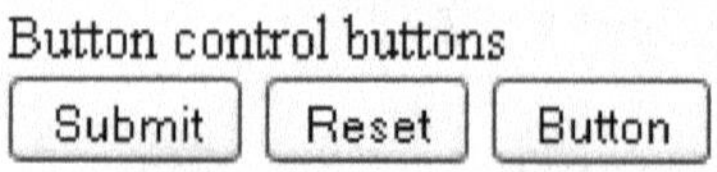

The Submit and Reset Button

These are special buttons which can be created using **<input>**. When **submit** button is clicked on, the form's data is submitted to the back-end application. When **reset** button is clicked on, all the forms control are reset to default state. You already have seen **submit** button above, Listing 11.7 is an example of a **reset** button, which produces the output in Figure 11.7.

Listing 11.7: submit_form.php

```
<form action="reset.php" method="get">

   First name:    <input type="text" name="first_name"
/><br>
   Last name:     <input type="text" name="last_name" />
                  <input type="submit" value="Submit" />
                  <input type="reset" value="Reset" />

</form>
```

This will produce the following result.

Figure 11.7:
Displays submitting and resetting of a form.

Checkbox Input Control

Checkboxes are used when more than one option is required to be selected. They are created using **<input>** tag as shown below.

Syntax:

<input type="checkbox">

Listing 11.8 is an example HTML code for a form with two checkboxes. The output generated from this script is shown in Figure 11.8.

Listing 11.8: checkbox.php

```
<form action="checkbox.php" method="get">

 <input type="checkbox" name="maths" value="on"> Maths
 <input type="checkbox" name="physics" value="on"> Physics
 <input type="submit" value="Select Subject" />

</form>
```

The result of this code is the following form

Figure 11.8: Display checkbox controls

Maths Physics Select Subject

Following is the list of important checkbox attributes:

- **type:** Indicates that you want to create a checkbox.
- **name:** Name of the control.
- **value:** The value that will be used if the checkbox is selected. More than one checkbox should share the same name only if you want to allow users to select

several items from the same list.

- **checked:** Indicates that when the page loads, the checkbox should be selected.

Radio-button Input Control

Radio buttons are used when only one option is required to be selected. They are created using **<input>** tag with other attributes as shown in Listing 11.9.

Syntax:

<input type="radio">

Here is an example HTML code for a form with two radio buttons:

Listing 11.9: radio_button.php

```
<form action="radio_button.php" method="post">

 <input type="radio" name="subject" value="maths" /> Maths
 <input type="radio" name="subject" value="physics" /> Physics
 <input type="submit" value="Select Subject" />

</form>
```

Figure 11.9 shows the form generated after running the above codes.

Figure 11.9:
Display radio button input controls

Maths Physics Select Subject

Following is the list of important radiobox attributes:

- **type:** Indicates that you want to create a radiobox.
- **name:** Name of the control.
- **value:** Used to indicate the value that will be sent to the server if this option is selected.

- **checked:** Indicates that this option should be selected by default when the page loads.

Select or Drop-Down Boxes

Drop-down box is used when we have many options available to be selected but only one or two will be selected.

The select option statement can be categorized in two ways:

- **Single option:** list of items are displayed in a drop-down menu to enable the user to select choose.
- **Group option:** in this case, the items listed in the drop-down menu are group under different headings for the user to select.

Single Select Option

Syntax:

```
<select>
    <option> … option item ….  </option>
    <option> … option item ….  </option>
    <option> … option item ….  </option>
    …
    …
</select>
```

Listing 11.10 is an example of HTML code for a form with one dropdown box. The output of this script is shown in Figure 11.10.

Listing 11.10: select_box.php

```
<form action="select_box.php" method="post">

  <select name="dropdown">
        <option value="Maths" selected >Maths</option>
        <option value="Physics">Physics</option>
  </select>

  <input type="submit" value="Submit" />

</form>
```

Figure 11.10 shows the form generated after running the above codes.

Figure 11.10:
Display a select box input control

Following is the list of important attributes of <**select**>:

- **name:** This is the name for the control.
- **size:** This can be used to present a scrolling list box.
- **multiple:** This allows the user to select multiple items from the menu.

Following is the list of important attributes of <**option**>:

- **value:** The value that is sent to the server if this option is selected.
- **selected:** Specifies that this option should be the initially selected value when the page loads.
- **label:** An alternative way of labeling options.

Group Select Option Control (Optgroup)

The **<optgroup>** tag is used to group together related options in a select list. If you have a long list of options, grouping of related options is easier for the user to select items.

Syntax:

<select>

<optgroup>

<option> ...option item... </option>
<option> ...option item... </option>
......

<optgroup>

</**select**>

Listing 11.11 is an example of HTML code for a form with one dropdown box with optgroup.

Listing 11.11: optgroup.php

```
<select>

  <optgroup label="West Africa">
      <option value="Ghana">Ghana</option>
      <option value="Togo">Togo</option>
  </optgroup>

  <optgroup label="East Africa">
      <option value="Uganda"> Uganda </option>
      <option value="Kenya"> Kenya </option>
  </optgroup>

</select>
```

The result of the above code produces the form shown in figure 11.11

Figure **11.11:**
Display optgroup input control

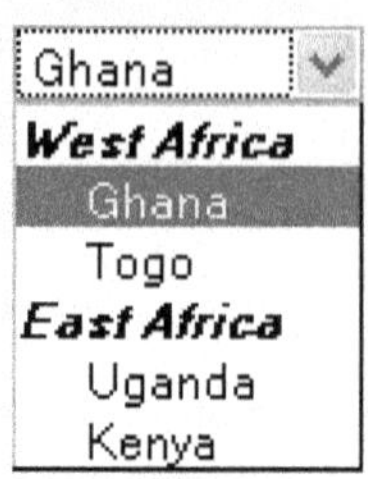

File Select (Upload) Boxes

If you want to allow a user to upload a file to your web site, you will need to use a file upload box, also known as a file select box. This is also created using the **<input>** element.

Syntax:

<input type="file" enctype="multipart/form-data">

Listing 11.12 describes an HTML code for a form with one file select box. After the execution of this script, automatically, a text input box and button with a prescription 'Browse…' are generated on the form that enables the user to upload the necessary files as shown Figure 11.12.

Listing 11.12: fileselect.php

```
<form action="fileselect.php" method="post" name="fileupload"
enctype="multipart/form-data">

    <input type="file" name="fileupload" />

</form>
```

The result of the above code produces the form below.

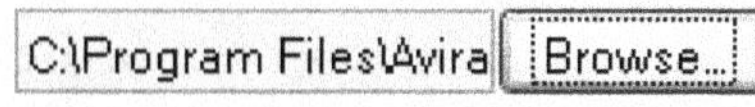

Figure 11.12: Display select file input control

Fieldset Controls

The <fieldset> tag is used to logically group together elements in a form. The <fieldset> tag draws a box around the related form elements. The <legend> tag defines a caption for the fieldset element.

Syntax:

```
< fieldset >
        <legend>write your section description here</legend>
</fieldset >
```

Example of HTML code for a form with fieldset is shown in Listing 11.13 and Figure 11.13 demonstrate the output.

Listing 11.13: fieldset.php

```
<html>
<body>
<form>

  <fieldset>
      <legend>Personal Info</legend>
      Customer Name:<input type="text" size="60"/><br/>
      Email Address:<input type="text" size="100"/><br />
      Date of birth: <input type="text" size="10" />
  </fieldset>

</form>
</body>
</html>
```

The result of the above code produces the form below.

Figure 11.13:
Display a fieldset around input boxes

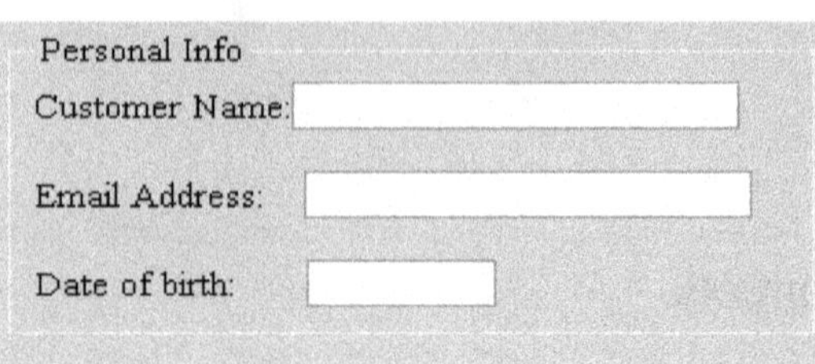

Detailed Examples

Q1. Form Handling: Member Login

This first example of form processing is a logon application. It involves two pages. The first page, named "**logonform.php**," contains a form for submitting username and password. The visitor enters the information and clicks the "**Submit**" button to submit the form information for checking.

Here is the code for the form as shown in Listing 11.14.

The form generated by the script (Listing 11.14) for user input is shown in figure 11.14.

Figure 11.14:
Member Login

Member Login

User Name: hightelsoft

Password: ●●●●●●●●●●

Submit

Listing 11.14: loginform.php

```
<html>
<body bgcolor="#F5F5F5">
<h3>Member Login</h3>
<pre>

<!-- The form starts here -->
<form name="Logon" action="welcome.php" method="post">
   <table border="0">
   <tr>
       <td>User Name: </td>
       <td><input type="text" name="username" size="20"></td>
   </tr>
   <tr>
       <td>Password: </td>
       <td><input type="password" name="Password"
   size="20"></td>
   </tr>
   <tr>
       <td> </td>
       <td><input type="submit" name="submit" value="Submit">
   </td>
   </tr>
   </table>
</form>

</pre>
</body>
</html>
```

The second page is a site welcome page named "**welcome.php**". The page displays the user name when the submit button is clicked. This is to just demonstrate how form fields are moved from one page to another as shown in Listing 11.15. In a more real-life application, which we shall see in our later chapters, the form information will be submitted through the **loginform.php** page to the **welcome.php** page. The **welcome.php** will have to check for valid user account. If the correct username and password is submitted, then the page will be displayed. If either the username or password is incorrect, the visitor is returned to the **logonform.php** page.

Listing 11.15: welcome.php
```
<html>
<body>

<?php

/* this is a simple example, as such the script to check
whether username and password are valid are not coded here.
*/

// display the username entered on the form.
$username=$_POST['username'];
echo "Welcome, $username!";

?>
</body>
</html>
```

The code above will output: **Welcome, Hightel!**.

Q2. Form Handling: Membership Registration Form

The following example shows a typical HTML form page that can be processed by PHP. In this example, users are asked to fill in a registration form. After the form is completed and the user clicks the "Register" button, the **process.php** file is activated and the user information is displayed on the screen as shown in Listing 11.16.

When the **Register** button in the above example is clicked, all of the form data entered by the user is passed to the page, **process.php**, for processing. Since this form is using the POST method, all form data is passed using the PHP **$_POST** variable. Each input control is uniquely identified by the value assinged to its name attribute. The form control's name attribute value becomes the index value of the **$_POST** array. The form page passes data using the following PHP **$_POST** variables:

$_POST["Fname"] = Eranus Frisaland

$_POST["Lname"] = Amoakoko

$_POST["City"] = Accra

$_POST["Region"] = Greater Accra

$_POST["Comments"] = PHP is interesting to learn.

Since the PHP **$_POST** and **$_GET** variables use the value associated with the form control's name attribute, it is important that all form elements be assigned a unique name value.

Listing 11.16: registerform.php

```
<html>
<body bgcolor="#F5F5F5">
<h3> Membership Registration Form </h3>
<pre>

<form action="process.php" method="post">

First Name:    <input type="text" name="Fname" size="30"
               /><br/>
Last Name:     <input type="text" name="Lname"
               size="30"/><br/>
City:          <input type="text" name="City" size="30"/><br/>
Region:        <input type="text" name="Region"
               size="30"/><br/>
Comments:      <textarea name="Comment" cols="23" rows="5">
               </textarea><br/>
               <input type="submit" name="submit"
               value="Register"/>
</form>
</pre>
</body>
</html>
```

In Figure 11.15, the form is displayed and the user enters data to be processed.

Figure 11.15: **Membership Registration Form**

Membership Registration Form

First Name: Eranus Friseland

Last Name: Amoakoko

City: Accra

Region: Greater Accra

Comments: PHP is interesting to learn.

Register

The HTML form page above is processed by the page **process.php** as shown in Listing 11.17. Data entered into the form are passed using the **$_POST** variable to a PHP script that displays the information to the browser window.

Listing 11.17: process.php

```
<html>
<body>
<?php

 // diaplay form data
echo "Your First Name is: " . $_POST["Fname"] . "<br/>";
echo "Your Last Name is: " . $_POST["Lname"] . "<br/>";
echo "Your City is: " . $_POST["City"] . "<br/>";
echo "Your Region is: " . $_POST["Region"] . "<br/>";
echo "<br/>";
echo "Your Comment: " . $_POST["Comment"];

?>
</body>
</html>
```

The PHP parses the XHTML form data and uses the **echo** statement to display the results in the browser window. The output would appear as:

Your First Name is: Eranus Frisaland
Your Last Name is: Amoakoko
Your City is: Accra
Your Region is: Greater Accra

Your Comment: PHP is interesting to learn.

If the get method is used instead of the post method **<form method="get" action="process.php/>,** the **$_POST** array will be replaced by the **$_GET** array. We can also use the **$_REQUEST** array. This array can be used to collect data submitted through either the **post** or **get** method. At this point you may question whether it is better to use the get or post method with PHP form processing. Although both specify the manner in which form information is transmitted to the page identified in the **action** attribute, the POST method is recommended. The differences between **post** and **get** were presented earlier in this chapter.

Q3. Combined Form Tags and PHP Script in One File: Membership Registration Form

While separation of HTML and PHP codes is a practice used by many developers, it is also possible to combine HTML and PHP codes into a single PHP file. This practice produces only a single file, simplifying the coding and error detection process. Listing 11.18 shows the previous example (**registerform.htm** and **process.php**) combined into a single PHP called **registerform_process.php**.

Listing 11.18: registerform_process.php

```
<?php

 // display form data
 echo "Your First Name is: " . $_POST["Fname"] . "<br/>";
 echo "Your Last Name is: " . $_POST["Lname"] . "<br/>";
 echo "Your City is: " . $_POST["City"] . "<br/>";
 echo "Your State is: " . $_POST["Region"] . "<br/>";
 echo "<br/>";
 echo "Your Comment: " . $_POST["Comments"];
?>
```

Continuation of Listing 11.18: registerform_process.php

```
<! -- HTML for start from here -- >
<html>
<head>
<title>Membership Registration Form</title>
</head>
<body>
<h3> Membership Registration Form </h3>
<pre>

<form action="registerform_process.php" method="post">

 First Name:    <input type="text" name="Fname" size="30"/>
 Last Name:     <input type="text" name="Lname" size="30"/>
 City:          <input type="text" name="City" size="25"/>
 Region:        <input type="text" name="Region" size="30"/>
 Comments:      <textarea name="Comment" cols="40" rows="5">
                </textarea>
                <input type="submit" name="submit"
                value="Register"/>
</form>

</pre>
</body>
</body>
</html>
```

The PHP code block is placed at the beginning section of the page. Also, the form tag **action** is changed to "**registerform_process.php**". Now, the page will post to itself and not to a separate PHP page. When you run this script, you will likely see some **Notice** similar to as shown below. Therefore, a final step is required in order for the page to work properly. Take a look at the generated page output below. Here the HTML form section displays properly. However, PHP code block has been executed prior to form submission (or before the **submit** button is clicked). This causes the string values in the **echo** statements to be display when the page loads. The concatenated **$_POST[]** values are missing because the form has not been submitted.

The solution to this problem is to prevent any of the PHP code block from executing until the form is submitted or until the submit button is clicked. This is possible using an **if** construct. When the page loads, we use an **if** statement to determine if the submit button has been clicked, using **if (isset($_POST['submit'])**. This statement is **true** only after a form submission has been triggered as a result of the submit button being clicked. The previous page is now shown in Listing 11.19 and Figure 11.16 using the **if** statement to check for form submission.

Notice: Undefined index: Fname in **c:\program files\easyphp1-8\www\phpcodes\registerform_process.php** on line **3**
Your First Name is:

Notice: Undefined index: Lname in **c:\program files\easyphp1-8\www\phpcodes\registerform_process.php** on line **4**
Your Last Name is:

Notice: Undefined index: City in **c:\program files\easyphp1-8\www\phpcodes\registerform_process.php** on line **5**
Your City is:

Notice: Undefined index: Region in **c:\program files\easyphp1-8\www\phpcodes\registerform_process.php** on line **6**
Your State is:

Notice: Undefined index: Comments in **c:\program files\easyphp1-8\www\phpcodes\registerform_process.php** on line **8**
Your Message is:

Figure 11.16: Membership Registration Form

Membership Registration Form

First Name: Eranus Frisaland

Last Name: Amoakoko

City: Accra

Region: Greater Accra

Comments: PHP is interesting to learn.

Register

Listing 11.19: registerform_notice_corrected_process.php

```
<html>
<head>
<title>Membership Registration Form</title>
</head>

<?php

// check whether the user clicks on the submit button
if(isset($_POST['submit']))
{
        // print form data
        echo "Your First Name is: " . $_POST["Fname"]."<br/>";
        echo "Your Last Name is: " . $_POST["Lname"]."<br/>";
        echo "Your City is: " . $_POST["City"] . "<br/>";
        echo "Your State is: " . $_POST["Region"] . "<br/>";
        echo "<br/>";
        echo "Your Comment: " . $_POST["Comment"];
}

?>

<body bgcolor="f3f3f3">
<h3> Membership Registration Form </h3>

<! -- HTML for start from here -- >
<form action="registerform_notice_corrected_process.php"
method="post">
   <table width="40%" border="0" cellspacing="4"
    cellpadding="3">
     <tr>
           <td width="29%">First Name:</td>
           <td width="71%"><input type="text" name="Fname"
            size="30"/></td>
     </tr>
```

Continuation of Listing 11.19: registerform_notice_corrected_process.php

```
        <tr>
              <td>Last Name: </td>
              <td><input type="text" name="Lname"
               size="30"/></td>
        </tr>
        <tr>
              <td>City:</td>
              <td><input type="text" name="City"
               size="25"/></td>
        </tr>
        <tr>
              <td>Region:</td>
              <td><input type="text" name="Region"
               size="30"/></td>
        </tr>
        <tr>
              <td>Comments:</td>
              <td><textarea name="Comment" cols="40" rows="5">
               </textarea></td>
        </tr>
        <tr>
              <td> </td>
              <td><input type="submit" name="submit"
              value="Register"/></td>
        </tr>
     </table>

</form>
</body>
</html>
```

Now the code in the PHP section of the page is only displayed after the condition **isset($_POST['submit'])** validates to **true,** meaning that the submit button has been clicked and the form submission process has begun.

Q4. Form Handling: Employee Data Capture Form

Figure 11.17 is a sample HTML form for inserting an employee record into a database.

Figure 11.17: **Employee Record Form**

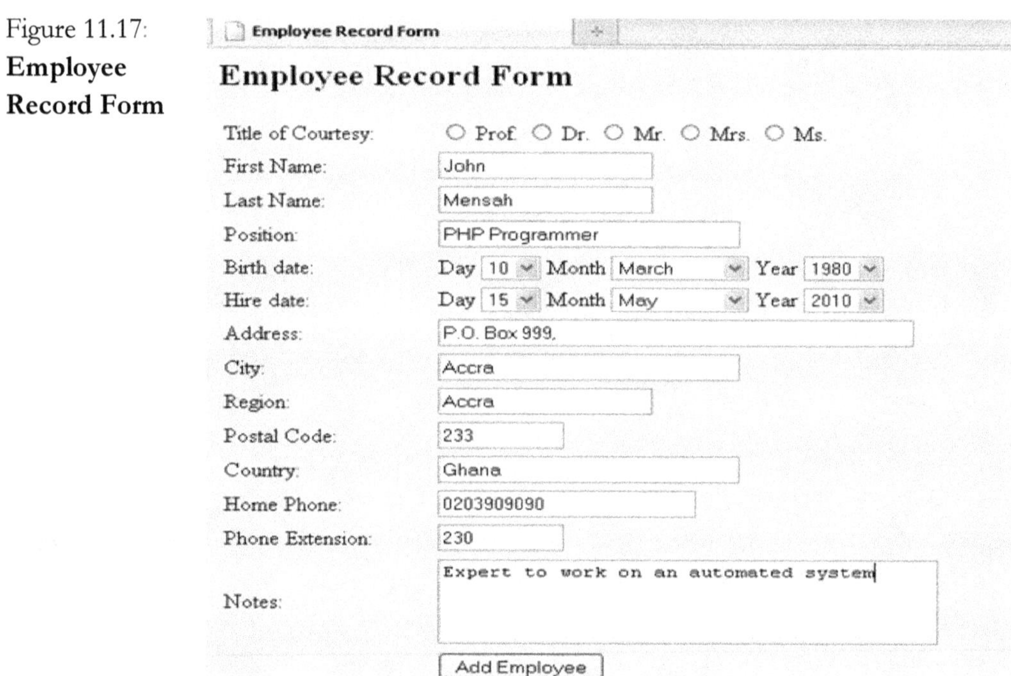

The HTML tags used to create the form (in Figure 11.17) are shown in the program Listing 11.20.

Listing 11.20: employee.php

```
<html>
<head>
<title> Employee Record Form</title>
</head>
<body bgcolor="#f3f3f3">
<h2>Employee Record Form</h2>

<form method="post" action=" process_employee.php ">
<table width="627" cellpadding="2">
<tr>
   <td>Title of Courtesy:</td>
   <td>
     <input type="radio" name="TitleOfCourtesy" value="Prof."/> Prof.
```

Continuation of Listing 11.20: employee.php

```
<input type="radio" name="TitleOfCourtesy"
  value="Dr."/> Dr.
  <input type="radio" name="TitleOfCourtesy"
   value="Mr."/>Mr.
  <input type="radio" name="TitleOfCourtesy"
   value="Mrs."/>Mrs.
  <input type="radio" name="TitleOfCourtesy"
   value="Ms."/>Ms.
</td>
</tr>
<tr>
      <td>First Name:</td>
      <td><input type="text" name="FirstName"
       size="20"/></td>
</tr>
<tr>
      <td>Last Name:</td>
      <td><input type="text" name="LastName"
       size="20"/></td>
</tr>
<tr>
      <td>Position:</td>
      <td><input type="text" name="Position"
      size="30"/></td>
</tr>
<tr>
      <td>Birth date:</td>
      <td>Day

      <select name="BirthDay">
      <?php
      // a for-loop to display the days in drop-down menu
      for($i=1; $i<=31; $i++)
      {
          echo "<option value='$i'>$i</option>";
      }
      ?>
```

Continuation of Listing 11.20: employee.php

```
        </select>
         Month
         <select name="BirthMonth">
            <option value="1">January</option>
            <option value="2">February</option>
            <option value="3">March</option>
            <option value="4">April</option>
            <option value="5">May</option>
            <option value="6">June</option>
            <option value="7">July</option>
            <option value="8">August</option>
            <option value="9">September</option>
            <option value="10">October</option>
            <option value="11">November</option>
            <option value="12">December</option>
          </select>

          Year
          <select name="BirthYear">
          <?php
          // a for loop to display the years from 1940 to now
          $currentYear=date('Y');
          for($i=$currentYear; $i>=1940; $i=$i-1)
          {
             echo "<option value='$i'>$i</option>";
          }
          ?>
          </select> </td>
</tr>
<tr>
        <td>Hire date:</td>
        <td> Day
        <select name="HireDay">
        <?php
```

Continuation of Listing 11.20: employee.php

```
        // a for loop to display days
        for($i=1; $i<=31; $i++)
        {
           echo "<option value='$i'>$i</option>";
        }
        ?>
        </select>
        Month
        <select name="HireMonth">
            <option value="1">January</option>
            <option value="2">February</option>
            <option value="3">March</option>
            <option value="4">April</option>
            <option value="5">May</option>
            <option value="6">June</option>
            <option value="7">July</option>
            <option value="8">August</option>
            <option value="9">September</option>
            <option value="10">October</option>
            <option value="11">November</option>
            <option value="12">December</option>
          </select>
          Year
          <select name="HireYear">
          <?php
             // set current year
             $currentYear=date('Y');
              // a for loop to display the years from 1940
             for($i=$currentYear; $i>=1940; $i=$i-1)
             {
                echo "<option value='$i'>$i</option>";
             }
          ?>
          </select> </td>
</tr>
```

Continuation of Listing 11.20: employee.php

```
<tr>
      <td>Address:</td>
      <td><input type="text" name="Address"
      size="50"/></td>
</tr>
<tr>
      <td>City:</td>
      <td><input type="text" name="City" size="30"/></td>
</tr>
<tr>
      <td>Region:</td>
      <td><input type="text" name="Region" size="20"/></td>
</tr>
<tr>
      <td>Postal Code:</td>
      <td><input type="text" name="PostalCode"
       size="10"/></td>
</tr>
<tr>
      <td>Country:</td>
      <td><input type="text" name="Country"
       size="30"/></td>
</tr>
<tr>
      <td>Home Phone:</td>
      <td><input type="text" name="HomePhone"
      size="25"/></td>
</tr>
 <tr>
      <td>Phone Extension:</td>
      <td><input type="text" name="Extension"
      size="10"/></td>
</tr>
<tr>
      <td>Notes:</td>
      <td><textarea name="Notes" cols="40" rows="3"></textarea></td>
</tr>
```

Continuation of Listing 11.20: employee.php

```
   <tr>
         <td>  </td>
         <td><input type="submit" name="add"
          value="Add Employee"/></td>
   </tr>
</table>
</form>
</body>
</html>
```

The above code, which contains some embedded PHP code, outputs a simple HTML form (Figure 11.17). Its action page is **process_employee.php**, which will eventually contain PHP code to process the submitted form.

The **process_employee.php** processing form is shown in Listing 11.21.

Listing 11.21: process_employee.php

```
<html>
<head>
<title> Employee Record </title>
</head>
<body bgcolor="#F5F5F5">
<h3>Employee Record </h3>
<?php
// checks whether the form has been submitted.
if(isset($_POST['add']))
{
     /* converts the new line characters (\n) in the text
     area into HTML line breaks (the <br /> tag)*/
     $_POST['Notes'] = nl2br($_POST['Notes']);

     // assign form values to new variables
     $TitleOfCourtesy = $_POST['TitleOfCourtesy'];
     $LastName = $_POST['LastName'];
     $FirstName = $_POST['FirstName'];
```

Continuation of Listing 11.21: process_employee.php

```
        $Position = $_POST['Position'];
        $Notes = $_POST['Notes'];
        $Region = $_POST['Region'];

        // print out some of the values in the browser.
        echo "Your Last Name: $LastName<br />";
        echo "Your First Name: $FirstName<br />";
        echo "Your Position: $Position<br />";
        echo "Your Comments:  $Notes<br />";
        echo "You are from: $Region<br />";
}
else
{
        echo "The submit button not clicked.";
}
?>

</body>
</html>
```

Q5. Internet Service Provider

An Internet service provider offers three subscription packages to its customers, plus a discount for nonprofit organizations:

Package A 10 hours of access for $9.95 per month. Additional hours are $2.00 per hour.

Package B: 20 hours of access for $14.95 per month. Additional hours are $1.00 per hour.

Package C: Unlimited access for $19.95 per month.

Nonprofit Organization: The service provider gives all nonprofit organizations a 20% discount on all packages.

Your form should look like Figure 11.18.

The user should select the package the customer has purchased (from a set of radio buttons) and enter the number of hours used. A check box captioned "Nonprofit Organization" should also appear on the form. The application should calculate and display the total amount due. If the user selects the "Nonprofit Organization" check box, a 20% discount should be deducted.

Input validation: The number of hours used in a month cannot exceed 740.

Suggested Solution

The HTML tag that generates the form and the PHP script that does the computation are shown in Listing 11.22.

Figure 11.18: Displays a form generated for an Internet Service Provider.

Internet Service Packages

Internet Services

Package A
Nonprofit Organization
Package B
Package C

Number of Hours: 44
Total Amount: 62.36
Compute

Listing 11.22: internet_services.php

```
<html>
<head>
<title>Internet Service Packages</title>
</head>
<body bgcolor="f3f3f3">
<h2>Internet Service Packages</h2>
```

Continuation of Listing 11.22: internet_services.php

```
<?php

//declare variables
$noofHours=' ';
$totalAmountDue=' ';

// check whether the user clicks on compute button
if(isset($_POST['compute'])){

// assign constant value to discount
define(DISCOUNT,0.20);

// assign form values to variables
$selectedPackage = $_POST['package'];
$nonprofit=$_POST['nonprofit'];
$noofHours=$_POST['noofHours'];
$totalAmount=$_POST['totalAmount'];
$nonprofit=$_POST['nonprofit'];

// if user selects package A
if($selectedPackage == "packageA"){
   if($nonprofit == "nonProfit"){
     if($noofHours <= 10){
          $amountWithoutDiscount = 9.95;
     }
     else{
          $amountWithoutDiscount = 9.95+(($noofHours-10)*2.00);
     }

    $discount = $amountWithoutDiscount * DISCOUNT;
    $totalAmountDue = $amountWithoutDiscount - $discount;
  }
  else{
    $totalAmountDue = 9.95 + (($noofHours - 10) * 2.00);
  }
 }
```

Continuation of Listing 11.22: internet_services.php

```
// if user selects package B
if($selectedPackage == "packageB"){
 if($nonprofit == "nonProfit"){
    if($noofHours <= 20){
        $amountWithoutDiscount = 14.95;
    }
    else{
        $amountWithoutDiscount = 14.95+(($noofHours-20)*1.00);
    }
    $discount = $amountWithoutDiscount * DISCOUNT;
    $totalAmountDue = $amountWithoutDiscount - $discount;
 }
 else{
    $totalAmountDue = 14.95 + (($noofHours - 20) * 1.00);
 }
}
 // if user selects package C
if($selectedPackage == "packageC"){
 if($nonprofit == "nonProfit"){
    $amountWithoutDiscount = 19.95;
    $discount = $amountWithoutDiscount * DISCOUNT;
    $totalAmountDue = $amountWithoutDiscount - $discount;
 }
 else{
    $totalAmountDue = 19.95;
 }
  }
}
?>

<! -- the form starts from here -->
<form action="internet_services.php" method="post">
<fieldset style="width: 30%; "><legend>Internet
Services</legend>
<table width="100%" border="0">
```

Continuation of Listing 11.22: internet_services.php

```
    <tr>
          <td><input type="radio" name="package"
           value="packageA">Package A</td>
          <td height="22"><input type="checkbox" name="nonprofit"
          value="nonProfit">Nonprofit Organization</td>
    </tr>
    <tr>
          <td colspan="2"><input type="radio"
          name="package">Package B</td>
    </tr>
    <tr>
          <td colspan="2"><input type="radio" name="package"
          value="packageC">Package C</td>
    </tr>
    <tr>
          <td colspan="2" nowrap> </td>
    </tr>
    <tr>
          <td width="34%" nowrap>Number of Hours:</td>
          <td width="66%" nowrap><input type="text"
           name="noofHours" value="<?php echo $noofHours ?>"
           size="10"></td>
    </tr>
    <tr>
          <td nowrap>Total Amount:</td>
          <td nowrap><input type="text" name="totalAmountDue"
           readonly="readonly" value="<?php echo $totalAmountDue
           ?>" size="10"></td>
    </tr>
    <tr>
          <td nowrap> </td>
          <td nowrap><input type="submit" name="compute"
          value="Compute"> </td>
    </tr>
</table>
</fieldset>
</form>
</body>
</html>
```

Programming Challenge

Q1. Theater Revenue

A theater keeps a percentage of the revenue earned from ticket sales. The remainder goes to the movie company. Write a script that calculates and displays the following figures for one night's business at a theater:

a) Gross revenue for adult tickets sold. This is the amount of money taken in for all adult tickets sold.
b) Net revenue for adult tickets sold. This is the amount of money from adult ticket sales left over after the payment to the movie company has been deducted.
c) Gross revenue for child tickets sold. This is the amount of money taken in for all child tickets sold.
d) Net revenue for child tickets sold. This is the amount of money from child ticket sales left over after the payment to the movie company has been deducted.
e) Total gross revenue. This is the sum of gross revenue for adult and child tickets sold.
f) Total net revenue. This is the sum of net revenue for adult and child tickets sold.

Your form should resemble Form A.

Assume the theater keeps 20% of its receipts. Use a named constant in your code to represent this percentage.

Q2. Stadium Seating

There are three seating categories at an athletic stadium. For a baseball game, Class A seats cost $15 each, Class B seats cost $12 each, and Class C seats cost $9 each. Write a script that allows the user to enter the number of tickets sold for each class. The script should be able to display the amount of income generated from each class of ticket sales and the total revenue generated. The form should resemble Form B.

Form A

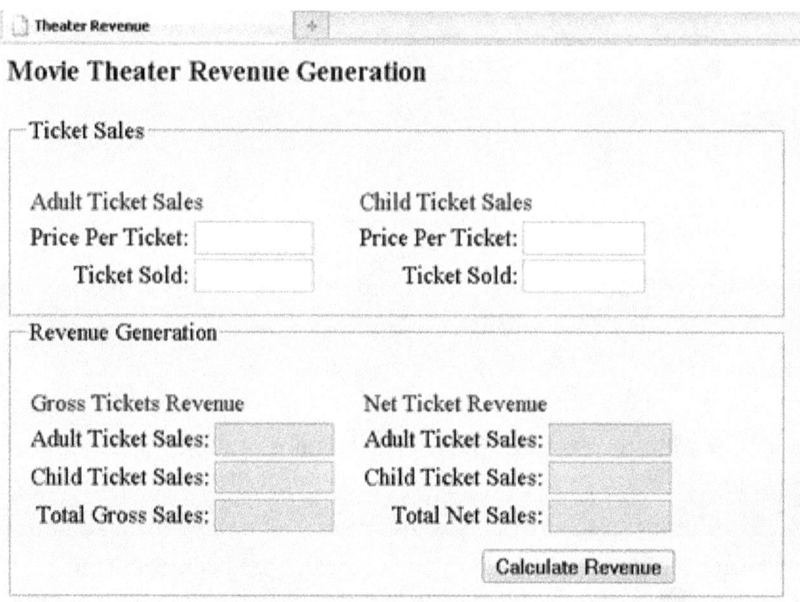
Theater Revenue
Movie Theater Revenue Generation
Ticket Sales
Adult Ticket Sales
Price Per Ticket:
Ticket Sold:
Child Ticket Sales
Price Per Ticket:
Ticket Sold:
Revenue Generation
Gross Tickets Revenue
Adult Ticket Sales:
Child Ticket Sales:
Total Gross Sales:
Net Ticket Revenue
Adult Ticket Sales:
Child Ticket Sales:
Total Net Sales:
Calculate Revenue

Form B

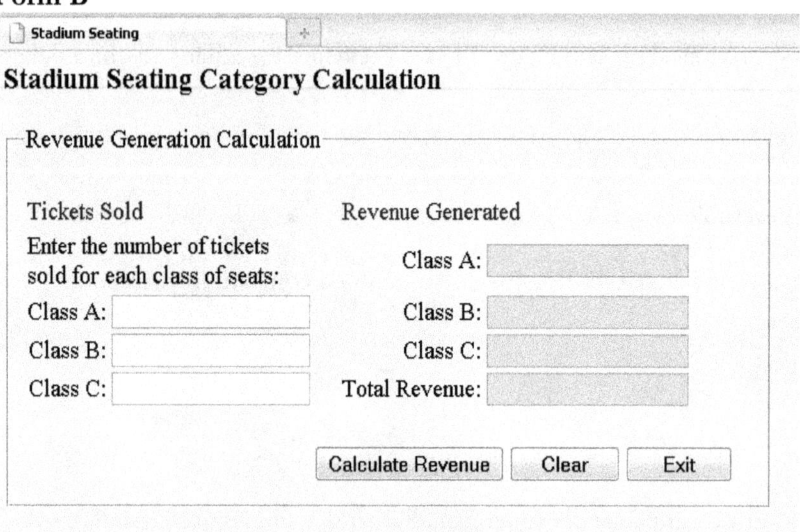
Stadium Seating
Stadium Seating Category Calculation
Revenue Generation Calculation
Tickets Sold
Enter the number of tickets sold for each class of seats:
Class A:
Class B:
Class C:
Revenue Generated
Class A:
Class B:
Class C:
Total Revenue:
Calculate Revenue
Clear
Exit

Q3. Test Average

Write a script that allows the user to enter five test scores. It should be able to calculate and display the average score. The form should resemble **Form C**.

Form C

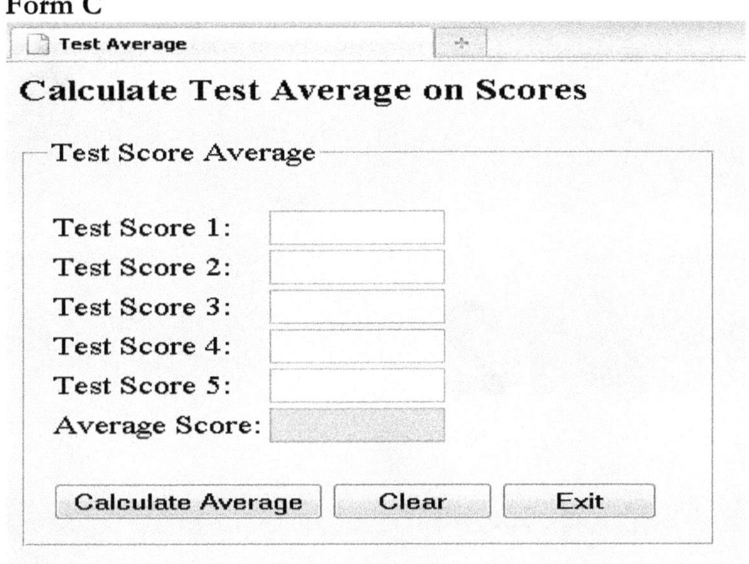

12

Sessions

A programming language is a tool that has a profound influence on our thinking habits.
- Edsger Dijkstra

Learning Objectives

After studying this chapter, you should be able to:

- Understand the concepts behind session management.
- Learn how sessions work.
- Apply sessions in scripts to track user activities.
- Use simple examples of sessions in scripts such as page counters.

Introduction

When you get to a stage where your website needs to pass along user data from one page to another, it might be the time to start thinking about using PHP sessions. In this chapter, you will learn how to work with sessions in PHP. You will also learn how to start a session, set session variables, display session data, transfer information over multiple pages, and destroy a session. A detailed example of how to use sessions in real-world applications is presented at the end of the chapter.

What is a Session

A session, according to php.net, is "a way to preserve certain data across subsequent accesses". A normal HTML website will not pass data from one page to another. In other words, all information on the previous page is forgotten when a new page is loaded into the browser. This makes it quite a problem for tasks like login information (username) or shopping cart, which requires data (the user's selected product) to be remembered (carried along) from one page to the next.

A PHP session solves the above problem by allowing you to store user information on the server, enabling that information to be used from one page to the other. However, this session information is temporary and is usually deleted very quickly after the user has left the website that uses sessions.

How Sessions Work

Before you can begin storing user information in your PHP session, you must first start the session. Whenever PHP session is started, it generates a session ID. The code to start the session must be at the very beginning of your script, before any HTML or text is sent. This tiny piece of code will register the user's session with the Web server and allow you to start saving user information for that user's session.

To store user data in a session, a session variable is used. A session variable is a special type of variable whose value is maintained across subsequent web pages. With session variables, user-specific data can be preserved from page to page as the user interacts with the web application.

Session variables normally exist until one of the following events occurs:

- The user closes the browser window.
- The maximum time set on the Web server for session lifetime is exceeded. PHP runs a garbage collecting process that destroys all sessions that have been inactive for twenty-four minutes (by default - this value can be changed)
- The PHP functions such as **session_destroy()** is executed to free all session variables currently registered.

PHP stores the session data on the Web server in some kind of database or a text file. Thus, sessions are a way of storing user data on the Web server.

Uses of Session

A session presents a few benefits. For instance, every time a PHP script accesses a session, the garbage collector (PHP built-in facility) resets its twenty-four minute (default session which can be changed) countdown for deletion of the session. Thus, a user cannot leave a site and come back in an hour or two and expect the session to still be alive. In addition, a user's computer deletes all session IDs every time the user closes the browser.

Thus, the only real advantage of using sessions is that they allow a PHP programmer to hide information being stored from the users and hackers. PHP programmers should use sessions only for things that require short-term preservation of data, such as a shopping cart. PHP programmers should not use sessions for things that require the long-term preservation of data, such as setting user preferences.

Overall, sessions serve as a short-term method for preserving data across pages while hiding information from users and hackers.

Session Keywords

PHP supports a number of session handlers. We will look at the most commonly used session handlers and their specific usage. They are defined in Table 12.1.

Table 12.1: Session Keywords

Keywords	Description
session_start()	Initializes session data. This function is called prior to creating a new session variable using $_SESSION[ ].
$_SESSION[ ]	PHP superglobal array variable that contains currently registered session.
session_destroy()	Destroys all data registered to a script's current session.
session_id()	Used to get the id value for the current session.

Using `header` Function

This section introduces you to the PHP "Location" **header()** function. Although this is an HTTP function and not a session function, it is commonly used in session scripts to redirect user's during existing sessions. The function is defined below:

header("Location: http://www.i-church.net")

Header function is used to redirect the browser page to the **Location** parameter provided, in this case http://www.i-church.net.

Using `isset` Function

When you create a variable and store it in a session, you probably want to use it in the future. However, before you use a session variable, it is necessary that you check to see if it already exists.

This is where PHP's **isset** function comes in handy. The **isset** is a function that takes any variable you want to use and checks to see if it has been **set**. That is, whether it has already been assigned a value.

Starting a PHP Session

The following code block demonstrates how the **session id** is created, session variable is inititalized, and how to retrieve (display) value held in the session variable.

Example 1:

In this example, **session_start()** is first called to initialize session data. The **session_start()** must be called before creating and assigning values to session variables. Next, an **if** statement is used to check the value of the session variable *counter*. If the session is **null** or contains no value, it is intialized to 1. Otherwise, the value of the session variable is incremented by 1. In this case, the session variable *counter* is used to count the number of visits to the page. Session variables provide an ideal way of creating page counters since each user represents a unique session.

Listing 12.1: counter1.php

```
<html>
<body bgcolor="#F5F5F5">
<?php

    // creates session Id
    session_start();

    // tests the existence of a session
    if ($_SESSION['counter'] == "")
    {
        // assigns 1 to session variable 'counter'
        $_SESSION['counter'] = 1;
    }else{
        // increments the session variable
        $_SESSION['counter'] = $_SESSION['counter'] + 1;
    }
?>
```

Continuation of Listing 12.1: counter1.php

```
<p>
  Hello, you are the visitor number
 <?php echo $_SESSION['counter']; ?>  to this page.
</p>

</body>
</html>
```

The tag **echo $_SESSION['counter']** then displays the number of times a visitor visits the page.

Figure 12.1
Simple page counter example with sessions.

Hello, you are the visitor number 1 to this page.

Example 2

The example 1 above can be re-coded using the ***isset*** function. We can create a very simple page view counter by using ***isset*** to check if the *counter* variable has already been created. If it has, we can increase the *counter*. If it does not exist, we can create a *counter* and set it to 1. Here is the code to do this (Listing 12.2).

The first time you run this script on a **newly opened browser**, the *if statement* will result in a *false* because no session variable would have been stored yet. However, if you refresh the page the **if statement** would be **true** and the *counter* would increase by 1. Each time you re-run this script you would see an increase in the *counter* by 1. Finally, the script outputs the value of the session variable and the session id.

Figure 12.2
Example to display visitor number and session id.

Hello, you are the 1 visitor to the page.
Display Session ID: q5ncen288hdksjopukp520i2i2

Web applications that use session data may be accessed my multiple users simultaneously. For each user to have unique session, a unique id value is associated with the session. In PHP, this unique session id value can be retrieved using the **session_id()** function. A unique **session_id()** value is maintained for each user and is stored in the ***sessiondata*** sub directory located on the Web server.

Since the **session_id()** value is unique for every user, it can be used to identify users without the need to create individual user names and passwords.

Listing 12.2: counter2.php

```
<html>
<body bgcolor="#F5F5F5">

<?php

// session starts
session_start();

// the use of isset function
if(isset($_SESSION['counter']))
{
        //assign value to the session
        $_SESSION['counter'] = 1;
}
else
{
        $_SESSION['counter'] = $_SESSION['counter'] + 1;
}
?>

<p>
<!--display message -->
Hello, you are the <?php echo $_SESSION['counter']; ?>
visitor to the page.<br>
Display Session ID: <?php echo session_id(); ?>
</p>

</body>
</html>
```

Destroying and Cleaning a Session

Although a session's data is temporary and does not require that you explicitly clean it yourself, you may wish to delete the data for various reasons. Imagine that you were running an online business and a user used your website to purchase some goods. The user has just completed a transaction on your website and you now want to remove everything from their shopping cart. In this case you will completely destroy the session entirely by calling the ***session_destroy*** function.

Example 3

Destroying a session can be achieved through **unset()** or **session_destroy()** functions as shown in Listing 12.3.

Listing 12.3: destroy_session.php

```
<?php

        // session starts
        session_start();

        // the use of isset function
        if(isset($_SESSION['counter']))
        {
                // destroy the session
                unset($_SESSION['counter']);
        }

        // we can also use this
        session_start();

        // destroy the session
        session_destroy();

?>
```

Destroying a session will reset your session, so do not call that function unless you are entirely comfortable losing all your stored session data.

Detailed Example

User Login Session

In this example, a session variable will be created after a user successfully enters the credentials needed to access a restricted site. In this case the session variable contains a value that is passed from page to page indicating that the user has permission to access any resources associated with the site. When the user exits or chooses to "logout", the session variable should be reset. This is accomplished by using **session_destroy()** keyword.

The HTML to create the form is shown below. When the user clicks on the **Login** button, the session starts and then redirects the user to the **admin.php** script (Listing 12.4).

This example consists of two pages, **login.php** and **admin.php**. Before a user can view the contents of **admin.php**, they must pass **login.php**. A session is created to ensure that the user is authenticated. After the user enters a valid username and password, the "Login" button is clicked. The PHP script ensures that the password and username are correct.

Next, a session variable is created which is assigned a value of **"yes"**. The user is then redirected to **admin.php**. A script, **($_SESSION['access'] != "yes")** , in **admin.php** file checks to ensure that the session exists. If the session exists, the user is granted access to view the contents of **admin.php** file. If the session does not exist, the **header(Location:login.php)** is used to redirect the user back to **login.php** and prevents viewing of **admin.php** contents.

Figure 12.3
The script below will create this login form.

Enter username:

Enter Password:

Login

The **admin.php** contains a second script that is used to destroy the session variable by calling **session_destroy()**. The script is executed after the user clicks the **"Logout"** button (which actually was not provided on Figure 12.3).

Listing 12.4: login.php

```
<html>
<body bgcolor="#F5F5F5">

<form method="post" action="login.php"/><p>
 Enter username: <input type="text" name="uname"/><br>
 Enter Password: <input type="password" name="pass"/><br>
 <input type="submit" name="login" value="Login"/>
</form>

<?php

if(isset($_POST['login']))
{

 // script to check username and password here.
 // if authentication is successful.
 session_start();
 $_SESSION['access'] = "yes";

  // redirect to admin.php script
 header("Location:admin.php");
}

?>
</body>
</html>
```

Listing 12.5: admin.php

```
<html>
<body bgcolor="#F5F5F5">
<?php
/* if the user accesses this page, make sure she has been
authenticated through login.php */

/* if the user has not login properly, the session variable
will differ from "yes" and she will be redirected to the login
screen. */
if($_SESSION['access'] != "yes")
{
        header("Location:login.php");
}

// an example of destroying the session when logging out
if(isset($_POST['logout']))
{
        // destroy the current session.
        session_destroy();
        echo "You have Logout Successfully.";
}
?>
Click here to Logout
<form>
<input type="submit" name="logout" value="Logout"/>
</form>
</body>
</html>
```

Programming Challenge

Q1. Login Page

A session variable is a special type of variable whose value is maintained across subsequent web pages. With session variables, user-specific data can be preserved from page to page, delivering customized content as the user interacts with the web application. Session variables normally exist until one of the follow criteria is met: (1) the user closes the browser window; (2) the maximum time allotment set on the server for session lifetime is exceeded; (3) using PHP functions such as **session_destroy()** to free all session variables currently registered.

You are required to write two pages, **login.php** and **access.php**. Your scripts should perform the tasks described in the paragraph below:

Before users can view the contents of **access.php**, they must login properly through **login.php**. A session is created to ensure that the user is authenticated. After the user enters a valid username and password, the "**Login**" button should be clicked. The PHP script ensures that the password and user name are correct. Next, a session variable is created and assigned a value of "**yes**". The user is then redirected to **access.php**. A script in **access.php** file checks to ensure the session exists. If the session does not exist, the **header()** function is used to redirect the user back to **login.php** and prevents viewing of **access.php** contents.

Login.php contains a second script that is used to destroy the session variable by calling **session_destroy().** The script is executed after the user clicks the "**Log Out**" button.

Q2. Password Verification

a. Create a login page that asks the user for a username and password. Trim the username and password to remove any unwanted whitespace. The **action** attribute of the **form** tag should redirect you to a new page, called **verify.php**.

b. The **verify.php** page will start a **session** and check that the username and password fields are not empty and also that they are correct. If not, the user will be informed and redirected back to the login page. If the username and the password are correct, the user will be directed to your home page.

c. When the user logs out, end and destroy the **session**.

13

Cookies

Practice is the best of all instructors. – Anonymous

Learning Objectives

After studying this chapter, you should be able to:

- Understand the concepts behind cookies.
- Learn how cookies work.
- Apply cookies in scripts to track user activities.
- Use simple examples of cookies in scripts such as page counters.

Introduction

Cookies can be easily and simply used by a web application developer to achieve many useful tasks when creating websites. Although cookies are well known to users, some developers are not really sure what they are used for. Others might be put off, thinking that cookies must be difficult to use. But in reality, cookies can be set and used by a simple command in most scripting languages. In this chapter, you will cover setting and using cookies in PHP as well as giving some basic information on how cookies can be used. The chapter ends with a more comprehensive example of how to use Cookies in the real-world application.

What is a Cookie

A cookie is an information that a website puts on your hard disk so that it can remember something about you at a later time. It is a piece of information the Web server stores on the client computer (in the users browser). Using the web's Hypertext Transfer Protocol (HTTP), each request for a web page is independent of all other requests. For this reason, the web server cannot remember the pages it has sent to a user previously or anything about the user's previous visits. A cookie is a mechanism that allows the server to store its own information about a user on the user's own computer.

You can view the cookies that have been stored on your hard disk (although the content stored in each cookie may not make much sense to you). The location of the cookies file depends on the browser. Internet Explorer stores each cookie as a separate file under a Windows subdirectory. Netscape stores all cookies in a single **cookies.txt** file. Opera stores them in a single **cookies.dat** file.

A cookie is a mechanism that allows the Web server to store its own information about a user on the user's own computer.

Uses of Cookie

Why would anyone want to store 4Kb (normally the size of a cookie file) characters of text on a user's computer? It is not enough to put anything really worthwhile in there. The power of the cookie, though, is to recognise a site user over and over again. The list below gives a few uses of cookies:

- Visitor tracking and statistics systems often use cookies to track visitors. By assigning the visitor a cookie, the visitor will be counted only once even if he visits the page a number of times. Thus, unique visitor statistics can accurately be obtained.
- As a unique cookie is assigned to a user, the system can track the user activities on a website, showing the webmaster exactly where the user has been and in what order. This is good for audit trail purposes.
- Many portals and search engines use cookies to provide customized pages to their users, allowing such features as My Yahoo, My Student Center, etc.
- Many websites use cookies to log in users automatically. By storing a few pieces of information about the user, the website can automatically authenticate the user and allow the user login into the system without having to go through the usual login process. This saves users time having to log in always into a particular site.

How Cookies Work

A cookie is a very basic data file. It has a name, a value, and an expiry time. It can also store the address of websites which are allowed to access it. Basically, a website will set a cookie and give it a name and value. This name is used by the website to refer to it, and no other website can access the cookie, even if they know it's name. The name should be unique to the website, but it does not matter if it clashes with the name of a cookie from another website.

In most cases, cookie can only store up to 4000 characters of data. This is enough to store lots of information about a user so if, for example, you wanted to store the user preferences for a search engine (much like Google does), you could simply list the preferences in the cookie. To retrieve data, the website simply has to request if the user has a cookie with a particular name.

Every cookie is assigned an expiry date and time. It is up to the website developer to decide how long the cookie should exist. Many developers may just choose to set the cookie for an hour, meaning it is only available perhaps for the user's single session. This is common in visitor tracking. Other cookies could be set for much longer, maybe a week or a month (often used for affiliate program tracking) or even several years (often used for user preferences).

Cookies Security

Despite security concerns, cookies actually pose no real danger to users. Unless they are really worried about themselves being recognized by a website, cookies are harmless. It is the browser that actually writes and reads cookies from the computer when requested to by a website, so a malicious website cannot damage the computer.

When the cookies are set, the domain(s) which can access it are set. Usually this is just the website that set the cookies. This makes cookies relatively secure, as you can be sure that your competitor cannot load your cookie from one of your visitors' computers (they cannot even find out if it exists). However, one major security problem with cookies is that they can easily be read by anyone using the computer which stores the cookies. They are just a simple text file, so you should not under any circumstances store passwords in cookies.

Cookies Keywords and Parameters

Cookies are created using the **setcookie()** function. All cookie data is then stored in the PHP **$_COOKIE[ ]** global variable and accessible in subsequent pages. The syntax for setting a cookie is:

setcookie (name, value, expiration, path, domain, security)

This function defines a cookie to be sent along with the rest of the HTTP headers. Like other headers, cookies must be sent before any output from your script (this is a protocol restriction). This means that the ***setcookie***() function must be at the very beginning of your script, before any HTML or text is sent. This requires that you place calls to this function prior to any output, including tags as well as any whitespace. If any output exists prior to calling this function, **setcookie()** will fail and return **false**. If **setcookie()** successfully runs, it will return **true**.

The **setcookie()** parameters are listed and explained in Table 13.1.

Table 13.1: Cookies Keyword and Parameters

Parameter	Description
name	The **name** of the cookie. The identifier is kept in the global $_COOKIE and is accessible in subsequent scripts.
value	The **value** of the cookie. The value associated with the cookie identifier. The value is stored on the user's computer. For this reason, the value should not contain sensitive information.
expiration	The time at which the cookie value expires or is no longer accessible. The expiration time can be set using the **time()** function. Cookies without an expiration value expire when the browser is closed.
path	Indicates the paths on the server for which the cookie is available. A forward slash "/" indicates the cookie is available to all folders.
domain	The domain that the cookie is available. If no domain is specified, the default value is the value of the host on which the cookie is created. Domain values must contain at least two periods (..) in the string to be valid.
security	Indicates whether the cookie will be transmitted via **https**. A value of **1** means that the cookie is transmitted over a secure connection (**https**). A value of **0** denotes a standard **http** transmission.

Setting Cookies

The PHP function for setting cookies is:

setcookie()

It is a PHP function which can be used without returning a value (for example you can simply execute a **setcookie()**) command, or you can return a value which can be used. The **setcookie**() function returns a boolean (**true** or **false**) value depending on whether it is successful. Let us take a look at this example.

```
setcookie()

if(setcookie())
{
   echo "Cookie is set";
}
else
{
   echo "Cookie is not set";
}
```

The most basic information for a cookie is its name and its value. The name of the cookie must be something which you can refer to later. You do not need to worry about it conflicting with cookie names on other sites as cookie names are site specific. But you should try and use a descriptive and unique name for your cookies.

For this first example, assume that you have used PHP to load the user's name into the variable **$name** and want to greet the user in the future by their names. You would need to create a cookie which stores their names as follows:

setcookie("UsersName", $name);

This creates the most basic of cookies, storing the user's name in a cookie called **'UsersName'**. By setting cookies like this, you don't set any specific options, so by default the cookie will be available to the domain in which it was set (e.g. yoursite.com) and will be deleted when the user closes the browser.

Although the above code would allows you to set a simple cookie on the user's computer, it is not very powerful because, for example, it is lost when the browser closes. One of the most powerful features of cookies is the ability to set an expiry date for the cookie. The cookie will remain on the user's computer until the expiry date, then it will automatically delete itself.

Setting Cookies with Optional Parameters

To set a cookie with an expiry date, use:

```
setcookie("UsersName", $name, time()+3600);
```

This code takes the current time (using **time()**) and then adds 3600 seconds to it, and uses this value to set the expiry time for the cookie. Basically this means that the cookie will remain on the user's computer for an hour (it expires 3600 seconds (1 hour) from the current time). For one week, for example, you would set the cookie as:

```
setcookie("UsersName", $name, time()+604800);
```

There are three other options which can be used when setting cookies. Firstly, the path which refers to where in the domain you are able to access the cookie in future. By default this is the current directory (so if you set the cookie at the page: **www.mysite.com/scripts/setcookie.php**, it would only be available to scripts in the **scripts** directory and below). You can set this in any part of your site, which can be useful in some situations.

A second setting you can change is the domain. By default, a cookie is only available in the domain you set it in. For example if you set the cookie on **www.mysite.com** you can only ever access it from **www.mysite.com** (and not **mail.mysite.com** domain). The most common need to change this setting is to allow the cookie to be viewed across all sub domains of a site. This can be done by setting the domain to **.yoursite.com**. By doing this **anything.yoursite.com** is accepted, not just **www.yoursite.com**.

Finally, a cookie has the option to be set as a secure cookie. If this is turned on, the cookie will only ever be available to the site over a secure connection, not an insecure one. The following code shows the implementation of a cookie with all settings specified:

```
setcookie("UsersName", $name, time()+3600, "/", ".mysite.com", 1);
```

The cookie set here is called **'UsersName'** and stores the value **$name**. It will expire in an hour from the current time. It is available in all directories of the site (/ is the root directory). It is available across any subdomain of the site **mysite.com**, as **'.mysite.com'** has been given as the domain. The final parameter, **1** means that this is a secure cookie, and can only be transmitted over a secure connection. This can be changed to **0** for a standard (non-secure) cookie.

Reading Cookie Values

PHP makes it extremely simple to read the value of a cookie. In PHP, reading form values are achieved using **$_GET** and **$_POST**. PHP has a similar global variable for cookies:

```
$_COOKIE['CookieName'];
```

This variable contains the value of the cookie with name 'CookieName'. So on your website, if you want to display the name of the user, you could simply use the following:

```
echo "Hello, ".$_COOKIE['UsersName']."! Welcome back!";
```

Of course, the user may not already have the cookie, so you should use the PHP function **isset**. This returns **true** if a variable has been set and **false** if not. Using this, your site could do the following:

```
if(isset($_COOKIE['UsersName'])
{
  echo "Hello, ".$_COOKIE['UsersName']."! Welcome back!";
}
else
{
  setcookie("UsersName",$name);
}
```

Deleting Cookies

There are occasions on which you may wish to delete a cookie from a user's computer. This could be if, for example, you want to log the user out of a system. Deleting a cookie is quite simple to do because all you have to do is to set the expiry time in the past. By doing this, the cookie will be automatically deleted as soon as it is created, and will remove any data that already exists there. The simplest way is using:

setcookie("UsersName", "", time()-3600);

This sets the expiry time in the past so it should be deleted immediately. There is a known problem with this, though. Although it works in most cases, there can be problems if a user's timezone is set wrongly. The safest way to completely delete a cookie is to use the following:

setcookie("UsersName", "", mktime(12,0,0,1, 1, 1990));

The **mktime()** function is a PHP function for setting up a time specified. The time specified here is in the year 1990, so even a badly configured computer should still delete the cookie immediately.

Detailed Example

The following example demonstrates how a cookie is used to retain a visitor's user name.

Initially, a user is required to enter a user name in order to access a restricted site. Once a user name is entered, a cookie containing the user name is created and stored on the user's computer. Future access to the restricted site is possible by retrieving the cookie from the user's computer.

In this example, we shall use the login form, **login.php** and **access.php** to illustrate the usage of the concept of cookies.

Enter username:

Enter Password:

Login

The example consists of two pages, **login.php** and **admin.php**. Before users can view the contents of **login.php**, they must pass **login.php**. After the user enters a valid username and password, the "**Login**" button is clicked. The PHP script ensures that the user name and password are correct and the cookie is created. The user is redirected to **access.php**. A script, **isset($_COOKIE['user'])** in **access.php** file checks to ensure that the cookie exists. If the cookie exists, the user is granted access to view the contents of **access.php** file. If the cookie does not exist, the **header(Location:login.php)** is used to redirect the user back to **login.php** and prevents viewing of **access.php** contents.

Listing 13.1: login2.php

```
<html>
<body bgcolor="#F5F5F5">
<pre>

<form method="post" action="login2.php" /><p>
  Enter username: <input type="text" name="username"/><br>
  Enter Password: <input type="password" name="pass"/>
                  <input type="submit" name="login"
                  value="Login"/>
</pre>
</form>
```

Continuation of Listing 13.1: login2.php

```
<?php
if(isset($_POST['login']))
{
    // check user name and password would be coded here.

    // if authentication is successful.
    $cookie_name = "user";
    $cookie_value = $_POST[username];
    $cookie_expire = time() + 3600;
    setcookie($cookie_name,$cookie_value,$cookie_expire, "/");

    // redirect the page to admin.php page.
    header("Location:access.php");
}
else
{
    echo  "Cookie is not set";
}
?>
</body>
</html>
```

Listing 13.2: access.php

```
<?php
// check whether a cookie has been created.
if(isset($_COOKIE['user']))
{
    // access to the restricted file is granted.
    echo "You are granted access to the restricted site" ."<br>";
    echo "Welcome, ".$_COOKIE['user']."! to the site!";
}
else
{
    /* user redirected back to the login form as cookie has not
    been set. */
    header("Location:login2.php");
}
?>
```

14

File and Folder Manipulation

Nothing will ever be attempted, if all possible objections must first be overcome.
- Samuel Johnson

Learning Objectives

After studying this chapter, you should be able to:

- Understand how to manage files in PHP.
- Create, rename, and delete folders and files.
- Write scripts to open, read, and write to files.
- Write scripts to copy and retrieve contents from files.

Introduction

File manipulation is necessary in programming. PHP gives you a great deal of tools for creating, uploading, appending, deleting, and editing files. This chapter is entirely dedicated to showing you how PHP can interact with files and folders. After completing this section you should have a solid understanding of different types of file manipulation techniques in PHP. This chapter begins with how to create, open, and close a file. After establishing those basics, we will then cover other important file tasks, such as: read, write, append, and delete.

When to Use Files

You can use files(eg. files saved with **.txt** extension) to store data. When you use PHP and learn how to work with files and databases, your work will become easier. Bur files should only be used to store temporary data or data which is insensitive in nature. If you need to store user data or sensitive data, database should be used instead of files. You should never use files to store huge amounts of data. Files can only hold certain amount of data in them. Files are generally used to store logs for audit trail purposes and monitoring of system activities, static data, and xml data for parsing.

Working with Folders

Using PHP commands, you can create and delete folders. Let us look at how this can be done.

Creating a New Folder

The PHP function to create a directory (folder) is **mkdir()**. This function returns TRUE on success, or FALSE on failure.

The syntax is

mkdir(path, mode, recursive, context)

Creating new directories (folders) in PHP is accomplished using the **mkdir()** function, which takes four parameters. The first two parameters are, in order, a directory name you want to create and a permission mode for a new directory (folder), which must be an octal number. The mode parameter is optional and has an effect only on Unix systems.

The table below describes the parameters of the **mkdir()** function.

Table 14.1: Creating a Folder

Parameter	Description
path	Required parameter. Specifies the name of the directory to create.
mode	Optional parameter. Specifies permissions. By default, the mode is 0777 (widest possible access). The mode parameter consists of four numbers: - The first number is always zero. - The second number specifies permissions for the owner. - The third number specifies permissions for the owner's user group. - The fourth number specifies permissions for everybody else. - Possible values (to set multiple permissions, add up the following numbers): 1 = execute permissions 2 = write permissions 4 = read permissions
recursive	Optional parameter. Specifies if the recursive mode is set (added in PHP 5)
context	Optional parameter. Specifies the context of the file handle. Context is a set of options that can modify the behavior of a stream (added in PHP 5)

The following example shows how to create a folder called "**scripts**" on drive **C**: on Windows operating system.

Listing 14.1: create_folder1.php

```
<?php
// check whether folder exists.
if(!is_dir("c:/scripts"))
{
        mkdir("c:/scripts",0777);
}
else
{
        echo "Folder exists";
}
?>
```

Always verify that the folder does not already exist. The above PHP statement presumes that the "**scripts**" folder will be created at the root (**c:/**).

By default, the **mkdir()** function only creates a folder if its parent folder exists. In PHP 5 the recursive parameter was added, which should be either **true** or **false** depending on whether you want to create parent directories or not. In the following example, we pass **true** as a third parameter to **mkdir()**, so this makes the function act recursively to create any missing parent directories(folders).

Listing 14.2: create_folder2.php

```
<?php

 // creating scripts, lessons and section folders if not exist
 mkdir("c:/scripts/lessons/section",0777, true);
 echo "Folders created";

?>
```

Deleting a Folder

PHP has the **rmdir()** function that takes a folder name as its only parameter and will remove the specified folder from the file system, if the process running your script has the right to do so. However, the **rmdir()** function works only on empty folders (folders with no files in them). The example below deletes an empty folder named "**scripts**":

Listing 14.3: delete_folder.php

```
<?php

// check whether the folder exists
if(is_dir("c:/scripts"))
{
      rmdir("c:/scripts");
}
else
{
      echo "Folder does not exist";
}

?>
```

Opening Files

PHP provides access to files on both Windows and Unix based operating systems for the purpose of reading, writing, or appending content. This section describes how to use PHP to open files on Windows systems.

Basic Syntax

PHP includes the **fopen()** and **fclose()** functions for working with files. Both functions are defined below:

fopen() Function

fopen(filename, mode)

This function is used to open a file. The function requires a **filename** and **mode**. It returns a file pointer which provides information about the file and is used as a reference.

The file name is the full path to the file that you want to create or open. The path can be a relative path to the file: "**/scripts/myfile.txt**" or an absolute path to the file: "**c:/script/myfile.txt** ". For each folder specified, you must have the proper permissions to create, modify, and delete files. The mode can be any of the following, as explained in Table 14.2.

fclose(resource handle)

This function is used to close a file. The function requires the file pointer which was created when the file was opened using the **fopen()** function. It returns TRUE on success or FALSE on failure.

The following example shows how to open a file for reading and writing.

Listing 14.4: open_file_reading.php

```
<?php

$filename = "c:/scripts/myfile.txt";

// open the file
$newfile = fopen($filename, "w+");

// close the file
fclose($newfile);

?>
```

It is necessary to create the folders **scripts** as in this path "**c:/scripts/**"

The first step is to create a variable to hold the full path to the file that will be opened:

$filename = "c:/scripts/myfile.txt";

The path to the text file, **myfile.txt**, is stored in the variable called **$filename**. Next, a file pointer, called **$newfile**, is created and used with the **fopen()** function to open the file. A file pointer is a PHP reference variable used to refer to the just-opened file:

$newfile = fopen($filename, "w+");

The file pointer will be used later as a reference to read and write content to the opened file.

Table 14.2: Modes Used with fopen()

Mode	Usage
r	Opens an existing file for the purpose of reading data from it. The file pointer is placed at the beginning of the file.
r+	Opens an existing file for the purpose of reading or writing data. The file pointer is placed at the beginning of the file.
w	Opens a file for writing. If the file does not exist, it is created. If the file exists, the file pointer is placed at the beginning of the file and the function deletes all existing content.
w+	Opens a file for reading and writing. If the file does not exist, it is created. If the file exists, the file pointer is palced at the beginning of the file and the function deletes all existing content.
a	Opens a file for writing. If the file does not exist, it is created. If the file exists, the file pointer is placed at the end of the file.
a+	Opens a file for reading and writing. If the file does not exist, it is created. If the file exists, the file pointer is placed at the the end of the file.

Checking Errors in File Open

In some instances, the **fopen()** function may not be able to successfully open a file as a result of an invalid file path, security permissions, or other unforseen issues. For these reasons, it is recommended that a special PHP function be used to handle such errors. These functions can be used in combination with the PHP error control operator "@" to terminate the script, supress PHP generated errors, and display a more user-friendly message. The PHP error control functions are described below:

exit(error message)

This terminates the current script and outputs the error message provided to the function.

die(error message)

This is an alias of the **exit()** function.

The following script demonstrates the use of the error control functions:

Listing 14.5: open_file_error.php

```
<?php

    $filename = "c:/scripts/myfile.txt";

    // opening the file with @ error suppressor
    $newfile = @fopen($filename, "w+") or
    exit("Could not open or create the file");

    // closing the file.
    fclose($newfile);

?>
```

If the file cannot be opened, the **exit()** function displays the message "**Could not open or create the file**" and the script terminates.

If the file is opened successfully, content can be read from the file, written to the file, or appended to the file depending on the mode used with the **fopen()** function. Details on these actions will be discussed in the following sections. When the file processing is completed, the **fclose()** function is used to close the opened file.

Reading Files

This section describes how to use PHP to read file contents on Windows operating system.

Read File Contents

Basic Syntax

PHP includes the **fread(), fgetcsv(),** and **filesize()** functions for reading files. The functions are defined below:

fread(resource handler, length)

This function is used to read the contents of a file. Reads up to length bytes from the file pointer referenced by resource handler. Reading stops when length bytes have been read, EOF (end of file) is reached. The function requires two parameters - a file pointer that is created when the file is opened with **fopen()** and a filesize that specifies how much of the file contents to read.

fgetcsv(resource handler, length, delimiter)

The function used to read the contents of a file and parses the data to create an array. Data is parsed on the delimiter parameter supplied to the function.

filesize(filename)

This returns the size of a file. If an error occurs the function returns a **false** value.

Reading Entire File Contents

The following example (Listing 14.6) illustrates how to read the entire contents of a file.

The first step is to create a variable to hold the full path to the file that will be opened for reading:

```
$filename = "c:/scripts/myfile.txt";
```

The path to the text file, **myfile.txt**, is stored in the variable called **$filename**. Next, a file pointer, called **$newfile**, is created and used with the **fopen()** function to open the file.

A file pointer is used to refer to the just-opened file:

```
$newfile = fopen($filename, "r");
```

The file pointer is a PHP variable that contains a reference to the opened file (in this case it is **$newfile**). It will be used later with the **fread()** function to read content from the opened file.

Next, a variable called **$file_contents** is created and used to store the contents of the text file, **myfile.txt**. The first parameter of the **fread()** function refers to the name of the file whose contents will be read. The second parameter specifies the length of the file. If the length of the file is unknown, a special PHP function - **filesize()** can be used. The **filesize()** function retrieves the entire contents of a file. It requires a single parameter - the name or path of the file currently being read.

$file_contents = fread($newfile, filesize($filename));

The entire contents of the text file are now stored in the variable **$file_contents**. This data can be displayed to the screen using the **echo** statement or can be written to another text file.

Listing 14.6: fileread.php

```
<?php

$filename = "c:/scripts/myfile.txt";

// Opening the file with @ error suppressor
$newfile = @fopen($filename, "r") or exit("Could not open
file");

// read file content
$file_contents = @fread($newfile, filesize($filename)) or
exit("Could not read file ");

// display file content
echo $file_contents;

// close the file
fclose($newfile);

?>
```

Reading Individual Items in the File

In some cases, it may be necessary to read and work with individual parts of the text file content. When using **fread()** the entire contents of the file is stored in a single variable, making it difficult to work with individual pieces of the file. If the text file contains delimiters to separate individual pieces of data, an alternative read function, **fgetcsv()**, can be used instead. This function reads the file contents and creates an array making specific parts of the text accessible.

Assume the text file, **myfile.txt**, exists and contains the following data:

10, 20, 30, 40, 50

The following script demonstrates the use of the **fgetcsv()** function to read the contents of the text file.

Listing 14.7: fileread_individual.php

```
<?php

 $filename = "c:/scripts/myfile.txt";
 $newfile = @fopen($filename, "r") or
                exit("Could not open file");

 // reading the file with comma as the delimiter
 $file_contents = @fgetcsv($newfile, filesize($filename),",")
                      or exit("Could not read file contents");

 // display file content
 for($i=0; $i < sizeof($file_contents); $i++)
 {
    echo $file_contents[$i];
    echo "<br/>";
 }

 // close the file
 fclose($newfile);

?>
```

The script will produce the following output

10
20
30
40
50

After opening the file, the **fgetcsv()** reads the entire contents of the file creating an array - **'$file_contents'**. The third parameter of **fgetcsv()** function specifies that each element separated by the "," delimiter will become an element of the new array. Since **myfile.txt** contains the delimiter values 10,20,30,40,50, $file_contents[0] = 10, $file_contents[1] = 20, $file_contents[2] = 30, $file_contents[3] = 40, $ile_contents[4] = 50. Once the array is created, the values can be manipulated using any of the PHP array functions. In this example, a **for** loop iterates through the **$file_contents()** array and displays each number.

After the file processing is complete, the **fclose()** function is used to close the opened file.

Writing to File

This section describes how to use PHP to write content to files on Windows systems.

PHP includes the **fwrite()** function for writing files. The function is defined below:

fwrite(resource handle, string)

This writes the contents of string to the file stream pointed to by resource handler. If the length argument is given, writing will stop after length bytes have been written or the end of string is reached, whichever comes first.

Writing Contents to File

Listing 14.8 illustrates how to write the entire contents of a file.

The first step is to create a variable to hold the full path to the file that will be opened or created:

$filename = "c:/scripts/myfile.txt";

The path to the text file, **myfile.txt**, is stored in the variable called **$filename**. Next, a file pointer, called **$newfile**, is created and used with the **fopen()** function to open the file specified. A file pointer is used to refer to the just-opened file. The file is opened in write mode:

$newfile = fopen($filename, "w");

The file pointer is a PHP variable that contains a reference to the opened file. It will be used later to write content to the opened file.

Next, a variable called **$file_contents** is created and is assigned a string value that will be written to the text file, **myfile.txt**.

Finally, the **fwrite()** function is called. The first parameter of the **fwrite()** function refers to the name of the file to which content will be written. The second parameter contains the text that will be written to the opened file.

fwrite($newfile, $file_contents);

After the file processing is complete, the **fclose()** function is used to close the opened file.

Listing 14.8: filewrite.php

```
<?php

 $filename = "c:/scripts/myfile.txt";

 // open the file to be written into
 $newfile = fopen($filename, "w") or
    exit("Could not open file");

 // string to write to file
 $file_contents = "Add this string to the text file";

 // writing the contents of $file_contents to myfile.txt file
 fwrite($newfile,$file_contents);

 fclose($newfile);

?>
```

Writing Contents of One File into Another File

In some cases it may be necessary to write the contents of an existing file to a new file. This process requires the use of the **fopen(), fread(), and fwrite()** functions. The first file is opened, its content is read, and is written to a new file which has also been opened. Listing

14.9 illustrates this process.

This script copies the contents of "**myfile1.txt**" to a new file, "**myfile.txt**". First, two variables, **$fileAname** and **$fileBname** are declared and assigned the directory paths for the existing and the new file. The **fopen()** function is used to open the current file to read its content. The opened file is assigned to the file pointer **$currentfile**.

The contents of the opened file are read using the **fread()** function and assigned to the variable **$fileAcontents**. Next, the **fopen()** function is used again to open the new file. The opened file is assigned to the file pointer **$newfile**. The **fwrite()** function is used to write the contents of the original file to the new file. Once the copy process is complete, both files are closed with the **fclose()** function.

Listing 14.9: filewrite_other.php

```
<?php

$fileAname = "c:/scripts/myfile1.txt";
$fileBname = "c:/scripts/myfile2.txt";

// open the two files for reading and writing respectively
$currentfile = fopen($fileAname,"r") or
 exit("Could not open file");
$newfile = fopen($fileBname,"w");

// read the contents of $fileAname
$fileAcontents = fread($currentfile,filesize($fileAname));

/* write the contents of $fileAname(myfile1.txt) to
   $fileBname(myfile2.txt) */
fwrite($newfile, $fileAcontents);

// close the two files
fclose($newfile);
fclose($currentfile);

echo "Contents copied from myfile1.txt to myfile2.txt";

?>
```

Copying Files

This section describes how to use PHP to copy files on Windows systems. PHP includes the **copy()** function for copying files. The function is defined below:

copy(original filename, new filename)

This copies the contents of an original file defined by the first parameter to a new file defined by the second function parameter. The function returns a **true** or **false** value to indicate success or failure of the copying process.

The following example illustrates how to copy the contents of one file to another file:

Listing 14.10: filecopy.php

```
<?php

$orig_filename = "c:/scripts/myoldfile.txt";
$new_filename = "c:/scripts/mynewfile.txt";

 /* Copy contents of $orig_filename (myoldfile.txt) to
$new_filename (mynewfile.txt) */
$status = copy($orig_filename, $new_filename) or
die("Could not copy file contents");

echo "Contents sucessfully copied";

?>
```

The first step is to create a variable to hold the full path to the original file whose contents will be copied:

$orig_filename = "c:/scripts/myfile.txt";

Next, a second variable is created to hold the full path to the new file that will be created:

$new_filename = " c:/scripts/mynewfile.txt ";

The **copy()** function is executed, accepting two parameters, the path of the original file - **$orig_filename**, and the path of the new file - **$new_filename**. The **copy()** function returns a value of **true** if the copy is completed successfully; otherwise a value of **false** is returned. The returned value is stored in the variable **$status**.

$status = copy($orig_filename, $new_filename) or die("Could not copy file contents");

If the **copy()** function fails, the **die()** function executes and displays an error message. Otherwise, success message is displayed using the **echo** statement.

echo "Contents sucessfully copied";

In Listing 14.9, the **fwrite()** function was used along with the **fread()** function to read the contents of one file and write the contents to a new file. Unless the contents of the original file are being appended to an existing file, the **copy()** function provides a more straightforward approach for copying content from an existing file to a new file.

Deleting Files

This section describes how to use PHP to delete files on Windows systems. PHP includes the **unlink()** function for deleting files. The **unlink()** function should be used with caution. Once a file is deleted, it cannot be retrieved. The function is defined below:

unlink(filename)

This deletes the file defined by the first parameter. The function returns a **true** or **false** value. The following example demonstrates how to delete a file using the **unlink()** function:

Listing 14.11: filedelete.php

```
<?php

 // assign file path to a variable
 $filename = "c:/scripts/mynewfile.txt";

 // delete mynewfile.txt file.
  $status = unlink($filename) or
  exit("Could not delete the file");

  echo "File deleted successfully";

?>
```

The first step is to create a variable to hold the full path to the file whose contents will be deleted:

```
$filename = "c:/scripts/mynewfile.txt";
```

The **unlink()** function is executed, accepting one parameter; the path of the original file - **$filename**. The **unlink()** function returns a value of **true** if the file is deleted successfully; otherwise a value of **false** is returned. The returned value is stored in the variable **$status**.

```
$status = unlink($filename) or exit("Could not delete the file");
```

If the **unlink()** function fails, the **exit()** function executes and displays an error message. Otherwise, a success message is displayed using the echo statement.

```
echo "File deleted successfully";
```

Renaming Files

This section describes how to use PHP to rename files on Windows systems. PHP includes the **rename()** function for renaming files. The function is defined below:

```
rename($orig_filename, $new_filename)
```

This function renames the file defined by the first parameter to the name defined in the second parameter. The function returns a **true** or false **value**.

The following example (Listing 14.12) demonstrates how to rename a file using the **rename()** function.

The first step is to create a variable to hold the full path to the file that will be renamed:

```
$orig_filename = "c:/scripts/myoldfile.txt";
```

The second step is to create a variable to hold the full path to the file that will be created when the old file is renamed:

```
$new_filename = "c:/scripts/mynewfile.txt ";
```

The **rename()** function is executed, accepting two parameters; the path of the original file - **$orig_filename** and the path to the file that will be created when the old file is renamed -

$new_filename. The **rename()** function returns a value of **true** if the file is deleted successfully; otherwise a value of **false** is returned. The returned value is stored in the variable **$status**.

$status = rename($orig_filename, $new_filename) or exit("Could not rename the file");

If the **rename()** function fails, the **exit()** function executes and displays an error message. Otherwise, success message is displayed using the echo statement.

echo "File renamed successfully";

Listing 14.12: filerename.php

```
<?php

 // assign file locations to variables
 $orig_filename = "c:/scripts/myoldfile.txt";
 $new_filename = "c:/scripts/mynewfile.txt";

 /* rename the $orig_filename(myoldfile.txt) to
  $new_filename(mynewfile.txt)*/
 $status = rename($orig_filename, $new_filename) or
              exit("Could not rename the file");

echo "File renamed successfully";

?>
```

Detailed Example

Writing Form Data into Text File

In most cases, form data entered by users are written to a relational database management systems (RDMS) such as MS Access and MySQL using the ODBC and MySQL functions. In a similar fashion, form data can be written to a text file. This example describes how to use PHP to collect form data and write it to a text file.

Consider the form page shown below.

Form data successfully written to file

Writing Form Data To A File

First Name becky

Last Name amponsah

Submit

In this example, the HTML form page contains a textbox for the user's first name and last name. A hidden field is also coded which includes the current date and time using the PHP **date()** function. When the form's submit button is clicked, a new text file called **'myfile.txt'** is created and opened in append mode:

```
$file_name = "c:\myfile.txt";

$open_file = fopen($file_name, "a+");
```

Next, the variable, **$file_contents**, is assigned the values of the POST superglobal variables, containing the user's first name, last name, and the current date/time value. Commas are concatenated to the strings to create delimiters separating each value. The newline character is added to create a carriage return at the end of each line:

```
$file_contents= $_POST['FName'] . "," . $_POST['LName'] . "," .
$_POST['DateTime'] ."\n";
```

Finally, the contents of the variable, **$file_contents**, are written (appended) to the text file. The file is closed and the **echo** statement is used to display a confirmation message to the browser window:

```
fclose($open_file);

echo "Form data successfully written to file";
```

The following listing shows how to write the submitted form data to the text file.

Remember to enable write access on your drive C:/. This will allow the creation of **myfile.txt** and permit the user to write form data into it.

Listing 14.13: saveform_to_flatfile.php

```
<?php

if(isset($_POST['save'] ))
{
   // open the file in append mode
   $file_name = "c:\myfile.txt";
   $open_file = @fopen($file_name, "a+") or
                exit("Could not open or create the file");

   $file_contents= $_POST['fName'] . "," . $_POST['lName'] . ","
   . $_POST['dateTime'] ."\n";

   // write the form data to $open_file(myfile.txt)
   fwrite($open_file,$file_contents);

   // close the file
   fclose($open_file);
   echo "Form data successfully written to file";
}
?>
<html>
<body bgcolor="#F5F5F5">
<p>Writing Form Data To A File</p>
<form method="post" action="saveform_to_flatfile.php">

  First Name  <input type="text" name="fName"/><br/><br/>
  Last Name   <input type="text" name="lName"/><br/><br/>
             <input type="hidden" name="dateTime"
             value="<?php echodate('g:i a') ?>"/>
             <input type="submit" name="save" value="Submit"/>
</form>
</body>
</html>
```

Programming Challenge

Q1. Random Number File Generation and Number Analysis

Create an application that generates a series of 100 random numbers in the range of 1 through 10000. Save the series of numbers to a text file.

Write a script that reads the numbers from the text file and perform the following:

- Display the total of the numbers.
- Display the average of the numbers.
- Display the highest number in the file.
- Display the lowest number in the file.

Your form may look like the figure below.

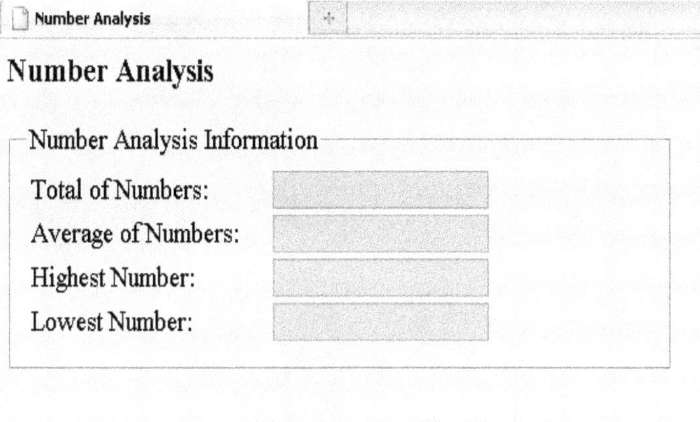

Q2. Saving Employee Data into Text File

Write a script that allows the user to enter the following employee data: first name, middle name, last name, employee number, department, telephone number, telephone extension, and e-mail address. The department dropdown menu contains the Accounting, Administration, Marketing, MIS, and Sales options.

Employee Data Capturing

Employee Data Capturing

Enter Employee Data

First Name:

Middle Name:

Last Name:

Employee Number:

Department:

Telephone:

Extension:

E-mail Address:

Add Record

You may design a form similar to above. The user enters the data and clicks on the **Add Record** button to write the record to the text file. The text file name should be coded within your script.

15

Uploading Files

First, solve the problem. Then, write the code. - John Johnson

Learning Objectives

After studying this chapter, you should be able to:

- Understand how to write scripts to upload files (including images, pictures, etc) to the web server.
- Learn how to write scripts to upload multiple files with one submission.
- Learn error tracking techniques in file upload.

Introduction

In dynamic Web applications it is necessary to allow users to upload files from their local computers to the Web server. Such an application may allow users to share files with others or simply provide a mechanism for storing files on the Web server for later use. This chapter discusses PHP functions for uploading files.

The `move_uploaded_file()` Function

The **move_uploaded_file()** function moves an uploaded file to a new location.

This function returns TRUE on success, or FALSE on failure.

The syntax is stated as:

move_uploaded_file(filename, destination)

The parameters represent

filename	-	Required parameter. Specifies the file to be moved.
destination	-	Required parameter. Specifies the new location for the file.

It should be noted that this function only works on files uploaded via HTTP POST and if the destination file already exists, it will be overwritten.

The `$_FILES` Array Functions

There is one global PHP variable called **$_FILES**. This variable is an associative double dimension array and keeps all the information related to uploaded file. So if the value assigned to the input box name attribute in uploading form is **fileUpload**,

```
<input type="file" name="fileUpload">
```

then PHP would create the following five variables:

Table 15.1: Array Functions

Function	Description
$_FILES['fileUpload']['tmp_name']	Directory on the web server where the file is temporarily stored. By default this is the **uploadtemp** directory located in the PHP folder.
$_FILES['fileUpload']['name']	Name of the file on the user's computer.
$_FILES['fileUpload']['size']	The size in bytes of the uploaded file.
$_FILES['fileUpload']['error']	The error code associated with the file upload. 0 - successful upload, 1 - file exceeds maximum upload size, 2 - file exceeds maximum file size, 3 - file partially uploaded, 4 - no file uploaded)
$_FILES[' fileUpload '][type']	The MIME type of the uploaded file

The user defined variable '**fileUpload**' which appears in the functions (such as **$_FILES['fileUpload']['tmp_name'**] in the table above represents the name of the text box, **(<input type="file" name="fileUpload">)**, which holds the path and filename of the uploaded file. The parameters **'name'**, **'tmp_name'**, **'size'** and **'error'** in the function are keywords.

File Upload Procedure

A PHP script can be used with an HTML form to allow users to upload files to the server.

Initially, files are uploaded into a temporary directory and then relocated to a target destination by a PHP script.

The process of uploading a file follows these steps:

- The user opens the page containing a HTML form showing a text box, a browse button and a submit button.
- The user clicks the browse button and selects a file to upload from the local PC.
- The full path to the selected file appears in the text field. The user clicks the submit button.
- The selected file is sent to the temporary directory on the server.
- The PHP script that was specified as the form handler in the form's action attribute checks that the file has arrived and then copies the file into an intended directory.
- The PHP script confirms the successful upload of the file to the user.

As usual, when writing files, it is necessary for both temporary and final locations to have permissions set that enable file writing. If either is set to be read-only then the process will fail.

An uploaded file could be a text file or image file or any document.

Uploading a File to the Web Server

Before we look at the details of the PHP code, lets explain the form controls needed to create the file upload page.

Create an Upload-File Form

To allow users to upload files from a form can be very useful. Look at the following HTML form for uploading files (Listing 15.1).

The code block begins with a standard XHTML **<form>** tag. In addition to the **action** and **method** attributes, a form used for file uploads must include the encode type "**enctype**" attribute. The value of the enctype attribute "**multipart/form-data**" should be included when a form is used to upload files.

Following the **<form>** is an **<input>** text box control. This control is used to specify the location and name of the file that will be uploaded. The control includes a name and type attribute. The type attribute must be set to "**file**". The name is a user-defined value that will be used by the server to identify the source file during the upload process. The file text box also includes a "Browse..." button when viewed in the browser window. See Figure 15.1. When the browse button is clicked, a dialog window appears and allows the user to browse the local computer for the file that will be uploaded.

Listing 15.1: upload_form.php

```
<html>
<head>
<title>File Upload Form</title>
<meta http-equiv="Content-Type" content="text/html;
                 charset=iso-8859-1">
</head>
<body>
<h3>Upload Files from Web Client to Web Server: </h3>

<form enctype="multipart/form-data" action="upload_form.php"
      method="post">

   Select File:  <input type="file" name="fileUpload">
                 <input name="fileUploadButton" type="submit"
                 value="File Upload">
</form>
</body>
</html>
```

The final control is a submit button. The submit button is used to initiate the form submission process. When the button is clicked, the file information is posted to the **fileupload.php** page which contains the PHP code to upload the file to a folder located on the Web server.

Create the Upload Script

After the form is coded, a PHP script can be added to the page to handle the file upload. When a file is uploaded using the **move_uploaded_file()** function, it is briefly stored in a temporary location on the Web server. To move the file to its final destination and manipulate its various properties, we use the PHP **$_FILES** super global array. The **$_FILES** array uses the name value provided in the **<input type="file" name="fileUpload">** to identify the file being uploaded.

Listing 15.2 shows how the **$_FILES** array is used with the **move_uploaded_file()** function to create a simple upload procedure.

Listing 15.2: uploadfile.php

```
<?php

// if the user clicks the upload button
if(isset($_POST['fileUploadButton']))
{
    move_uploaded_file($_FILES['fileUpload']['tmp_name'],
    "C:/{$_FILES['fileUpload']['name']}");
    echo "File uploaded Successfully.";
}

?>
```

When the " File Upload " button is clicked, the file specified in the **<input type="file" name="fileUpload">** is automatically posted to a temporary folder on the webserver.

The **move_uploaded_file()** function is then called to move the file. The first parameter of the function - **$_FILES['fileUpload'] ['tmp_name']**, becomes a reference (source) to the file as the function prepares to move it to its final destination. The second parameter - " **C:/{$_FILES['fileUpload'] ['name']}**", is an absolute path to the folder were the file will be permanently saved. In this case the file will be saved directly on the C drive. The last part of the path includes the code - **{$_FILES['fileUpload']['name']}**. This can be interpreted as the name of the file which was entered into the file text box named "**fileUpload**".

In short, the **move_uploaded_file()** function moves the file from a temporary upload folder (**$_FILES['uploadFile'] ['tmp_name']**) to the C drive (C:/) and the file is saved with the same name as entered or selected by the user (**{$_FILES['uploadFile'] ['name']}**). In fact, files can be uploaded to any directory on the Web server, however, the destination folder must have "write" access permissions.

Error Tracking in File Upload

The previous code example illustrates the ease of uploading a file but the assumption is that the file upload process will always work and errors will never occur. We have not considered what happens when a user attempts to upload a file that exceeds size limits, if the upload folder does not have appropriate security permissions, or some unforseen network issue that will prevent the entire file from being uploaded. To improve the file upload code above, we must provide routines that check for errors and provide feedback to the user on how to correct these problems.

The next block of codes show a modified version of the previous upload routine which includes error checking. We shall revisit and apply the the error checking function:

$_FILES['UploadFile']['error'] - the error code associated with the file upload

0 - successful upload,
1 - file exceeds maximum upload size,
2 - file exceeds maximum file size,
3 - file partially uploaded,
4 - no file uploaded

When the "File Upload" button is clicked, the file specified in the **<input type="file" name="fileUpload">** is automatically posted to a temporary folder on the Web server.

The **move_uploaded_file()** function is then called to move the file. The first parameter of the function - **$_FILES['fileUpload'] ['tmp_name']**, becomes a reference (source) to the file as the function prepares to move it to its final destination. The second parameter **../scripts/{$_FILES['fileUpload'] ['name']}",** is now a relative path to the folder were the file will be permanently saved. It is important to note that the folder **scripts** is already created and in existence, otherwise an error message will be encountered.

Listing 15.3: fileupload_error.php

```
<?php

// when the user clicks the File Upload button
if(isset($_POST['fileUploadButton']))
{
       // move the file to the server
       move_uploaded_file($_FILES['fileUpload']['tmp_name'],
       "../scripts/{$_FILES['fileUpload']['name']}");

      // error checking script
      if($_FILES['fileUpload'] ['error'] > 0)
      {
           switch($_FILES['fileUpload '] ['error'])
           {
           case 1: echo 'File exceeded max server upload size';
           break;

           case 2: echo 'File exceeded max file size';
           break;

           case 3: echo 'File only partially uploaded';
           break;

           case 4: echo 'No file uploaded';
           break;
           }
      }
      else
      {
           // no error occurred.
           echo 'File successfully uploaded';
      }
}
?>
```

Continuation of Listing 15.3: fileupload_error.php

```
<!- the HTML table -->
<!DOCTYPE HTML PUBLIC "-//W3C//DTD HTML 4.01
Transitional//EN">
<html>
<head>
<title>File Upload</title>
<meta http-equiv="Content-Type" content="text/html;
charset=iso-8859-1">
</head>
<body bgcolor="#F5F5F5">
<pre>

Upload Files from Web Client to Web Server:

<form enctype="multipart/form-data"
      action="fileupload_error.php" method="post">

 Select File: <input type="file" name="fileUpload">
 <input type="hidden" name="MAX_FILE_SIZE" value="1000000">
 <input name="fileUploadButton" type="submit"
  value="File  Upload">

</form>
</pre>
</body>
</html>
```

The updated code includes an **if** statement and a **switch/case** statement to check the status of the file upload. After the **move_uploaded_file(),** an **if** statement checks the value of the **$_FILES['fileUpload"] ['error']** array. If the value is greater than 0, an error has occured. The value of **$_FILES['fileUpload'] ['error']** is passed to a **switch** statement and is evaluated. When the value is determined, the appropriate error message is displayed. If the value of **$_FILES['fileUpload'] ['error']** is equal to 0, the **else** statement displays a success message.

Another new feature included in this example is a hidden text box called "MAX_FILE_SIZE". This is a special hidden tag that can be used with the file tag **<input type="file" name="fileUpload">** to set a maximum file size. If the file exceeds the specified value, an error will occur. The value is measured in bytes. Here the maximum file size is set to 1,000,000 bytes (approximately 1 MB). It is also possible to set a maximum server upload size. This is the maximum file size set on the server in the **php.ini** file.

Figure 15.1
The screen to browse for file to be uploaded.

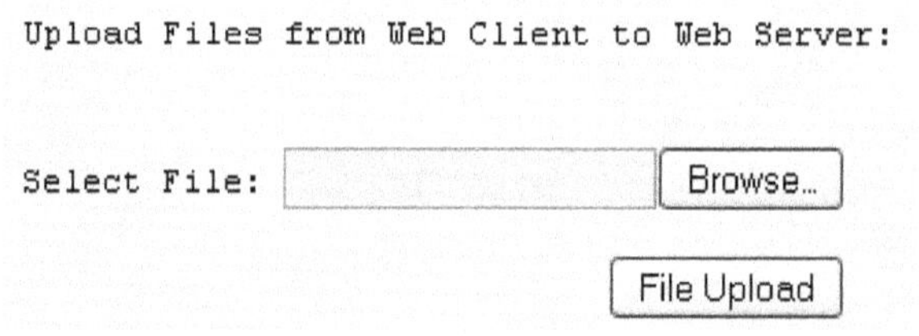

```
Upload Files from Web Client to Web Server:

Select File: [          ] [Browse...]

                          [File Upload]
```

Multiple File Uploading

In this section we will learn how to upload multiple files using a single form. This is required if you are allowing users to upload more than one file and you do not know how many files they may want to upload. Before we delve into the scripts, we will take a quick look at the **copy()** function which we shall use to upload the file.

The copy() Function

The **copy() function** copies a file. This function returns TRUE on success and FALSE on failure.

Syntax

copy(source, destination)

where

source - Required parameter. Specifies the file to copy

destination - Required parameter. Specifies the file to copy to

During the copying process, if the destination file already exists, it will be overwritten.

Create Multiple File Upload Scripts

In this first script, the user is required to state the number of files to be uploaded. For example, if a user wants to upload up to 8 files the user will be allowed to set the number in the text box and this value will provide the number of uploaded boxes the user can use to select the files to be uploaded.

Listing 15.4: upload_files_needed.php

```
<html>
<head>
<title>State Number of Files to Upload</title>
<meta http-equiv="Content-Type" content="text/html;
charset=iso-8859-1">
</head>
<body bgcolor="#F5F5F5">

<form method="post" action="upload_files_needed.php">
        <p>Enter the number of files you want to upload.
        <p><input type="text" name="noUploadNeed"
        maxlength="1">
        <p><input type="submit" name="Submit" value="Submit">
</form>
</body>
</html>
```

Having set the **noUploadNeed** input **maxlength** to 1, the maximum upload boxes the user can get is 9. The developer can change this value by increasing or decreasing the number of uploads required. When the user clicks on the **Submit** button, the **uploadForm.php** script is activated.

In this second script, we will be using the **for loop** to create the needed text boxes.

Listing 15.5: uploadForm.php

```
<html>
<head>
  <title>Untitled Document</title>
  <meta http-equiv="Content-Type" content="text/html;
  charset=iso-8859-1">
</head>

<body>
<form enctype="multipart/form-data" method="post"
      action="uploadForm.php">

<?php
// assign the form field to $uploadNeed variable
$noUploadNeed = $_POST['noUploadNeed'];

// create number text boxes
for($x=0;$x<$noUploadNeed;$x++)
{
    ?>
      Select File for Upload:
      <input name="uploadFile<?php echo $x;?>" type="file"
     id="uploadFile<?php echo $x;?>"><br>
    <?php
}
?>
     <input name="noUploadNeed" type="hidden" value="<? echo
      $noUploadNeed;?>">
     <input type="submit" name="Submit" value="Submit">
</form>

</body>
</html>
```

In this page, a simple HTML form with the value of the attribute "**type**" set to "**file**" has been created. Within the form there is a block of code to start the **for loop**. The $x has been set to 0 and made to stop at the value of **$noUploadNeed** less 1 (this is because the $x starts at 0). Next, the value of **$noUploadNeed** has been put into a hidden input field to be carried over to the next page.

The key to making this all work however is the **$x** variable that is echoing right next to the **uploadFile** name. What this will do is to append a number starting with 0 to the name. This in turn will make each upload field's name unique. We shall have **uploadFile0, uploadFile1, uploadFile2, uploadFile3, etc,** upto the specified number of files. Here is the last page to complete our multiple upload tasks.

Listing 15.6: processUploadFiles.php

```
<?php

$noUploadNeed = $_POST['noUploadNeed'];

// start the loop to upload files
for($x=0;$x<$noUploadNeed;$x++)
{
   $file_name = $_FILES['uploadFile'. $x]['name'];

   // strip file_name of slashes
   $file_name = stripslashes($file_name);
   $file_name = str_replace("'","",$file_name);

   $copy =
   copy($_FILES['uploadFile'.$x]['tmp_name'],$file_name);

   // check if successfully copied
   if($copy)
   {
       echo "$file_name uploaded sucessfully!<br>";
   }
   else
   {
       echo "$file_name  could not be uploaded!<br>";
   }
}

?>
```

The first thing we do in this page is to grab the **noUploadNeed** from **uploadForm.php**. We setup our **for loop** in the same fashion as the previous script. The difference here though is we get the **$_FILES** name within the **for loop**. This is assigned to a local variable named **$file_name**. Next, we do a little parsing by adding the **stripslashes()** and **str_replace()** functions. The reason we add the **stripslashes** is due to files that may have apostrophes in their names; otherwise this will generate a parse error and prevent that file from being uploaded.

Notice once again how we added the **$x** variable, which in turn is a number, to the name of the **$_FILES**. By doing this the script now knows which file it is uploading.

We will use the **copy()** function now to actually begin the upload process. The last thing we added was a simple **if** statement to check that the copy was successful and **echo** the appropriate message to the screen.

Detailed Example

Picture Upload

You have been asked by your supervisor to upgrade your company's website. The company's clients are required to upload their pictures to you, which will be used to process electronic ID Cards. Given the form below, you are required to write PHP script to perform picture upload from client computers to the Web server.

Upload Picture from Web Client to Web Server:

Suggested Solution

The listing to upload the picture is as below:

Listing 15.7: upload_photo.php

```
<html>
<head>
<title>Photo Upload</title>
</head>
<body bgcolor="#f6f6f6">

<?php

// when the user clicks the File Upload button
if(isset($_POST['fileUploadButton']))
{
        $photo_name = $_FILES['fileUpload'] ['name'];
       $new_filename = strtolower($photo_name).'.jpg';

       $status=rename($new_filename,$orig_filename);

       // move the file to the server
       move_uploaded_file($_FILES['fileUpload'] ['tmp_name'],
       "images/{$new_filename}");

      // error checking script
       if($_FILES['fileUpload'] ['error'] > 0)
       {
           switch ($_FILES['fileUpload '] ['error'])
        {
        case 1: $msg = 'File exceeded maximum server upload size';
        break;

        case 2: $msg = 'File exceeded maximum file size';
        break;

        case 3: $msg = 'File only partially uploaded';
        break;
```

Continuation of Listing 15.7: upload_photo.php

```
         case 4: $msg = 'No file uploaded';
         break;
             }
        }
        else
        {
         // no error occurs.
         $msg = 'File successfully uploaded!';
        }
}
?>
<!—Start HTML form -->
<form enctype="multipart/form-data" action="upload_photo.php"
  method="post">
<table>
<tr>
   <td>Please select your photo file for upload: <br />
    <input type="file" name="fileUpload" size="30" /> 
    <input name="fileUploadButton" type="submit"
    value="Upload Photo" />
   <br />
   </td>
</tr>
</table>
</form>
</body>
</html>
```

Programming Challenge

Q1. Single File Upload

In some dynamic web applications, it is necessary to allow users to upload files from the local computer to the Web server. Such an application may allow users to share files including images with others or simply provide a mechanism for storing files for later use.

Given the form below, you are required to write PHP script to perform file upload from your client computer to the web server.

Upload File from Web Client to Web Server:

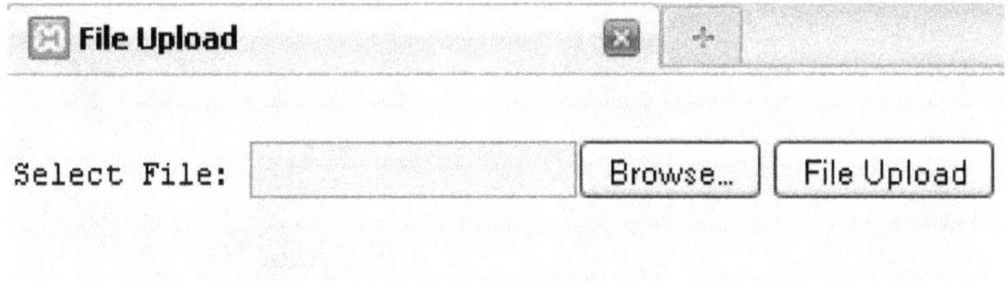

Q2. Multiple Files Upload

In this exercise you will write scripts to upload multiple files with one time submission (see Form A). You will use arrays in answering this question.

You will create 2 files:

a. multiple_upload.php
   The upload file screen is shown below. Your screen should be in this form.

b. process_multiple_upload.php
   This is the php scripts that should carry out the processing of the files to be uploaded.

Do the following:

- Create a file known as **multiple_upload.php**.
- Create another file known as **process_multiple_upload.php**
- Create a folder "**upload**" on drive C: to store uploaded files. Make sure the folder has read and write permissions.

Other requirements:

- The file sizes cannot exceed 500000.
- Check for the following and display appropriate message to the user:
  a. Successful file upload
  b. File exceeds maximum upload size

c. File partially uploaded
d. No file uploaded

Form A

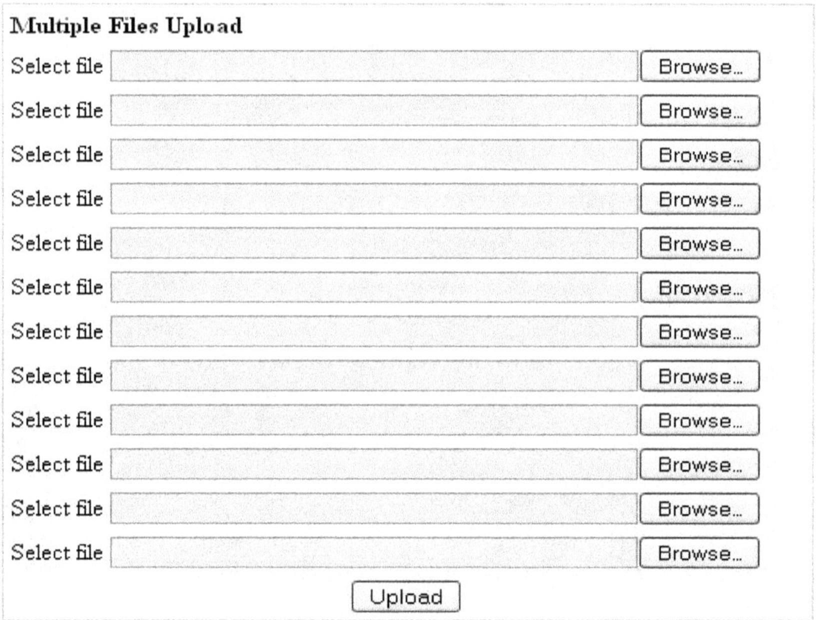
Multiple Files Upload
Select file
Browse...
Select file
Browse...
Select file
Browse...
Select file
Browse...
Select file
Browse...
Select file
Browse...
Select file
Browse...
Select file
Browse...
Select file
Browse...
Select file
Browse...
Select file
Browse...
Select file
Browse...
Upload

16

Sending E-Mail Message

The computers do what you tell them to do, not what you want them to do.
- Alexander Atanasov

Learning Objectives

After studying this chapter, you should be able to:

- Learn how to setup Windows and Linux platform for sending automated email.
- Write scripts to send simple automated email.
- Write scripts to send email with file attachment.

Introduction

Email is among the most popular Internet services today. A lot of emails are sent and delivered each day. The purpose of this chapter is to demonstrate how to generate and send emails in PHP. We shall learn how to send automated email messages from your PHP application. This can be in direct response to a user's action, such as signing up for your site, or a recurring event at a set time, such as a monthly newsletter or monthly bills, etc.

Sometimes email contains file attachments, both plain text and HTML portions, and so on. To understand how to send each variation that may exist on an email, we will start with a simple example and move to a more complicated example. It is important to note that to send email with PHP you need a working email server that you have permission to use: for Unix machines, this is often Sendmail; for Windows machines, you must set the Simple Mail Transfer Protocol (SMTP) directive in your **php.ini** file to point to your email server.

It is important to note that to send email with PHP you need a working email server.

The `Mail()` Function

PHP includes the **mail()** function for sending email. The function is defined below:

mail(to, subject, message, headers, parameters)

The function allows you to send mail. It returns **true** if the message is sent successfully, otherwise a value of **false** is returned.

Table 16.1 describes the parameters of the **mail()** function.

Table 16.1: Mail() Function

Parameter	Description
to	Required parameter. Specifies the receiver/receivers of the email.
subject	Required parameter. Specifies the subject of the email. This parameter cannot contain any newline characters.
message	Required parameter. Defines the message to be sent. Each line should be separated with a line feed (\n).
header	Optional parameter. Specifies additional headers, like From, Cc, and Bcc. The additional headers should be separated with a carriage return and line feed (\r\n).
parameters	Optional parameter. Specifies an additional parameter to the sendmail program.

Platform Setup

This section describes how to use SMTP services to send automated email messages from PHP applications. Email is sent from a Web server through its SMTP service. This is, as the name implies, a limited email service; however, it is sufficient for generating automated emails. It should be noted that SMTP server is required in order to take advantage of PHP's email functionality. On most Windows platforms SMTP services are bundled with Internet Information Services (IIS). On Linux/Unix, Sendmail and Qmail are popular SMTP packages.

Windows Platform Setup

If you are running PHP under a server using IIS SMTP services, you may need to configure it to permit relay of email messages. Perform the following steps:

Step 1:

1. Open IIS Administrative Tools.
   a) Open Control Panel
   b) Open Administrative Tools
   c) Open Internet Information Services
   d) Expand Default SMTP Virtual Server

2. Stop Default SMTP Virtual Server service.
   a) Right-click Default SMTP Virtual Server service and select Stop

3. Open properties window of Default SMTP Virtual Server and setup SMTP.
   a) Right-click Default SMTP Virtual Server service and select Properties
   b) Click "Access" tab and click "Relay..." button.
   c) Click "Only the list below" button and add the single computer IP address 127.0.0.1.
   d) Click "OK" buttons to close "Access" tabs and properties window.

4. Restart Default SMTP Virtual Server service.
   a) Right-click Default SMTP Virtual Server service and select Start

Step 2:

It is also necessary to make the following changes to the PHP configuration file - **php.ini** - so that PHP can use SMTP services. Open the **php.ini** file (located at Apache folder) with a text editor (Notepad) and locate the following lines:

[mail function]

For Win32 only
SMTP = **localhost**
; For Win 32 only
sendmail_from = **info@hightelsoft.net**

You will need to modify the SMTP directive to point to your SMTP server. If you are using local SMTP services, this value should be set to **localhost**. The second directive **sendmail_from** is the email address used in the **From** header of the out-going email. This should be set to a valid email address if users will be permitted to respond to auto generated email messages.

Linux Platform Setup

PHP must be configured correctly in the **php.ini** file with the details of how your system sends email. Open **php.ini** file available in **/etc/** directory and find the section headed **[mail function]**. Linux users simply need to let PHP know the location of their **sendmail** application. The path and any desired switches should be specified in the **sendmail_path** directive.

The configuration for Linux should look something like this:

```
[mail function]
; For Win32 only.
SMTP =

; For win32 only
sendmail_from =

; For Unix only
sendmail_path = /usr/sbin/sendmail -t -i
```

Sending Text Email

At first, let us consider how to send a simple text email message. We shall use the **mail()** function for sending email, which takes three basic and two optional parameters. These parameters are, in order, the email address to send to, the subject of the email, the message to be sent, additional headers you want to include, and finally an additional parameter to the Sendmail program. The **mail()** function returns True if the message is sent successfully and False otherwise. Have a look at the example:

Listing 16.1: email_hardcoded.php

```
<?php

  //define the receiver of the email recipient
  $to = 'youraddress@example.com';

  //define the subject of the email
  $subject = 'Online Registration';

  /* define the message. Each line should be separated
   with \n */
  $message = "Dear,\n\n We are pleased to register you.";

  /* define the headers. Note that they are separated
   with \r\n */
  $headers = "From: info@hightelsoft.net\r\n Reply-To:
              info@hightelsoft.net ";

  //send the email
  $mail_sent = @mail($to, $subject, $message, $headers );

  /* if the message is sent successfully display "Mail sent
  successfully". Otherwise display "Mail failed" */
  echo $mail_sent ? "Mail sent successfully" : "Mail failed";

?>
```

As you can see, it is very easy to send an email. You can add more recipients by either adding their addresses, comma separated, to the **$to** variable, or by adding **cc:** or **bcc:** headers. When you run this script and do not receive the mail, you have probably installed PHP incorrectly, or may not have permission to send emails.

Sending HTML Email

The next step is to examine how to send HTML email. However, some mail clients cannot understand HTML emails. Therefore, it is best to send any HTML email using a multipart construction, where one part contains a plain-text version of the email and the other part is HTML. If your customers have HTML email turned off, they will still get a nice email, even if they do not get all of the HTML markup. Let us have a look at the example:

The following function in Listing 16.2 will send out an HTML formatted email using the PHP built-in **mail()** function. In our **send_email** function, we set the content type headers to **text/html**. It is important to do so because it tells the email server that the email contains html code and to format and display the email correctly when it is opened.

Listing 16.2: html_email.php

```
<?php

// declare an email function with its parameters
function send_email($from, $to, $subject, $message){
    $headers = "From: ".$from."\r\n";
    $headers .= "Reply-To: ".$from."\r\n";
    $headers .= "Return-Path: ".$from."\r\n";
    $headers .= "Content-type: text/html\r\n";

    // send the email
    if (mail($to,$subject,$message,$headers) )
    {
            echo "Email sent successfully.";
    }else{
            echo "Could not send email.";
    }
}
// assign values to subject and message parameters
$subject = "Registration";
$message .= "<html><body>";
$message .= "<b>You have been successfully
registered!</b>";
$message .= "<br>Thanks";
$message .= "</body></html>";

// call the function
send_email("info@hightelsoft.net", "johnbaba@yahoo.com",
          $subject ,$message);
?>
```

Collecting User Input into Email Message

In most cases, the **to, subject,** and **message** parameters of the **mail()** function are not simply hardcoded as shown in the previous examples. Instead they are provided dynamically as a result of user input. For example, consider a page that allows a user to electronically register for a product or service. The user enters a first name, last name, email address, and telephone number. This information is passed to a PHP page that parses the information and sends the user a confirmation email. The following example (Listing 16.3) demonstrates this process.

Listing 16.3: email_form.php

```
<html >
<head>
<title>Email</title>
</head>
<body bgcolor="#F5F5F5">
<h3> Registration Page </h3>

<form name="registration" method="post"
      action="email_form.php">

      <!-- form input fields-->
      First Name:     <input type="text" name="fname"/><br>
      Last Name:      <input type="text" name="lname"/><br>
      Email Address: <input type="text" name="email"/><br>
      Telephone:      <input type="text"
                      name="telephone"/><br>

      <input type="submit" name="Registration"
      value="Send"/>

</form>
</body>
</html>
```

The script produces the following form:

The **email_form.php** page is a page that allows the user to enter a first name, last name, email address, and telephone number. When the "Send" button is clicked, the form data is passed to the PHP page - **email_dynamic.php** through $_POST[ ] variables:

$_POST['fname']	-	contains user's first name
$_POST['lname']	-	contains user's last name
$_POST['email']	-	contains user's email address
$_POST['telephone']	-	contains user's telephone number

The following script (see Listing 16.4) shows how the form information is parsed and used by the **mail()** function.

The **email_dynamic.php** page assigns the values of the **$_POST[ ]** superglobals (containing the values submitted from **email_form.php**) and assigns them to scalar variables which will be easier to work with. Next, a variable **$mailheaders** are created and the **mail( )** function is called. The scalar variables supply the function with the required parameters.

Listing 16.4: email_dynamic.php

```
<?php

  // form input fields from email_form.php
  $to = $_POST[email];
  $subject = "Member Registration Confirmation";
  $msg = "Dear: " . $_POST[fname]." ".$_POST[lname].",\n\n";
  $msg .= "You are now successfully registered."

  // header information
  $mailheaders = "From: Member Registration Site
                   <info@hightelsoft.net>";

  $mailheaders .= "Reply - To: info@hightelsoft.net";

  // sending the email
  if(mail($to, $subject, $msg, $mailheaders))
  {
    echo "Email sent successfully. ";
  }
  else
  {
     echo "Email could not be sent.";
  }

?>
```

Sending Email Attachments

To send an email with mixed content requires us to set **Content-type** header to **multipart/mixed**. The text and attachment sections can be specified within **boundaries**. A boundary is started with two hyphens followed by a unique number which can not appear in the message part of the email. A PHP function **md5()** is used to create a 32 digit hexadecimal number to create unique number. A final boundary denoting the email's final section must also end with two hyphens.

Attached files should be encoded with the **base64_encode()** function for safer transmission and are best split into chunks with the **chunk_split()** function. This adds **\r\n** inside the file at regular intervals, normally every 76 characters. Following is the example which will send a file **/scripts/test.txt** as an attachment. You can code your program to receive an uploaded file and send it.

Have a look at the example:

Listing 16.5: email_attachment.php
```
<html>
<head>
<title>Sending attachment using PHP</title>
</head>
<body>
<?php

        // assign message parameters to variables
        $to = "xyz@somedomain.com";
        $subject = "This is subject";
        $message = "This is test message.";

        // open a file
        $file = fopen("/tmp/test.txt", "r");
        if($file == false)
        {
        echo "Error in opening file";
        exit();
        }
        // read the file into a variable
        $size = filesize("/tmp/test.txt");
        $content = fread( $file, $size);

        /* encode the data for safe transit and insert \r\n
        after every 76 chars.*/
       $encoded_content = chunk_split(
       base64_encode($content));

        // get a random 32 bit number using time() as seed.
        $num = md5(time());
```

Continuation of Listing 16.5: email_attachment.php

```
        // define the main headers.
        $header = "From:xyz@somedomain.com\r\n";
        $header .= "MIME-Version: 1.0\r\n";
        $header .= "Content-Type: multipart/mixed; ";
        $header .= "boundary=$num\r\n";
        $header .= "--$num\r\n";

        // define the message section
        $header .= "Content-Type: text/plain\r\n";
        $header .= "Content-Transfer-Encoding:8bit\r\n\n";
        $header .= "$message\r\n";
        $header .= "--$num\r\n";

        // define the attachment section
        $header .= "Content-Type:  multipart/mixed; ";
        $header .= "name=\"test.txt\"\r\n";
        $header .= "Content-Transfer-Encoding:base64\r\n";
        $header .= "Content-Disposition:attachment; ";
        $header .= "filename=\"test.txt\"\r\n\n";
        $header .= "$encoded_content\r\n";
        $header .= "--$num--";

        // send email now
        $retval = mail ( $to, $subject, "", $header );
        if( $retval == true )
  {
     echo "Message sent successfully.";
  }
  else
  {
     echo "Message could not be sent.";
  }
?>
</body>
</html>
```

Programming Challenge

Q1. Sending Email Message

In this exercise you will write scripts to submit records. After a message is successfully submitted a confirmation email should be sent to the user confirming the registration.

a) Write HTML tags to create the form. The file name should be **contacts.php**.
b) When the form is submitted, create a new script **emailprocessing.php** that carries out the sending of the email.
c) Use server-side validation to ensure that the email address entered is valid.

Contact Form

Subject :

Detail :

Name :

Email :

Submit Reset

Q2. Sending Email Message

Web users are asked to register their names, emails and telephone numbers with a service provider online. After the user successfully sent the information, an automated confirmation email is delivered to the user. Using the form provided below, use the **mail()** function to write a script that delivers the information from info@hightel.com. A confirmation message should be sent back to the user to the email address provided in the address textbox.

The script produces the form below.

Customer Registration Page

Q3. Email with File Attachment

Write HTML tags and PHP scripts to design the form and send email with an attachment.

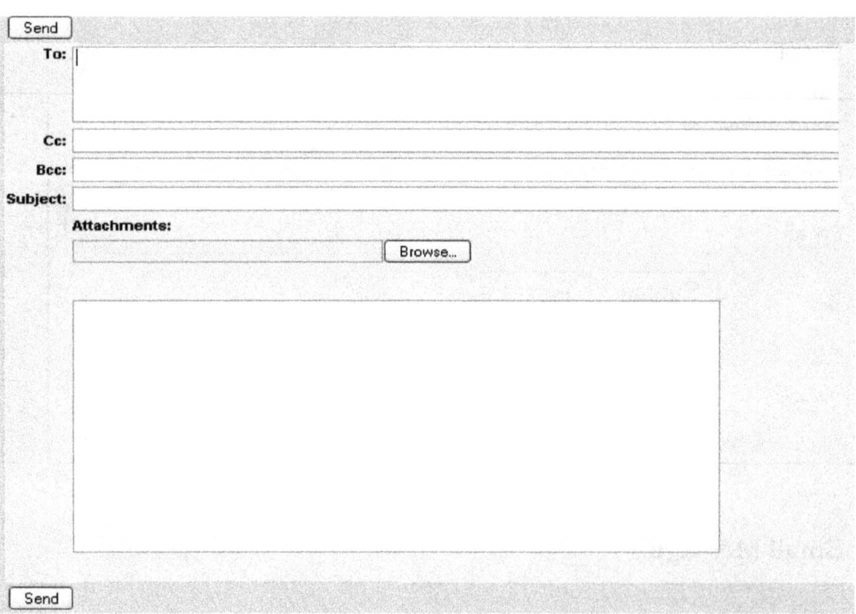

17

Server-Side Form Validation

Let he who has a bug free software cast the first stone. - Assaad Chalhoub

Learning Objectives

After studying this chapter, you should be able to:

- Understand the server-side validation and its application in PHP.
- Distinguish between server-side and client-side validation techniques.
- Write PHP script to validate various types of data fields including letters, numbers, email, date, and empty fields.
- Use Regular Expressions in server-side form validation.

What is Validation

Validation is a process of verifying that something is correct or conforms to a certain standard. In data collection or data entry, it is the process of ensuring that the data that are entered fall within the accepted boundaries of the application collecting the data. For example, if a program is collecting last names to be entered in a database, the program validates that only letters are entered and not numbers; or in a survey collecting data in the form of "yes" or "no" questions, the program validates that only those responses are used and not some other word.

Validation procedures typically are written into the program code and are therefore invisible to the user. Whenever you make a form you should not leave it alone without any form validation. This is because there is no guarantee that the input on the form is correct. Processing incorrect input values can make your application give unpredictable result.

Types of Validation

You can validate form inputs at two places, **server-side** and **client-side**. In this chapter, we shall look at how to write server-side validation script using PHP. In chapter 18, we shall discuss client-side validation.

What is Server-Side Validation

With the Server-side validation, the process of validation is undertaken by the Web server instead of the Web browser. Server-side validation means using a server-side scripting language such as PHP (or any other server-side scripting languages such ASP) to verify that acceptable values have been kept by the server. Server-side validation is more secure and works with all browsers. Because the validation is done by the Web server, it has a slightly higher server load and slower feedback for users. PHP comes with a wide variety of functions and language features to help you check and compare strings, check that numbers are within ranges, and so on..

What to Validate

The following are some pieces of data you may want to validate before you store them in the Web server or use them in your application.

- Empty values
- Letters only
- Numbers only
- Alphanumeric (numbers and letters)
- Input length
- Email address
- Date format
- Telephone number
- Selection has been made from dropdown, check box, radio button selectors.

Validation Using PHP Server-Side Functions

PHP includes numerous string and numeric functions that can be used to validate user input. The most common functions are explained below:

Table 17.1: Some Server-Side Validation Functions

Function	Description
is_string()	Determines whether a variable is a string. Returns a true or false value.
is_int() or is_integer()	Determines whether a variable is an integer. Returns a true or false value.
is_numeric()	Determines whether a variable is numeric. Returns a true or false value.
is_double() or is_float()	Determines whether a variable is a float. Returns a true or false value.
strlen()	Returns the length of a string.

Validation Using Regular Expression

In addition to PHP string and numeric values, we shall use Regular Expressions (regex) to validate certain input fields due to their flexibility of use. Regular Expressions are used for string matching. They are based on search and pattern matching of strings in text. Regular Expression is a way for a computer user or programmer to express how a computer program should look for a specified pattern in **text** and then what the program is to do when each pattern match is found. For example, a regular expression could tell a program to search for all text lines that contain the word "PHP" and then to print out each line in which a match is found or substitute another text sequence where any match occurs.

There are two ways to use regular expressions in PHP. One is the true PHP style in which case we have to use **ereg()** function and the other is to use Perl style syntax for our validations. In this chapter we shall use **preg_match()** function. The **preg_match()** is faster in most cases and also supports the most common regular expression syntax. The **preg_match()** function can be defined in the format:

preg_match(regex, variable).

The function **returns 0 if there is no match**. In that case we have to set our error variable, so we can show some meaningful message to the user if there is no match. We shall look at some specific Regular Expressions and discuss various data types and text formats. We shall create a class for our possible input values. The class is created when we enclose some symbols in parentheses. The following (see Table 17.2) are some basic classes we shall use in our examples.

Table 17.2: Validation Using Regular Expression

Regex Class	Description
/^ $/	Start and end characters. The forward slash (/) is used by **preg_match** to define the start and the end of our regexp. "^" means the start of the line and "$" means the end of it.
[a-z]	This contains only lower case letters.
[A-Z]	This contains only upper case letters.
[0-9]	This contains numbers from 0 to 9.
\w =[0-9A-Za-z_] (a predefined class equivalence)	This predefined class (\w) includes digits, letters and underscore character.
\d = [0-9] (a predefined class equivalence)	This predefined class (\d) includes only digits.
/^[A-Z][a-zA-Z -]+$/	This contains letters, dashes and spaces only and start with upper case letter

Server-Side PHP Form Validation

In this section we shall look at the commonly used validation functions that are used in PHP, write program segments to show you how to validate input values. Finally, we shall integrate all the various program segments to illustrate a complete usage of form validation.

We shall use the form in Figure 17.1 to validate various input data.

Figure 17.1: Form Validation

Form Validation

SERVER-SIDE FORM VALIDATION

Customer Name:	[required field]
User Name:	[letters only]
Password:	[must be least 8 characters]
Phone No:	[as of 233-21-254347 format]
Date:	[must be of dd-mm-yyyy format]
Address:	[letters, numbers, space . - etc]
Email:	[use email address format, ie xxxx@xxx.com]
Credit Card No:	[numbers only]
Continent:	[required field]
	Validate

Checking for Empty Value in Dropdown Selection

Checking for empty value is the most common type of form validation. You want to be sure that the users enter data into the HTML fields you have "required" for a valid submission. Listing 17.1 is the PHP script to perform this basic check to see if a given HTML input is empty or not.

When the submit button is clicked, the **if** statement is used to validate the content of the name field. First, the continent field (value of **$_POST['continent']** is checked for a NULL value. If **$_POST['continent']** contains a NULL value, this indicates the user did not select a continent in the 'continent' dropdown. An **echo** statement is used to request the user to select the continent. If the **$_POST['continent']** does contain a value, it is assigned to a scalar variable, **$continent**, which can be used later in the script when the data processing begins.

Listing 17.1: empty_values.php

```
<?php
/* determine if the submit button has been clicked. If so,
begin validating form data. */
if(isset($_POST['check']))
{
        // Check for empty field.
        if ($_POST['continent'] == "")
        {
                echo "Enter Your Continent" . "<br>";
                $valid_form = false;
        }
        else
        {
                $continent = $_POST['continent'];
                $valid_form = true;
        }
}
?>
```

Checking Validity of a Name Field

We will continue with validation of the name of the customer. We will allow only letters, space and a dash. So we create our regexp. We will make a class for our possible values. The class is created when we enclose some symbols in parenthesis. This is our class:

[a-zA-Z -]

Our class includes all letters between a-z (all lower case letters), A-Z (all upper case letters), space and a dash.

Now, we have to set this class to apply for every character that we enter. So we add a (+) plus sign after our class definition. We are still missing something. We have not defined the range of our validation test. We have to set which part of the text we are validating. If we do not do this our regular expression will be satisfied if it finds even one match in the characters that we enter, which is of no use for us. How do we do this? We put our string between /^ and $/ (start and end characters). The forward slash is used by **preg_match** to define the start and the end of our regexp. "^" means the start of the line and "$" means the end of it. We are ready to complete our class.

/^[a-zA-Z -]+$/

The way we defined our class allows the user to enter dash at the begining of the name. This is something we want to prevent. So we have to add something to our regexp, so it will disallow this.

[A-Z]

We define a new class for the first letter of the customer name. It can contain only upper case letters. Now we combine what we have done so far, to get the final result:

/^[A-Z][a-zA-Z -]+$/

Listing 17.2: name_field.php

```
<?php

/* determine if the submit button has been clicked. If so, begin
validating form data. */
If(isset($_POST['check']))
{
    /* full name must contain letters, dashes and spaces onlyand
    must start with upper case letter. */
    if(preg_match("/^[A-Z][a-zA-Z -]+$/", $_POST["name"]) == 0)
    {
            echo "Invalid Customer Name ". "<br>";
            $valid_form = false;
    }else{
            $name = $_POST['name'];
            $valid_form = true;
    }
}
?>
```

preg_match("/^[A-Z][a-zA-Z-]+$/", $POST['name']) returns **0** if there is no match.

Checking for Phone Number Field

In this example we shall check for a phone number to see whether it is in a particular format. The procedure is to define the number of digits in every part of the phone number and choose a delimiter. The delimiter can be any symbol you want to use to format the phone number, usually it is a dash (-) or a space. Remember the predefined class \d = [0-9].

Listing 17.3: phone_field.php

```
<?php

/* checks the click of the submit button. If yes, begin
validating form data. */
if(isset($_POST['check']))
{
   // phone number must comply with this mask: 233-21-3334444.
    if(preg_match("/^\d{3}-d{2}-\d{6}$/", $_POST["phoneNo"]) ==
    0)
    {
          echo "Phone No. format must be: 233-21-3334444 ". "<br>";
          $valid_form = false;
    }
    else
    {
          $phoneNo = $_POST['phoneNo'];
          $valid_form = true;
    }
}

?>
```

Again remember that preg_match("**/^\d{3}-d{2}-\d{6}$/**", **$_POST["phoneNo"]**) returns **0** if there is no match.

Checking for Validity of a Date Field

Now we will make a date mask. It will look like this: DD-MM-YYYY. Our date will be made up of digits only. You already know how to set the length of the year, but the month and day can be between 1 and 2 digits in length. We set this by separating the two values by comma {1,2}. This means that all the numbers in this interval are valid values.

Listing 17.4: date_field.php

```
<?php

/* determine if the submit button has been clicked. If
so, begin validating form data. */
if(isset($_POST['check']))
{
     // date mask  DD-MM-YYYY.
    if(preg_match("/^[0-9]{1,2}-[0-9]{1,2}-[0-9]{4}$/",
       $_POST["curDate"])==0)
    {
        echo "Date format must be: DD-MM-YYYY". "<br>";
        $valid_form = false;
    }
    else
    {
        $curDate = $_POST['curDate'];
        $valid_form = true;
    }
}

?>
```

Checking for Numbers Only

If the user is entering a Credit Card information (credit card number is required to be made up of numbers only) you want to be able to ensure that the input is all numbers. The quickest way to check if the input value is all numbers is to use a PHP function **is_numeric().** This is illustrated in Listing 17.5.

Here we want to see if the input value is all numbers so we use PHP's **is_numeric()** function to check for numbers [0-9]. If **$_POST['cardNo']** contains a letter or other character, an **echo** statement is used to display an error message to the user. If the **$_POST['cardNo']** does contain numbers, it is assigned to a scalar variable, **$cardNo**. The **$valid_form** is used to determine the state, whether the test was successful or not.

Listing 17.5: number_field.php

```
<?php

/* determine if the submit button has been clicked. If so,
begin   validating form data. */
if(isset($_POST['check']))
{
  // determine if the credit card no are all numbers.
  if(is_numeric($_POST['cardNo']))
   {
        $cardNo = $_POST['cardNo'];
        $valid_form = true;
  }
  else
  {
        echo "Card Number must be between 0-9. " . "<br>";
        $valid_form = false;
   }
}

?>
```

Checking for Letters Only

Here, the user enters the user name which is required to be letters. We shall use PHP function **preg_match()** which checks for letters in the regex: **/^[a-zA-Z]+$/.** In this example, we assume the user name will be made up of lower and upper case letters only

Listing 17.6: letter_field.php

```
<?php

/* determine if the submit button has been clicked. If so,
begin validating form data. */
if(isset($_POST['check']))
{
   /* determine if the User Name are all letters(lower case
   and upper case). */
 if(preg_match("/^[a-zA-Z]+$/", $_POST["userName"]) == 0)
 {
          echo "User Name must be letters only. " . "<br>";
          $valid_form = false;
 }
 else
{
          $userName = $_POST['userName'];
          $valid_form = true;
 }
}

?>
```

Checking an Address Field

Let us move forward to the next validation field, which is going to be the address. Address field can contain a lot of symbols. We just have to define one class that holds them all.

/^[a-zA-Z0-9 _-.,:\"\']+$/

We can explain this regexp as: From the beginning to the end of the address string, you should check if a character is one of the following **a-z, A-Z, 0-9, space, underscore, dash, dot, comma, semicolons, double and single quotes**. You can add any character that you think may be part of an address. The thing to notice here is that when we have quotes we have to put an escape character (\) before them.

Listing 17.7: address.php

```
<?php

/* begin validating form data. */
if(isset($_POST['check']))
{
   /* determine if the address is Address which must be only
   letters, numbers or one of the following _ - . , : ' */
 if(preg_match("/^[a-zA-Z0-9 _-.,:\"\']+$/",
       $_POST["address"])== 0){
         echo "Invalid address, must be letters, numbers,
                spaces, dash, dot, ... " . "<br>";
         $valid_form = false;
 }else{
         $address = $_POST['address'];
         $valid_form = true;
 }
}
?>
```

Checking for Input Length

We can validate a password by checking its length. Validation of a password is a two step process: (1) checking that a password was entered, and (2) if a password was entered, make sure it contains at least 8 characters. The **if** statement checks whether a password was entered and that it is at least 8 characters in length using the **strlen()** function. This function returns the length of the password. The resulting length is compared to 8. If the value is less than 8 or no password entered, an error message is displayed. Otherwise, the password is correct and is assigned to the scalar variable, **$pass**.

Listing 17.8: input_length.php

```
<?php

/* determine if the submit button has been clicked. If so,
begin validating form data. */
If(isset($_POST['check']))
{
 // determine if the password is at least 8 characters.
 if(strlen($_POST['pass'] < 8) || ($_POST['pass'] == ""))
 {
         echo "Invalid password. " . "<br>";
         $valid_form = false;
 }
 else
 {
         $pass = $_POST['pass '];
         $valid_form = true;
 }
}

?>
```

Checking for Email Address

Our next task is to create a regexp for email validation. Here we are going to include another feature of the expressions that represents predefined classes. Here is a list of those that we will use:

\w = [0-9A-Za-z_] Class includes digits, letters and underscore character.

\d = [0-9] Class includes only digits

These predefined constants (**\w** and **\d**) save a lot of typing and make source code easier to read and understand. What is the mask for an email? The first part of the username in an email can contain letters, digits, dots and underscore character. It has to begin with a letter and if we have dot, it must be followed by a letter. Then it must be followed by @ sign. At the end we must have a dot followed by 2 to 4 letters. Whenever we have a character that has special meaning in regexp and we want to use it as character, we have to escape it with backslash (\).

Listing 17.9: email.php

```
<?php

// determine if the user enters a valid email address.
If(isset($_POST['check']))
{
   // determine whether a valid email is entered.
   if(preg_match("/^[a-zA-Z]\w+(\.\w+)*\@\w+(\.[0-9a-zA-
      Z]+)*\.[a-zA-Z]{2,4}$/", $_POST["email"] == 0))
   {
         echo "Invalid email Address. " . "<br>";
         $valid_form = false;
   }
   else
   {
         $email = $_POST['email'];
   }
}

?>
```

Detailed Example

We shall use Figure 17.2 to illustrate the use of server-side form validation as discussed in various program segments above.

Validating Customer Input Form

This form page requires that the user enters a name(this is a required field), user name(which should be letters only), and a password (at least 8 characters in length), address (which must be made up of letters, numbers, etc), email (valid email address), credit card number(must be numbers only), and country(required field) before form processing occurs. This type of form validation is important because it helps ensure that user input is in a proper format to be written to a database, text file, used to produce an automated e-mail message, or re-displayed to the user.

The following steps are involved in processing the form:

1. the user enters form data and clicks the **Validate** button.
2. the validation script validates the input data on the form.

We shall demonstrate this process in the following sections. Note that the script to process the form is not shown in this example.

Figure 17.2: Form validation

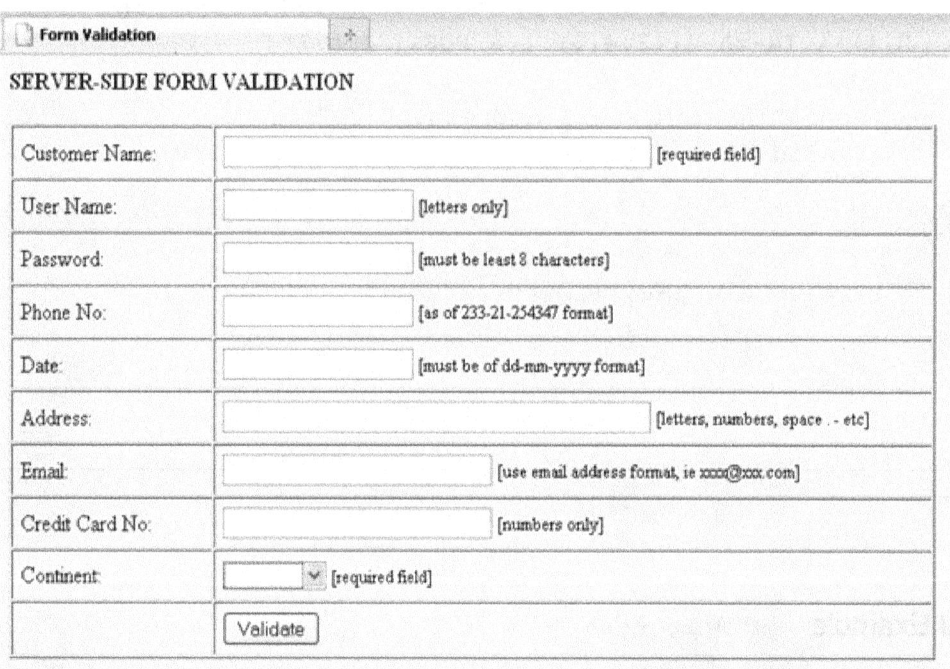

HTML Input Form and PHP Listing

The HTML tags that produce the above form is presented below. It is very necessary to pay a particular attention to the *name* and *id* parameters of the input fields. This include name="name", *id="nameId", name="userName" id="userNameId", name="continent" id="continentId",* to mention but a few. The **name** and **id** parameters will be used in the validation scripts in Chapter 18.

If all form fields contain valid data, form processing can begin. A flag can be set to help keep track of the validation. First, a flag is set **($valid_form = true**) at the beginning of the code block. If any of the form fields do not contain valid data, the flag **($valid_form)** is set to **false**. After all form fields have been checked, a final **if** statement is used to check the status of the flag **($valid_form)**. If the value of **$valid_form** is **true** (all form fields contain valid data), form processing can begin. Otherwise, the form processing block is skipped. The user is presented with the error message presented during the validation process, requiring the user to make corrections.

Listing 17.10: validation.php

```
<?php

/* Determine if the sumbit button has been clicked. If so, begin
validating form data. */
if(isset($_POST['check']))
{
   /* Set a flag $valid_form to hold true value initially. If any
   of the tests fails, the flag is set to false. */
  $valid_form = true;

   /* Full Name must contain letters, dashes and spaces only and
   must start withupper case letter. */
  if(preg_match("/^[A-Z][a-zA-Z -]+$/", $_POST["name"]) == 0)
  {
   echo "Invalid Customer Name ". "<br>";
   $valid_form = false;
  }
  else
  {
   $name = $_POST['name'];
  }

  // Phone number must comply with this mask: 233-21-3334444.
  if(preg_match("/^\d{3}-d{2}-\d{6}$/", $_POST["phoneNo"])==0)
  {
   echo "Phone no must comply with this mask: 233-21-3334444 ". "<br>";
   $valid_form = false;
  }
  else
  {
   $phoneNo = $_POST['phoneNo'];
  }
```

Continuation of Listing 17.10: validation.php

```
// Check  date mask  of DD-MM-YYYY.
     if(preg_match("/^[0-9]{1,2}-[0-9]{1,2}-[0-9]{4}$/",
         $_POST["curDate"]) == 0)
{
 echo "Date must comply with this mask:DD-MM-YYYY". "<br>";
 $valid_form = false;
}
else
{
 $curDate = $_POST['curDate'];
}

//Determine if the credit card no are all numbers.
if(is_numeric($_POST['cardNo']))
{
 $cardNo = $_POST['cardNo'];
 $valid_form = true;
}
else
{
 echo "Credit card Number must be between 0-9. " . "<br>";
}

//Determine if the User Name are all letters(lower case and upper case).
if(preg_match("/^[a-zA-Z]+$/", $_POST["userName"]) == 0)
{
 echo "User Name must be letters only. " . "<br>";
 $valid_form = false;
}
else
{
 $userName = $_POST['userName'];
}
```

Continuation of Listing 17.10: validation.php

```
/* Determine if the address is Address must be only letters,
numbers or one of the following _ - . , : \ */
if(preg_match("/^[a-zA-Z0-9 _-.,:\"\']+$/",
    $_POST["address"]) == 0)
{
 echo "Invalid address, must be letters, numbers, spaces,
         dash,dot, … " . "<br>";
  $valid_form = false;
}
else
{
 $address = $_POST['address'];
}

// Check if the password is entered and the is at least 8 characters.
if(strlen($_POST['pass'] < 8) || ($_POST['pass'] == ""))
{
 echo "Invalid password, enter correct password." . "<br>";
 $valid_form = false;
}
 else
{
 $pass = $_POST['pass'];
}

//Determine whether a valid email is entered.
if(preg_match("/^[a-zA-Z]\w+(\.\w+)*\@\w+(\.
 [0-9a-zA-Z]+)*\.[a-zA-Z]{2,4}$/", $_POST["email"] == 0))
{
 echo "Invalid email Address. " . "<br>";
 $valid_form = false;
}
 else
{
 $email = $_POST['email'];
}
```

Continuation of Listing 17.10: validation.php

```
    /* Determine if a continent has been selected. Check for empty
    field. */
   if($_POST['continent'] == "")
   {
    echo "Enter Your Continent" . "<br>";
    $valid_form = false;
   }
   else
   {
        $continent = $_POST['continent'];
    }

   // If all input form fields are correct, begin processing
   if($valid_form == true)
   {
    echo "Congrats, all fields are entered correctly!" ;
   }
}
?>

<!--Form processing codes start from here. -->
<html>
<head>
    <title>Form Validation</title>
    <meta http-equiv="Content-Type" content="text/html;
    charset=iso-8859-1" />
</head>

<body bgcolor="#f3f3f3">
<strong>SERVER-SIDE FORM VALIDATION</strong>

<form method="post" action="validation.php">
<table width="70%" border="1" cellspacing="1" cellpadding="6">
<tr>
      <td width="22%">Customer Name:</td>
      <td width="78%"> <input name="name" type="text" id="nameId"
       size="50" /><font size="2">[required field]</font></td>
</tr>
```

Continuation of Listing 17.10: validation.php

```
<tr>
      <td>User Name:</td>
      <td><input type="text" name="userName" id="userName" />
      <font size="2">[letters only] </font></td>
</tr>
<tr>
      <td>Password:</td>
      <td><input type="password" name="pass" id="pass" />
      <font size="2">[must be least 8 characters]</font></td>
</tr>
<tr>
      <td>Phone No: </td>
      <td><input type="text" name="phoneNo" id="phoneNo" />
      <font size="2">[as of 233-21-254347 format]</font></td>
</tr>
<tr>
      <td>Date:</td>
      <td><input type="text" name="curDate" id="curDate" />
      <font size="2">[must be of dd-mm-yyyy format]</font></td>
</tr>
<tr>
      <td>Address:</td>
      <td><input name="address" type="text" id="address"
      size="50" /><font size="2">[letters, numbers, space . -
      etc]</font></td>
</tr>
<tr>
      <td>Email: </td>
      <td><input name="email" type="text" id="email" size="30" />
      <font size="2">[use email address format, ie xxxx@xxx.com]
      </font></td>
</tr>
<tr>
      <td>Credit Card No:</td>
      <td><input name="cardNo" type="text" id="cardNo"
       size="30" />
      <font size="2">[numbers only] </font></td>
</tr>
```

Continuation of Listing 17.10: validation.php

```
<tr>
      <td>Continent: </td>
      <td><select name="continent" id="select">
           <option></option>
           <option>Africa</option>
           <option>America</option>
           <option>Asia</option>
           <option>Australia</option>
           <option>Europe</option>
          </select> <font size="2">[required field]</font></td>
</tr>
<tr>
      <td> </td>
      <td><input type="submit" name="check" value="Validate"
      id="check"></td>
</tr>

</table>

</form>
</body>
</html>
```

Programming Challenge

Q1. Form Field Validation

In this exercise you will write scripts to validate form fields. You will use PHP functions and regular expressions extensively. Write an HTML tags to create the form. The file name should be **employee.php**.

Employee Record Form

Employee Record Form

Title of Courtesy: ○ Prof. ○ Dr. ○ Mr. ○ Mrs. ○ Ms.
First Name:
Last Name:
Position:
Birth date: Day 7 Month March Year 1980
Hire date: Day 10 Month March Year 1992
Address:
City:
Region:
Postal Code:
Country:
Home Phone:
Phone Extension:
Notes:
Add Employee

Use server-side validation to ensure that numeric values are not entered into the database for fields supposed to be all alphabets (First Name, Last Name, City, etc). Also, check for alpha-numeric fields (address etc) and character fields (Notes, etc).

Q2. Password Verifier

You are developing a software package that requires users to enter their passwords. Your software requires that user's passwords meet the following criteria:

- The password should be at least eight characters long.
- The password should contain at least one numeric digit, one alphabetic character, and one uppercase character.

Design a form that asks the user to enter the password. The application should use a PHP function named **IsValid** to verify that the password meets the criteria. The **IsValid** function should accept a string as its argument and return a Boolean value. The string argument is the password that is to be checked. If the password is valid, the function should return **true**; otherwise, it should return **false** and hence display a message indicating whether the password is valid or invalid.

Q3. User Login Information Setup

Whenever you make a form, you should not leave it alone without any form of validation. This is because there is no guarantee that the input is correct; and processing incorrect input values can make your application give unpredictable result. In this exercise you would create a login form shown below and write a script to carry out validation of the fields.

This form requires the user to enter a name, user name, and a password (at least 8 characters) in length before form processing occurs. In addition, the user will not be allowed to save empty fields into the database. This type of form validation is important because it helps ensure that user input is in a proper format before written to the database.

You are required to write **server side PHP scripts** that will validate all the input fields before data will be processed. Do not write any processing script (only the validation segment is required).

18

Client-Side Form Validation

There is no programming language - no matter how structured - that will prevent programmers from making bad programs. - Larry Flon

Learning Objectives

After studying this chapter, you should be able to:

- Understand the client-side validation and its application in PHP.
- Distinguish between server-side and client-side validation techniques.
- Write PHP script to validate various types of data fields including letters, numbers, email, date, and empty fields.
- Use JavaScripts in client-side form validation.

Client-Side Validation

Client-side form validation is usually done with JavaScript. Client-side validation means that the validation is carried out by the browser, but not the Web server. You can write scripts (most commonly using JavaScript) that will verify that form fields contain good data before being submitted to the server.

The advantages of using client-side validation are two-fold: (a) users receive feedback quicker (no need to go off to the server, process the information, then download another HTML page), and (b) it saves overhead on the server - more work is done on the client-side rather than the server. The disadvantage, however, is that the client-side support for scripting languages varies wildly: some browsers support client-side scripts very well, others partly support the scripts, and others do not support client-side scripts. Furthermore, some users can disable client-side checking on their browsers. When this happens, validation mechanism will fail. In this chapter we will be discussing JavaScript form validation. We shall show you how to write validation scripts for various data inputs.

Client-Side JavaScript Form Validation

The idea behind JavaScript form validation is to provide a method to check the user entered data before they are submitted to the server. JavaScript lets you display messages to inform the users what information they have entered incorrectly and how they can correct it. In JavaScript, most client-side validation is accomplished using the special "**onSubmit**" event of a form. This event allows you to run JavaScript code to handle form validation when your visitor attempts to submit the form. If it returns **false** from your code in **onSubmit**, Web browsers will not proceed with submitting the form, but prompt users to correct any errors before submission.

What to Validate on the Form

Some input data you need to check are:

- Empty values

- Numbers only
- Letters only
- Alphanumeric (numbers and letters)
- Input length (necessary when restricting the length of a username or password)
- Email address.
- Selection has been made from dropdown, check box, radio button selectors.

The form below is used in our examples.

Figure 18.1: Form validation

Form Validation

SERVER-SIDE FORM VALIDATION

Customer Name:	[required field]
User Name:	[letters only]
Password:	[must be least 8 characters]
Phone No:	[as of 233-21-254347 format]
Date:	[must be of dd-mm-yyyy format]
Address:	[letters, numbers, space . - etc]
Email:	[use email address format, ie xxx@xxx.com]
Credit Card No:	[numbers only]
Continent:	[required field]
	Validate

Checking for Empty Values

This is the most common type of form validation. You want to be sure that your users enter data into the HTML fields you have "required" for a valid submission. The following is the JavaScript code to perform this basic check to see if a given HTML input is empty or not.

The function *emptyField* will check to see that the *name* text input that we send has a value in it. *fieldName* is a HTML text input that we send to this function. JavaScript strings have built-in properties, one of which is the **length** property which returns the length of a string. The code **fieldName.value.length** will check for how long the string is.

So long as *fieldName.value.length* is 0, an alert with an *errorMessage* will inform the user of the error and return *false*, otherwise the input box is not empty and the function returns *true*.

```
<script type='text/javascript'>

// determine whether a name was entered or is empty.
function emptyField(fieldName, errorMessage)
{
   if(fieldName.value.length == 0)
   {
          alert(errorMessage);
          // set the focus to the same input field
          fieldName.focus();
          return false;
   }
   else
   {
          return true;
   }
}
</script>
```

Checking for Numbers Only

If someone is entering a credit card information, you may want to ensure that the input is all numbers. The quickest way to check if an input value is all numbers is to use a regular expression **/^[0-9]+$/** that will only *match* if the string is all numbers and is at least one character long. JavaScript has an existing framework that we can use to perform this task. A function called **match** can be used to see if the string matches a certain regular expression. We accessed this function by **fieldName.value.match(numberOnly).**

We wanted to see if the input value was all numbers so we made a regular expression to check for numbers [0-9] and stored it as *numberOnly*.

We then used the **match** function with our regular expression. If it is numeric then **match** will return **true**, making our **if** statement pass the test and our function *isNumberField* will also return true. However, if the expression fails because there is a letter or other character in our input value then we will display an *errorMessage* and return false.

```
<script type='text/javascript'>

// determine whether the credit card no are all numbers.
function isNumberField(fieldName, errorMessage)
{
    var numberOnly = /^[0-9]+$/;
    if(fieldName.value.match(numberOnly)){
            return true;
    }else{
            alert(errorMessage);
            // set the focus to the same input field
            fieldName.focus();
            return false;
    }
}
</script>
```

Checking for Letters Only

This function is identical to *isNumberField* as above except for the change to the regular expression we use inside the *match* function. Instead of checking for numbers we will check for all letters. If we want to see if a string contains only letters we need to specify an expression that allows for both lowercase and uppercase letters: **/^[a-zA-Z]+$/.**

```
<script type='text/javascript'>

// determine whether the user name is all letters.
function isLettersField(fieldName, errorMessage){
    var lettersOnly = /^[a-zA-Z]+$/;
    if(fieldName.value.match(lettersOnly)){
            return true;
    }else{
```

Continuation

```
            alert(errorMessage);
            // set the focus to the same input field
            fieldName.focus();
            return false;
    }
}
</script>
```

Checking for Numbers and Letters

By combining both the *isLettersField* and *isNumberField* functions into one we can check to see if a text input contains only letters and numbers. If we want to see if a string contains letters and numbers we need to specify the regular expression: **/^[0-9a-zA-Z]+$/.**

```
<script type='text/javascript'>

// check if the address consists of numbers and  letters
function isAphaNumericField(fieldName, errorMessage)
{
   var lettersOnly = /^[0-9a-zA-Z]+$/;
   if(fieldName.value.match(lettersOnly))
   {
            return true;
   }
   else
   {
            alert(errorMessage);
            // set the focus to the same input field
            fieldName.focus();
            return false;
   }
}
</script>
```

Checking for Input Length

Below we have created a *minimumLength* function that takes a text field. The input field must not be less than 8 characters in length and at the same time cannot be empty.

```
<script type='text/javascript'>

/* Determine if the password is at least 8 characters min is 8
characters from the calling function */
function minimumLength(fieldName, min)
{
  var minInput = fieldName.value;
  if(minInput.length >= min && minInput.length != 0)
         {
         return true;
         }
         else
         {
         alert("Password must be at least 8 characters");
         // set the focus to the same password input field
         fieldName.focus();
         return false;
    }
}

</script>
```

Checking for Email Address

We will be showing you how to check to see if a user's email address is valid. Every email is made up for 5 parts:

1. A combination of letters, numbers, periods, hyphens, plus signs, and/or underscores
2. The symbol @
3. A combination of letters, numbers, hyphens, and/or periods
4. A period
5. The top level domain (com, net, org, us, gov, gh, ...)

Valid Examples:

winfred.hi@hightelsoft.net
winfred+joshua@hightelsoft.com
winfred-me@hightelsoft.section.com

Invalid Examples:

@hightelsoft.net - no characters before the @
software@hightel_soft.com - underscores are not allowed in the domain name
hightel!soft@bravehe.art - invalid character !

The regular expression to check for all of this is **/^[\w\-\.\+]+\@[a-zA-Z0-9\.\-]+\.[a-zA-z0-9]{2,4}$/**.

```
<script type='text/javascript'>

// determine if the user enters a valid email address.
function isEmail(fieldName, errorMessage)
{
 var emailField = /^[\w\-\.\+]+\@[a-zA-Z0-9\.\-]+\.[a-zA-z0-
9]{2,4}$/;

        if(fieldName.value.match(emailField))
        {
                return true;
        }
        else
        {
                alert(errorMessage);
                fieldName.focus();
                return false;
        }
}
</script>
```

Checking for Dropdown Selection

By making the first option of your select input something like "Select Your Continent" you can direct the user to both make a selection and to see if the default option " Select Your Continent " is still selected when the submitting the form.

```
<script type='text/javascript'>

// Check if the user selects an item from the dropdown list.
function continentSelection(fieldName, errorMessage)
{
        if(fieldName.value == "Select Your Continent")
         {
                alert(errorMessage);
                errorMessage.focus();
                return false;
        }
        else
        {
                return true;
        }
}
</script>
```

Detailed Example

If you have made it this far I commend you, but we are not done yet. The final step is to be able to perform all of these validation steps when the user is ready to submit the data.

Validation Input Form

This form page requires that the user enters a name, user name, and a password , address, email, credit card number, and country before form processing occurs. This type of form validation is important because it helps ensure that user input is in a proper format to be written to a database, text file, used to produce an automated e-mail message, or re-displayed to the user.

The following steps are involved in processing the form:

1. the user enters form data and clicks the submit button,
2. the validation script validate the input data on the form using JavaScript,
3. a script to process (write to file, generate automated e-mail message, or re-display input) the data.

We shall demonstrate this process in the following sections. Note that the script to process the form is not shown in this example but only the validation script.

The form has a JavaScript event called **onSubmit** that is triggered when the *submit* button is clicked. If this event returns **0** or **false** then a form cannot be submitted, and if it returns **1** or **true** it will always be submitted.

The **validateForm** will check valid data before submission. But before we can decide what we want to check for, we need to have our form and fill it with the input values.

The first thing we want to check is that each field has been filled out. To check for completion we will ensure no fields are empty and that the dropdown field has a selection. Here are the starting pieces of our validation function **validateForm**.

Figure 18.2: Server-side form validation

Form Validation

SERVER-SIDE FORM VALIDATION

Customer Name:	[required field]
User Name:	[letters only]
Password:	[must be least 8 characters]
Phone No:	[as of 233-21-254347 format]
Date:	[must be of dd-mm-yyyy format]
Address:	[letters, numbers, space . - etc]
Email:	[use email address format, ie xxx@xxx.com]
Credit Card No:	[numbers only]
Continent:	[required field]
	Validate

Description of *validateForm* Function

- The first part of this function is where we create references to our HTML inputs using the **getElementById** function. These references will make our next block of code much easier to read.
- The second part uses a block of embedded **if** statements to see whether or not each field has the correct type of data. If every single one of those fields we check validates, then we will return **true** and the form will be submitted successfully.
- However, if just one of those **if** statements fails then the *return false* at the end of the function is reached and that prevents the form from being submitted.

As you can see in Listing 18.1, this function (***ValidateForm***) really does a lot. Notice how this one function references all of the functions we have covered in this section. By placing all of these checks in a central location, you make your code easier to read and easier to edit in the future.

The HTML and JavaScript Listing

Below we have taken the HTML form code and the new function ***ValidateForm*** and put together all the other form validation functions taught in this chapter.

Listing 18.1: client_side_validation.php

```
<html>
<head>
<title>Form Validation</title>
</head>
<script type='text/javascript'>

// the validateForm Function
function validateForm()
{
  // make quick references to the field Id on the form
  var name = document.getElementById('nameId');
   var cardNo = document.getElementById('cardNoId');
   var userName = document.getElementById('userNameId');
   var address = document.getElementById('addressId');

   var password = document.getElementById('passwordId');
   var email = document.getElementById('emailId');
   var continent = document.getElementById('continentId');

  // check each input in the order as it appears on the form!
  if(emptyField(name, "Name Field Cannot be Empty")){
     if(isNumberField(cardNo, "Enter only numbers for Credit
      Card")){
       if(isLettersField(userName, "Please enter only Letters for
         User Name")){
         if(isAphaNumericField(address, "Enter only Letters and
            numbers for Address")){
             if(minimumLength(password, 8)){
```

Continuation of Listing 18.1: client_side_validation.php

```
            if(isEmail(email, "Please enter Valid Email
                    Address")){
                     if(continentSelection(continent,"You must
                        select Your Continent")){
                    return true;
                         }
                }
                 }
              }
         }
     }
 }
 return false;

}
// functions to test the various input fields.

// determine if a name was entered. Check for non empty field.
function emptyField(fieldName, errorMessage)
{
   if(fieldName.value.length == 0)
  {
    alert(errorMessage);
    // set the focus to the same input field
    fieldName.focus();
    return false;
   }
  else
  {
    return true;
  }
}
```

Continuation of Listing 18.1: client_side_validation.php

```
 // determine whether the credit card no are all numbers.
function isNumberField(fieldName, errorMessage)
{
   var numberOnly = /^[0-9]+$/;
   if(fieldName.value.match(numberOnly))
  {
     return true;
   }
  else
  {
     alert(errorMessage);
     // set the focus to the same input field
     fieldName.focus();
     return false;
   }
}

// determine whether the user name is all letters.
function isLettersField(fieldName, errorMessage)
{
   var lettersOnly = /^[a-zA-Z]+$/;
   if(fieldName.value.match(lettersOnly))
  {
     return true;
   }
  else
  {
     alert(errorMessage);
     // set the focus to the same input field
     fieldName.focus();
     return false;
   }
}
```

Continuation of Listing 18.1: client_side_validation.php

```
// check whether the address consists of numbers and letters.
function isAphaNumericField(fieldName, errorMessage)
{
   var lettersNumbersOnly = /^[0-9a-zA-Z,.]+$/;
   if(fieldName.value.match(lettersNumbersOnly))
   {
     return true;
   }
  else
  {
     alert(errorMessage);
     // set the focus to the same input field
     fieldName.focus();
     return false;
   }
}

/* determine whether the password is at least 8 characters.
   Notice that min is 8 characters from the calling function */
function minimumLength(fieldName, min){
   var minInput = fieldName.value;
   if(minInput.length >= min && minInput.length != 0)
  {
     return true;
   }
  else
  {
     alert("Please password must be at least 8 characters");
     // set the focus to the same password input field
     fieldName.focus();
     return false;
   }
}
```

Continuation of Listing 18.1: client_side_validation.php

```
// determine whether the user enters a valid email address.
function isEmail(fieldName, errorMessage)
{
   var emailField = /^[\w\-\.\+]+\@[a-zA-Z0-9\.\-]+\.
  [a-zA-z0-9]{2,4}$/;
   if(fieldName.value.match(emailField))
  {
     return true;
   }
  else
  {
     alert(errorMessage);
     fieldName.focus();
     return false;
   }
}

/* determine whether the user selects an item from the dropdown
list. */
function continentSelection(fieldName,errorMessage)
{
   if(fieldName.value == "")
   {
     return true;
   }
   else
   {
     alert(errorMessage);
     fieldName.focus();
     return false;
   }
}
</script>
```

Continuation of Listing 18.1: client_side_validation.php

```
<! - - The form starts from here -->
<body>
<strong>FORM VALIDATION</strong>

<form onsubmit='return validateForm()'>

Customer Name: <input name="name" type="text" id="nameId"/><br />
User Name:  <input type="text" name="userName" id="userNameId"
            /><br />
Password: <input type="password" name="pass" id="passId" />
          <br />
Address:    <input name="address" type="text" id="addressId" />
            <br />
Email:      <input name="email" type="text" id="emailId"
            size="30"/><br />
Credit Card No:    <input name="cardNo" type="text" id="cardNoId"
                   size="30" /><br />
Country:    <select name="continent" id="continentId">
                      <option>Select Your Continent</option>
                      <option>Africa</option>
                      <option>America</option>
                      <option>Asia</option>
                      <option>Australia</option>
                      <option>Europe</option>
            </select><br />
<input type="submit" name="check"  value="Submit" id="checkId">

</form>
</body>
</html>
```

Programming Challenge

Q1. Form Field Validation

In this exercise you will write JavaScript to validate input fields. You will use JavaScript functions and regular expressions extensively. Do the following

a. Write an HTML tags to create the form below. The file should be named **employee.php**.

b. Use client-side validation to ensure that numeric values are not entered into the database for fields supposed to be all alphabets (First Name, Last Name, City, etc).

c. Also, check for alpha-numeric fields (address etc) and character fields (Notes, etc).

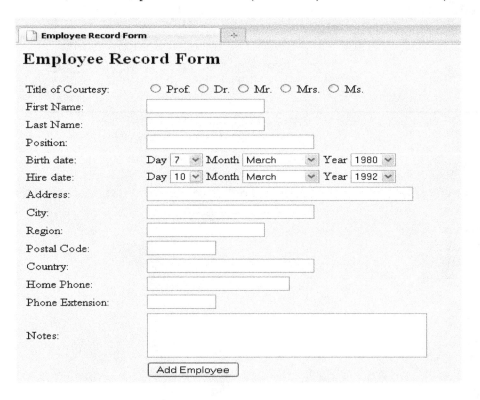

Employee Record Form

Employee Record Form

Title of Courtesy: ○ Prof. ○ Dr. ○ Mr. ○ Mrs. ○ Ms.

First Name:

Last Name:

Position:

Birth date: Day 7 Month March Year 1980

Hire date: Day 10 Month March Year 1992

Address:

City:

Region:

Postal Code:

Country:

Home Phone:

Phone Extension:

Notes:

Add Employee

Q2. Password Verifier

You are developing a software package that requires users to enter their passwords. Your software requires that users' passwords meet the following criteria:

a) The password should be at least eight characters long.

b) The password should contain at least one numeric digit, one alphabetic character, and one uppercase character.

Design a form that asks the user to enter a password. The application should use a JavaScript function named **IsValid** to verify that the password meets the criteria. The **IsValid** function should accept a string as its argument and return a Boolean value. The string argument is the password that is to be checked. If the password is valid, the function should return **true**; otherwise, it should return **false** and hence display a message indicating whether the password is valid or invalid.

Q3. User Login Information Setup

Whenever you make a form, you should not leave it alone without any form of validation. This is because there is no guarantee that the input is correct; and processing incorrect input values can make your application give unpredictable result. In this exercise you would create a login form shown below and write JavaScript to carry out validation of the fields.

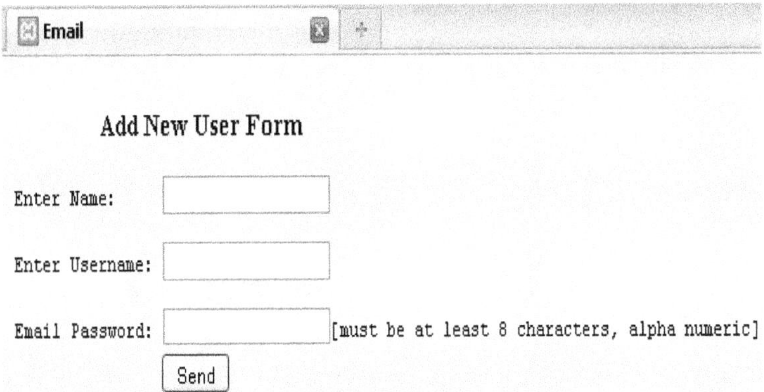

This form requires the user to enter a name, user name, and a password (at least 8 characters) in length before form processing occurs. In addition, the user will not be allowed to save empty fields into the database. This type of form validation is important because it helps ensure that user input is in a proper format before written to the database.

You are required to write JavaScript that will validate all the input fields before data will be processed. Do not write any processing script (only the validation segment is required).

19

PHP Errors and Exceptions Handling

As soon as we started programming, we found to our surprise that it wasn't as easy to get programs right as we had thought. Debugging had to be discovered. I can remember the exact instant when I realized that a large part of my life was going to be spent in finding mistakes in my own programs.
(Maurice Wilkes discovers debugging, 1949)

Learning Objectives

After studying this chapter, you should be able to:

- Understand the major causes of errors in programming, particularly, as they relate to PHP.
- Discover how to use simple die() and exit() functions to handle errors.
- Work with custom error handling techniques.
- Understand the object-oriented way of dealing with exceptions.
- Discover and write fine scripts that would take care of errors that may occur in your program.

Introduction

It is very important to have mechanisms in place that will help you deal with errors or unexpected events as they occur in your scripts. It is a professional practice to handle errors in your scripts. PHP provides methods to assist you properly manage errors. In this chapter, we will exhaustively discuss the major causes of errors in programming as they relate to PHP scripts. Further, we will discuss three main methods you can employ in dealing with errors, (a) simple **die()** or **exit()** statement, (b) custom errors and error triggers, and (c) exception handling using **try**, **throw**, and **catch** keywords.

Types of Errors in Programming

We shall begin by discussing the various types of errors that can occur in a program. Generally, there are three varieties of programming errors. These are:

1. Syntax errors
2. Logical errors
3. Run-Time errors

Syntax Errors

Syntax errors are generated as a result of not following the rules (syntax or grammar) of the programming language. These errors usually involve improper punctuation and spelling of keywords or improper formatting. Syntax errors are easier to solve since the compiler identifies the erroneous statement and may state the line number or underline the statement that contains the error. Syntax errors are sometimes referred to as compilation errors. To avoid syntax errors, you just have to review the rules of the language and make sure you are writing the statements properly

Logical Errors

Logical errors occur when your program is not doing what it is supposed to be doing. The program is giving you wrong results. This may simply mean that your algorithm fails to solve the problem the program was written to resolve. Logical errors are very difficult to resolve because you need to re-think and review your algorithm.

Run-Time Errors

Run-Time errors occur when your program is executing. The program passed the syntax or compiler test but fails during execution. Run-Time errors can be caused by the user entering a wrong data type via keyboard or performing some illegal operations (such as division by zero), program logic not doing what is supposed to do, or system errors (such as network or database connection errors). These problems are usually caused by improper arithmetic execution, attempting to access resources that are not available, etc.

Run-Time errors are difficult to resolve since they only show up when the program is running. When a run-time error occurs, the built-in default error-handling mechanism will trap the error and terminate the execution of the program and hence provide you a message indicating the nature of the error. Most often the error message cannot be understood by the users. In addition, the message does not provide action to be taken to deal with the error condition.

It is, therefore, the responsibility of the programmer to provide an alternate mechanism to trap or handle these errors in order to prevent the default error-handling mechanism from terminating the program execution. To protect users from viewing such strange error messages you have to provide users with friendly messages.

Common Types of Errors in PHP Script

PHP classifies errors into four different types, which are as follows:

1. Parse Error (Syntax Error)
2. Fatal Error
3. Warning Error

4. Notice Error

Parse Errors (Syntax Errors)

The parse errors occur if there is a syntax mistake in the script. A parse error stops the execution of the script. There are many reasons for the occurrence of parse errors in PHP. The most common reasons for parse errors are as follows:

1. Unclosed quotes - there is opening but not closing quotation mark or vice versa.
2. Missing or extra parentheses - there is opening but not closing parenthesis or vice versa; or there are many parentheses than required.
3. Unclosed braces - there is opening but not closing braces or vice versa; or there are many braces than required.
4. Missing semicolon – there is no semi-column to terminate a PHP statement as shown in Listing 19.1.

Listing 19.1: pass_error.php

```
<?php

// this statement ends with semi column
echo "Financial Institution";

// this statement does not end with semi column
echo "Utility Companies"

?>
```

In the above code we missed the semicolon in the statement **`echo "Utility Companies"`.** When that happens there will be a parse or syntax error which stops execution of the script and displays error message similar to one shown below:

Parse error: syntax error, unexpected T_ECHO, expecting ',' or ';' in **E:\xampp\htdocs\phpcodes\parse.php** on line **4**

Fatal Errors

Fatal errors occur when PHP understands what you have written (your script is grammatically correct), however, what you are asking the program to do cannot be done. Fatal errors stop the execution of the script. For instance, if you are trying to access undefined functions, the output will be a fatal error as shown in Listing 19.2.

In the above code, we defined a function **lovePHP()** but we call another function **dislikePHP().** The function **dislikePHP()** is not defined. So a fatal error will be produced, which will stop the execution of the script.

The output of the above script will be similar to the one below:

Fatal error: Call to undefined function dislikePHP() in **E:\xampp\htdocs\phpcodes\fatalerror.php** on line **10**

Listing 19.2: fatal_error.php

```
<?php

// define a function
function lovePHP()
{
	echo "I love PHP";
}

// trying to call a function that does not exist
dislikePHP();
echo "Fatal Error !!";

?>
```

Warning Errors

The main reason for warning errors are to include a missing file or using incorrect number of parameters in a function as shown in Listing 19.3. Warning errors will not stop execution of the script.

Listing 19.3: warning_error.php

```
<?php

    echo "Warning Error!!";

    // trying to include a file that does not exist
    include ("Welcome.php");

?>
```

In the above code, we include a **welcome.php** file, but the **welcome.php** file does not exist in the directory. So there will be a warning error. The error message will not stop the execution of the script, however you will see a message similar to the one below:

> Warning Error!! **Warning**: include(Welcome.php) [function.include]: failed to open stream: No such file or directory in **E:\xampp\htdocs\phpcodes\warning.php** on line **3**
>
> **Warning**: include() [function.include]: Failed opening 'Welcome.php' for inclusion (include_path='.;E:\xampp\php\PEAR') in **E:\xampp\htdocs\phpcodes\warning.php** on line **3**

Notice Errors

Notice errors occur when you try to access an undefined variable. Notice errors and warning errors are similar. Also, in the notice errors, execution of the script does not stop. Example of a notice error is shown in Listing 19.4.

Listing 19.4: notice_error.php

```
<?php

$quote="The god of small things";

// trying to display variable that does not exit
echo $great_quote;
echo "Notice Error !!";

?>
```

In Listing 19.4, we defined a variable named **$quote**. But we call another variable **$great_quote**, which has not been defined. So there will be a notice error produced but execution of the script does not stop. You will see a message similar to the one below:

> **Notice**: Undefined variable: great_quote in
> **C:\xampp\htdocs\phpcodes\Chapter19\notice_error.php** on line **6**
> Notice Error !!

Handling PHP Errors

PHP has embedded error-handling mechanism. When an error occurs, PHP displays the filename that contains the error, the line number, and a message describing the error on the user's browser. To help the programmer to handle the errors that may occur in the program, we shall discuss the three most common error handling methods in PHP. These are:

a) Simple **die()** or **exit()** statement
b) Custom errors and error triggers
c) Exception handling using **try**, **throw**, and **catch** keyword

Simple `die()` and `exit()` Statements

The **die()** function prints a message and exits the current script. It is an alias of the **exit()** function. The function takes on only one parameter. This is shown in Table 19.1.

Table 19.1: die() and Exit() parameter

Parameter	Description
message	Specifies the message or status number to write before exiting the script. The message will be displayed to the screen, but the status number will not be written to the screen.

A simple example is shown in Listing 19.5

Listing 19.5: die.php

```
<?php

$filename = "c:/scripts/myfile.txt";

// open the file that cannot be found on the system
$newfile = fopen($filename, "w") or
            die("Could not open file");
$file_contents = "Add this string to the text file";

 // writing the contents of $file_contents to file.
fwrite($newfile,$file_contents);
fclose($newfile);

?>
```

In this example, the script attempts to open **myfile.txt** located in **c:/scripts** folder which is not found. The **die()** function terminates script execution and displays an error message.

Output: **Could not open file**

Creating a Custom Error Handler and Error Trigger

Custom Error Handler is a special function that can be called when an error occurs in your PHP script. Creating a custom error handling involves three main steps:

1. Create the special function that will be called
2. Set the error-handler
3. Create a trigger that calls the function

The syntax of a Custom Error Handler function is shown below. The function requires a minimum of two parameters (error level and error message) but can accept up to five parameters (optionally: file, line-number, and the error context).

Syntax

error_function(error_level, error_message, error_file, error_line, error_context)

The parameters of the function are described in Table 19.2.

Table 19.2: Parameters of Custom Error handler function

Parameter	Description
error_level	Required parameter. Specifies the error report level for the user-defined error. Must be a number. See Table 19.3 for possible error report levels.
error_message	Required parameter. Specifies the error message for the user-defined error.
error_file	Optional parameter. Specifies the filename in which the error occurred.
error_line	Optional parameter. Specifies the line number on which the error occurred.
error_context	Optional parameter. Specifies an array containing every variable and their values in use when the error occurred.

Error Report Levels

The error report levels are the different types of errors that the user-defined error handler can use. Examples of such error reports are described in Table 19.3.

For example, you may create the following function which has all the five parameters.

function errorHandler($errno, $errstr, $errfile, $errline, $errcontext)

As you can see, **errorHandler** is the name the user gives to the function. The parameters **($errno, $errstr, $errfile, $errline, $errcontext**) are all user-defined, but each correspondingly represent (**error_level, error_message, error_file, error_line, error_context**).

Table 19.3: Some error report levels

Value	Constant	Description
2	E_WARNING	Non-fatal run-time errors. Execution of the script is not halted.
8	E_NOTICE	Run-time notices. The script found something that might be an error, but could also happen when running a script normally.
256	E_USER_ERROR	Fatal user-generated error. This is like an E_ERROR set by the programmer using the PHP function trigger_error()
512	E_USER_WARNING	Non-fatal user-generated warning. This is like an E_WARNING set by the programmer using the PHP function trigger_error()
1024	E_USER_NOTICE	User-generated notice. This is like an E_NOTICE set by the programmer using the PHP function trigger_error()
4096	E_RECOVERABLE_ERROR	Catchable fatal error. This is like an E_ERROR but can be caught by a user defined handle (see also set_error_handler())
8191	E_ALL	All errors and warnings, except level E_STRICT (E_STRICT will be part of E_ALL as of PHP 6.0)

We shall now look at the three steps involved in custom error-handling procedure:

Create the Custom Error-Handling Function

Now let us take a simple example to explain how to create a custom error function (program segment) shown in Listing 19.6.

The script above is an error handling function. When it is triggered, it gets the error level, an error message, the file name, and the line number. It then outputs the values of the parameters and terminates the script.

Listing 19.6: custom_error

```
<?php

// error handler function
function errorHandler($errno,$errstr,$errfile,$errline)
{
    // display the error code, message, filename, line number.
    echo "<b>Error:</b>[$errno] $errstr - $errfile:$errline";
    echo "<br />";

    echo "Terminating PHP Script";
    // terminate script execution
    die();
}
?>
```

Set the Error-Handler (set_error_handler)

Once you defined your custom error handler you need to set it using PHP built-in library **set_error_handler** function. You may recall from our earlier discussion that the default error handler for PHP is a built-in error handler. When you define your own error-handler, your function then acts as the default error handler for the duration of your script. In other words, the standard PHP error handler is completely bypassed if we use our own function.

The **set_error_handler()** function sets a user-defined function to handle errors. This function is used to create your own way of handling errors during runtime and has two parameters.

The syntax to set the error handler is as

set_error_handler(error_function, error_types)

Using the first parameter, let's see the following example

set_error_handler("errorHandler");

In this example **set_error_handler** is a reserved word (keyword) and the parameter**,** **errorHandler** is the name of your error handler function. Table 19.4 describes the parameters of the function.

Table 19.4: Set error handler

Parameter	Description
error_function	Required parameter. Specifies the name of the function to call.
error_types	Optional parameter. Specifies which error report levels the user-defined error will be shown. Default is "E_ALL".

Listing 19.7 adds **set_error_handler** to the error handler and tests how the script works:

Listing 19.7: error_handler.php

```
<?php

// error handler function
function errorHandler($errno,$errstr,$errfile,$errline)
{
   // display the error code, message, filename, line number.
   echo "<b>Error:</b>[$errno] $errstr:File Name: $errfile.
   Line No: $errline";
   echo "<br />";

   echo "Terminating PHP Script";

   // terminate script execution
   die();
}

// set error handler
set_error_handler("errorHandler");

// trigger error because $test variable has not been declared
echo $test;

?>
```

Output: **Error:**[8] Undefined variable: test: File Name: E:\xampp\htdocs\phpcodes\errorhandler.php. Line No: 19

Since we want our custom function to handle all errors, the **set_error_handler()** only needed one parameter (that is the name of our error function, **errorHandler**), a second parameter can be added to specify an error level.

Trigger Error Function (trigger_error)

The **trigger_error()** is a built-in function that creates a user-defined error message. It is used to trigger an error message at a user-specified condition. The **trigger_error()** can be used with the built-in error handler, or with a user defined function set by the **set_error_handler()** function.

The syntax is

trigger_error(error_message, error_types)

The function contains two parameters. The first parameter, **error_message**, is required as it represents the message to be sent to the user. The second parameter is the **error_type**. Table 19.5 describes the parameters.

Table 19.5: Parameters of trigger error function

Parameter	Description
error_message	Required parameter. Specifies the error message. Limited to 1024 characters in length.
error_type	Optional parameter. Specifies the error type for this error message. Possible error types: • E_USER_ERROR – This is a fatal user-generated run-time error. Errors that cannot be recovered from and the execution of the script is halted. • E_USER_WARNING – This is a non-fatal user-generated run-time warning. Execution of the script is not halted. • E_USER_NOTICE – This is the default. User-generated run-time notice. The script found something that might be an error, but could also happen when running a script normally.

We shall add **trigger_error** to the error handler and test how the script works, as can be seen in Listing 19.8.

Listing 19.8: trigger_error.php

```
<?php

// error handler function
function errorHandler($errno,$errstr)
{
        // display the error code and message.
        echo "<b>Error:</b>[$errno] $errstr";
        echo "<br />";
        // terminate script execution
        die();
}
```

Continuation of Listing 19.8: trigger_error.php

```
// set error handler
set_error_handler("errorHandler");

$testscore = 101;
if($testscore > 100)
{
        // trigger when testscore is greater than 100
        trigger_error("Score cannot be more than 100");
}

?>
```

Output: **Error:**[1024] Score cannot be more than 100

Exception Handling Using Try, Throw, and Catch

An exception is an abnormal termination of a program. Because exceptions occur at run-time, they are often referred to as run-time errors. To avoid the abnormal termination of a program, a mechanism is provided, known as exception handling, to deal with the situation. Ones exception occurs, the exception handling mechanism changes the normal flow of the script execution and deals with the error according to a specified error condition. In other words, exception handling is used to change the normal flow of the code execution if a specified error condition occurs. This condition is known as an exception. An exception handling was introduced into PHP and is an object oriented way of dealing with errors.

How Exception Works

The following shows the steps of what normally happens when an exception is triggered:

1. The current code state is saved.
2. The code execution will switch to a predefined (custom) exception handler function.
3. Depending on the situation, the exception handler may resume the execution from the saved code state, terminate the script execution, or continue the script from a

different location in the code.

PHP handles exceptions using different error handling methods. These are:

- Basic use of exceptions
- Creating a custom exception handler
- Multiple exceptions
- Re-throwing an exception
- Setting a top level exception handler

First of all, let us look at the keywords in exception handling. Exceptions use a **try…throw…catch** mechanism. The format is as follows:

```
try

   your scripts which can cause the exception.

   your regular scripts should be placed here.

Throw

   triggers when there is an exception in your regular script
      under the "try" block.

catch

   code statement for handling the exception here.

   you can have here many "catch" statements as necessary to
        handle the exception.

   you can also specify here what type of error to look for
```

The structure is quite easy to understand. That is, you **try** to do something (run your script), if a problem is detected, you **throw** an error (problem) and the **catch** receives it at the end of your code.

A simple rule on exception is: *If you throw something, you have to catch it.* This mean that a **throw** must always have a **catch.** The keywords are explained further in Table 19.6.

Table 19.6: Exception Handling

Keyword	Description
try	A script using an exception should be in a "try" block. If the exception does not trigger, the code will continue to run as normal. However, if the exception triggers, an exception is "thrown".
throw	This is how you trigger an exception. Each "throw" must have at least one "catch"
catch	A "catch" block retrieves an exception and creates an object containing the exception information.

There are a number of built-in functions in **Exception** class which you can use in your script. Some of the commonly used ones are summarized in the Table 19.7.

Table 19.7: Exception Class

Keyword	Description
getMessage()	The message of exception (error) to be displayed.
getCode()	The error code of the exception that has occurred.
getFile()	The source filename in which the error has occurred.
getLine()	The source line on which the error can be found.

Let us take this example to show how exceptions work, as shown in Listing 19.9.

The output from this program will be:

Message: An error has occurred!

File: E:\xampp\htdocs\phpcodes\exception.php

Line: 11

Within the **try** block in the script above, the value of **$num** is 0, which is an error (exception) because we cannot divide by 0. Immediately, the error is thrown to the **catch** block. The catch receives the exception and displays the error message, the file name of the script containing the error, and the line on which the error can be found.

Listing 19.9: exception.php

```
<?php

// the try block
try{
   $total = 4;
   $num = 0;

   // this will result in an error because of division by
   zero
   $average = $total/$num;

   // throw exceptions when an error occurs in the try
   block
   throw new Exception("An error has occurred!");

   // this line will not run because of the exception
   echo $average;
}

// catch the error thrown from the "throw"
catch(Exception $e) {
    // display messages
    echo "Message: " . $e->getMessage() . "<br />";
    echo "File: " . $e->getFile() . "<br />";
    echo "Line: " . $e->getLine();
}

?>
```

Now, we shall discuss each of the methods used in exception-handling and give examples to explain how they work.

Basic Use of Exceptions

In the basic use of exceptions, your script should be in three segments: a **function** that tests and **throw** the exception, the **try** block, and the **catch** block as shown in listing 19.10.

Listing 19.10: exception2.php

```
<?php

// create function with an exception
function validateNum($number)
{
      if($number <> 1)
      {
          throw new Exception("Value must be 1");
      }
          return true;
}

// trigger exception in a "try" block
try
{
      $total = 4;
      $num = 2;

      // this gives 2
      $average = $total/$num;

      // call the function
      validateNum($average);

      // if exception is thrown, this line will not be shown
      echo $average;
}

// catch exception
catch(Exception $e)
{
      echo 'Message: ' .$e->getMessage();
}

?>
```

The code above will display an error message like:

Message: Value must be 1

In the code above, you will observe that:

- The **validateNum()** function is created. The function checks if **$number** is different from 1. If it is, an exception is thrown.
- The **try** block calls the **validateNum()** function.
- The **validateNum()** function throws an exception because **$number** is different from 1.
- The **catch** block retrieves the exception and creates an object ($e) containing the exception information.
- The error message from the exception is echoed by calling **$e->getMessage()** from the exception object.

Creating a Custom Exception Handler

The problem with the basic exception handling described above is that for every **throw** you must have a **catch**. To avoid this, you must set a top level exception handler to handle errors that may occur. To do this we will create a special class with functions that can be called when an exception occurs. This class must be an extension of the built-in Exception class. The custom exception class inherits the properties from PHP's Exception class and you can add custom functions to it.

Now, let us examine in the following script how custom exceptions work, as shown in Listing 19.11.

The output from the program will be:

Error on line 35 in E:\xampp\htdocs\phpcodes\exceptioncustom.php:

Number must be 1

It is important to note that the new class, **customException**, extends the **Exception** class and contains an addition function called **errorMessage()**. Because the **customException** class extends the **Exception** class, all the properties and methods from the **Exception** class is available to it, including methods such as **getLine()** and **getFile()** and **getMessage().**

Listing 19.11: custom_exception.php
```
<?php

class customException extends Exception
{
   public function errorMessage()
   {
      // error message
      $errorMsg = 'Error on line '.$this->getLine().' in '.
      $this->getFile().': <b>'.$this->getMessage().'</b>';
      return $errorMsg;
   }
}

try
{
   $total = 4;
   $num = 2;

   // this gives 2
   $average = $total/$num;

   // custom message
   $msg ="Number must be 1";

   // check if $number <> 1
   if($number <> 1)
    {
      //throw exception
      throw new customException($msg);
    }
  }
```

Continuation of Listing 19.11: custom_exception.php

```
catch(customException $e)
{
        //display erromessage function
        echo $e->errorMessage();
}

?>
```

Multiple Exceptions

The previous scripts handle only one exception. It is very useful to have multiple exceptions in your script to check for multiple conditions. You may use several **if...else** blocks or a **switch** statement together with multiple exceptions. These exceptions can use different exception classes and return different error messages.

Let us modify our previous example to illustrate the use of multiple exceptions (Listing 19.12).

Listing 19.12: multiple_exception.php

```
<?php

// the custom class
class customException extends Exception
{
    // custom exception handler
   public function errorMessage()
   {
            //error message
            $errorMsg = 'Error on line '.$this->getLine().' in '.
             $this->getFile().': <b>'.$this->getMessage().'</b>';

            return $errorMsg;
     }
}
```

Continuation of Listing 19.12: multiple_exception.php

```
// the try block
try
{
   $number = 101;

   // check if $number is greater than 100
   if($number >= 100)
    {
          // custom message if $number is greater than 100
         $msg ="Number cannot be greater than 100";

         // throw custom exception
         throw new customException($msg);
    }

  // check if $number is less than -1
  if($number <= -1)
    {
         // throw exception
         throw new Exception("Number cannot be less than 0");
    }
}

// catch custom exception
catch (customException $s)
{
  //display erromessage function
  echo $s->errorMessage();
}

// catch exception
catch(Exception $e)
{
   // display error message
  echo $e->getMessage();
}

?>
```

The output from this program will be:

Error on line 30 in E:\xampp\htdocs\phpcodes\exceptionmultiple.php: **Number cannot be greater than 100**

Re-throwing an Exception

Sometimes, when an exception is thrown, you may wish to handle it differently from the standard way. You can do this by re-throwing an exception the second time within a **catch** block.

A script should hide system errors from users who may not understand them. System errors may be important for the programmer, but is of no interest to the user. To provide a more user-friendly message to the users, you can re-throw the exception to a custom error function.

We shall again modify our previous example to explain re-throwing exception (see Listing 19.13).

Listing 19.13: rethrow_exception.php

```
<?php

// the custom class
class customException extends Exception
{
  // custom exception handler
  public function errorMessage()
  {
          //error message
          $errorMsg = 'Error on line '.$this->getLine().' in '.
           $this->getFile().': <b>'.$this->getMessage().'</b>';
          return $errorMsg;
    }
}
```

Continuation of Listing 19.13: rethrow_exception.php

```
// the try block
try
{
        try
        {
        $number = 101;
        // check if $number is greater than 100
        if($number >= 100)
            {
                // custom message if $number is greater than 100
                $msg ="Number cannot be greater than 100";
                    // throw custom exception
                    throw new Exception($msg);
            }
         }

    // catch the exception and re-throws the custom exception
    catch(Exception $e)
    {
        // re-throw exception
        throw new customException($msg);
    }
}

// catch custom exception
catch (customException $e)
{
   // call and display erromessage function
   echo $e->errorMessage();
}

?>
```

The output will be:

> Error on line 45 in E:\xampp\htdocs\phpcodes\rethrow.php: **Number cannot be greater than 100**

In the above example, the **try** block contains another **try** block to make it possible to re-throw the exception. The exception is triggered since the **$number** is greater than 100. The

catch block catches the exception and re-throws the **customException** exception. The **customException** is caught and an error message is displayed.

Normally, PHP tries to catch the exception in its current **try** block, if the exception is not caught in this block, it will search for a **catch** block on "higher levels". In the above example, the exception is thrown from the current **try** block.

Setting a Top Level Exception Handler

The **set_exception_handler()** function sets a user-defined function to handle all uncaught exceptions. This is shown in Listing 19.14.

Listing 19.14: top_level_exception.php

```
<?php
// define a top-level exception handler
function topException($exception)
{
    echo "<b>Exception:</b> " , $exception->getMessage();
}

// set a user-defined function to all un catch exceptions
set_exception_handler('topException');
$filename = "c:/scripts/myfile.txt";

// error occurs since opening a file that cannot be found
$newfile = fopen($filename, "w");
$file_contents = "Add this string to the text file";

// error occurs since writing to a file that cannot be found
fwrite($newfile,$file_contents);

// error occurs since closing a file that cannot be found
fclose($newfile);

// throw exception
throw new Exception('All uncaught exceptions');

?>
```

The output of the script in Listing 19.14 will be something similar to this:

> **Warning**: fopen(c:/scripts/myfile.txt) [function.fopen]: failed to open stream: No such file or directory in **E:\xampp\htdocs\phpcodes\topexception.php** on line **16**
>
> **Warning**: fwrite() expects parameter 1 to be resource, boolean given in **E:\xampp\htdocs\phpcodes\topexception.php** on line **21**
>
> **Warning**: fclose() expects parameter 1 to be resource, boolean given in **E:\xampp\htdocs\phpcodes\topexception.php** on line **23**
> **Exception:** Uncaught Exception occurred

In Listing 19.14, there was no **catch** block. Instead, the top level exception handler is triggered. This function should be used to catch all uncaught exceptions.

Rules to remember when working with exceptions

1. Code may be surrounded in a **try** block, to help catch potential exceptions.
2. Each **try** block or "throw" must have at least one corresponding **catch** block.
3. Multiple **catch** blocks can be used to catch different classes of exceptions.
4. Exceptions can be thrown (or re-thrown) in a **catch** block within a **try** block.

Detailed Example

Bank Charges

A bank charges $10 per month, plus the following cheque fees for a commercial checking account:

$0.10 each for less than 20 cheques
$0.08 each for 20 through 39 cheques
$0.06 each for 40 through 59 cheques
$0.04 each for 60 or more cheques

Create a form that allows the user to enter the number of cheques written. Your script should compute and display the bank's service fees for the month.

Input validation: Do not accept a negative value for the number of cheques written.

Suggested Solution

This example shows how to work with custom error handling function (errorHandler) with **set_error_handler**() function and **trigger_error**()function. Figure 19.1 shows the form created by HTML tags. In this example, a button is used to illustrate the use of **if** constructs.

Figure 19.1:
The form and test output from the script. The PHP and HTML are listed in Listing 19.15.

Cheques Information

No. of Cheques : -10

Service Fee: 0.00

Charges[IF]

When you run the following script and enter a negative number such as -10, the following error message will be displayed:

Bank Charges

Error:[1024] Cheques written cannot be less than zero !

Listing 19.15: custombankcharges.php

```
<html>
<head>
  <title>Bank Charges</title>
</head>
<body bgcolor="f3f3f3">
<h2>Bank Bank Charges </h2>
```

Continuation of Listing 19.15: custombankcharges.php

```
<?php

// create custom error handler function
function errorHandler($errno,$errstr)
{
    // display the error code, message, filename, line no.
    echo "<b>Error:</b>[$errno] $errstr";
    echo "<br />";

    // terminate script execution
    die();
}

// check whether the user clicks on the IF button.
if(isset($_POST['calculateChargesIF']))
{
      // set the error handler
      set_error_handler("errorHandler");

      // assign form values to variables
      $noofCheques = $_POST['noofCheques'];
      $serviceFee = $_POST['serviceFee'];

      // assign the fixed monthly amount to a variables
      $fixedChargePerMonth = 10;

        // check whether the number of cheques is less than 0
        if($noofCheques < 0)
        {
        // trigger when cheque written is less than 0
        trigger_error("Cheques cannot be less than zero !");
        }
        // check whether the number of cheques is between 0 - 20
        elseif($noofCheques >= 0 && $noofCheques < 20)
        {
          $checkingFee = $noofCheques * 0.10;
        }
        // check whether the number of cheques is between 20 - 39
```

```
        elseif($noofCheques >= 20 && $noofCheques <= 39)
        {
          $checkingFee = $noofCheques * 0.08;
        }

        // check whether the number of cheques is between 40 - 59
        elseif($noofCheques >= 40 && $noofCheques <= 59)
        {
          $checkingFee = $noofCheques * 0.06;
        }
        // check whether the number of cheques is greater than 60
        elseif($noofCheques >= 60)
        {
          $checkingFee = $noofCheques * 0.04;
        }
        // if none of the conditions is satisfied
        else
        {
          echo "Invalid!";
        }

        // calculate the monthly service fees
        $serviceFee = $checkingFee + $fixedChargePerMonth;
}
?>
<!-- the form starts here. The form action calls itself
custombankcharges.php' -->
<form action=" custombankcharges.php" method="post">
<fieldset style="width: 30%; "><legend>Cheques
Information</legend>
<table width="60%" border="0" cellspacing="5">
<tr>
      <td width="26%" nowrap>No. of Cheques :</td>
      <td width="74%"> <input name="noofCheques" type="text"
      value="<?php echo $noofCheques ?>" size="15"></td>
</tr>
```

Continuation of Listing 19.15: custombankcharges.php

```
<tr>
      <td nowrap>Service Fee:</td>
      <td><input type="text" name="serviceFee"
       readonly="readonly"
      value="<?php printf("%.2f", $serviceFee) ?>" size="15">
      </td>
</tr>
<tr>
      <td nowrap> </td>
      <td nowrap>
      <input type="submit" name="calculateChargesIF"
      value="Charges[IF]">
      </td>
</tr>
<tr>
      <td> </td>
      <td>  </td>
</tr>
</table>
</fieldset>
</form>
</body>
</html>
```

Solution Using Try, Throw, and Catch

When you run the listing below and enter a negative number such as shown below, an error message would be displayed

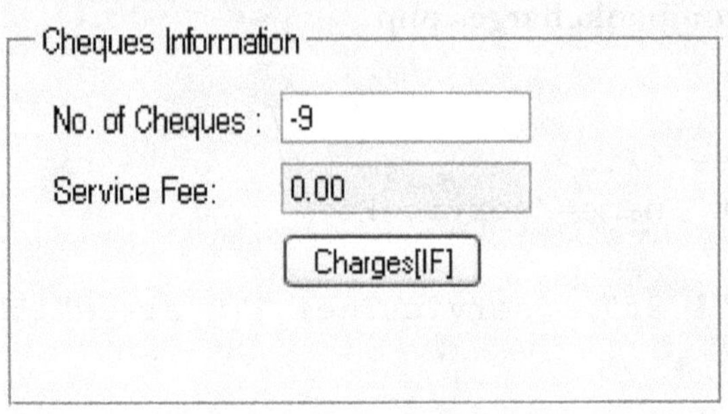

The output will be similar to the one below:

Bank Bank Charges

Error on line 46 in E:\xampp\htdocs\phpcodes\throwbankcharges.php: **Cheque written cannot be less than 0**

Listing 19.16: throwbankcharges.php

```
<html>
<head>
<title>Bank Charges</title>
</head>
<body bgcolor="f3f3f3">
<h2>Bank Bank Charges </h2>
<?php

// define custom exception and extend the Exception class
class customException extends Exception
{
     // create error function
     public function errorMessage()
     {
         //error message
         $errorMsg = 'Error on line '.$this->getLine().' in '.
          $this->getFile().': <b>'.$this->getMessage().'</b>';
         return $errorMsg;
     }
}
```

Continuation of Listing 19.16: throwbankcharges.php

```
// the try block begins from here
try
{
     // check whether the user clicks on the IF button.
     if(isset($_POST['calculateChargesIF']))
     {
        // assign form values to variables
        $noofCheques = $_POST['noofCheques'];
        $serviceFee = $_POST['serviceFee'];
        $msg = 'Cheque written cannot be less than 0';

        // assign the fixed monthly amount to a variables
        $fixedChargePerMonth = 10;

        // check if number of cheques is less than 0
        if($noofCheques < 0)
        {
           // throw an exception when cheque written < 0
           throw new customException($msg);
        }

        // check if number of cheques is between 0 and 20
        elseif($noofCheques >= 0 && $noofCheques < 20)
        {
           $checkingFee = $noofCheques * 0.10;
        }
        // check if number of cheques is between 20 and 39
        elseif($noofCheques >= 20 && $noofCheques <= 39)
        {
           $checkingFee = $noofCheques * 0.08;
        }
        // check if number of cheques is between 40 and 59
        elseif($noofCheques >= 40 && $noofCheques <= 59)
        {
           $checkingFee = $noofCheques * 0.06;
        }
```

Continuation of Listing 19.16: throwbankcharges.php

```
        // check if number of cheques is greater than 60
        elseif($noofCheques >= 60)
        {
            $checkingFee = $noofCheques * 0.04;
        }
        // if none of the conditions is satisfied
        else
        {
            echo "Invalid!";
        }

        // calculate the monthly service fees
        $serviceFee = $checkingFee + $fixedChargePerMonth;
    }
}

// the catch block
catch (customException $e)
{
    // call erromessage function and display error message
    echo $e->errorMessage();
}
?>

<!-- the form starts here. The form action calls itself
throwbankcharges.php' -->
<form action=" throwbankcharges.php" method="post">
<fieldset style="width: 30%; "><legend>Cheques
Information</legend>
<table width="60%" border="0" cellspacing="5">
<tr>
      <td width="26%" nowrap>No. of Cheques :</td>
      <td width="74%"> <input name="noofCheques" type="text"
      value="<?php echo $noofCheques ?>" size="15"></td>
</tr>
```

Continuation of Listing 19.16: throwbankcharges.php

```
<tr>
      <td nowrap>Service Fee:</td>
      <td><input type="text" name="serviceFee"
       readonly="readonly" value="<?php printf("%.2f",
       $serviceFee) ?>" size="15"></td>
</tr>
<tr>
      <td nowrap> </td>
      <td nowrap>
      <input type="submit" name="calculateChargesIF"
      value="Charges[IF]">
      </td>
</tr>
<tr>
      <td> </td>
      <td>  </td>
</tr>
</table>
</fieldset>
</form>
</body>
</html>
```

20

Introducing PHP and MySQL Interaction

Make it work, make it right, make it fast. - Kent Beck

Learning Objectives

After studying this chapter, you should be able to:

- Use PHP procedural and object-oriented functions to dynamically interact with MySQL Database.
- Learn how to write a script to connect to and close MySQL server.
- Create, truncate, and drop databases and tables from within your PHP scripts.
- Write scripts to count total number of records in a table.

Introduction

MySQL database has become the world's most popular open source database because of its consistent fast performance, high reliability, and ease of use. It is used in many installations in small to large organizations and also in specialised embedded applications. To allow interaction with MySQL server, PHP provides an array of functions that can be used to manipulate MySQL data. The purpose of this chapter is to introduce those functions commonly used in PHP data-driven applications for connecting to MySQL server and creating databases and tables using the PHP MySQLi extensions' Procedural style as well as Object Oriented style. The chapter also provides practical examples of database driven web application development.

In this chapter we would discuss both the Procedural and Object Oriented style of the MySQLi extension. In this regard under a topic we may come across terms and variables which are common to both the Procedural and Object Oriented style pertaining to that topic. In such a case we may explain the term or variable in the preceding style discussed and may not explain it in the next style. In cases where common terms have different meanings we will explain both of them distinctly. Also, it is worth noting that MySQLi is designed to work with MySQL version 4.1.13 or newer, or 5.0.7 or newer.

Why Use PHP MySQLi Extension

First of all PHP MySQLi stands for MySQL Improved. This tells us that it is an improved version of the PHP MySQL Extension. Let us look at a few reasons why I think the MySQLi extension is much better than the old MySQL extension of PHP.

- Developers of MySQL Server version 4.1.3 and above embedded new features in its design. Unlike the old PHP MySQL extension the MySQLi extension takes full advantage of the new MySQL Server features.

- The old MySQL extension was deprecated since PHP 5.5.0 and has been removed from PHP 7. It is safe to develop your new applications with the MySQLi extension

- Unlike the old extension, MySQLi extension supports Prepared Statemesnt. Use of this feature automatically protects web developers from SQL Injection attacks. This implies that you would not need to escape strings before executing queries.

These are but a few reasons why the PHP MySQLi extension is a preferred choice.

Common PHP MySQLi Functions

As mentioned above MySQLi has both Procedural and Object Oriented functions. **Table 20.1** and **Table 20.2** describes the common **Procedural** and **Object Oriented** functions respectively.

Table 20.1: MySQLi Procedural Functions

Function	Description
mysqli_connect(MySQL server name, username, password, database name)	Opens a connection to a MySQL server. The MySQL server name, username, password, and database name must be stated within the parenthesis. For example, *$link = mysqli_connect('localhost', 'root', 'mypassword', 'databasename');*
mysqli_query(connection identifier, sql query)	Sends a query to the currently active database. It executes SQL commands. For example, *$rs = mysqli_query($link, 'SELECT * FROM mytable');*
mysqli_fetch_array(resource resultset)	Returns an array that corresponds to the fetched row and moves the internal data pointer ahead. You can loop through the array to fetch individual records. Example is *$row = mysqli_fetch_array($rs);*
mysqli_num_rows(resource resultset)	Gets the number of rows in a query result. For example *$count = mysqli_num_rows($rs);*
mysqli_close(connection identifier)	Closes the result set. For example, *$link_close($link);*

The use of the functions will be demonstrated in the following sections.

Before you can use these functions to create data-driven application with MySQL, you will need to have appropriate user account and permission to MySQL objects, which includes:

1. MySQL server's name (host name) or IP address.
2. User account (password and username).
3. Permissions to the database and tables containing your web data.

For default values, the user account is root and blank (" ") password. The root account has full permission on tables and other objects. The sever name is the computer name or the computer's IP address. If your computer is not on a network, the **localhost** or **127.0.0.1** should be used.

Table 20. 2: MySQLi Object Oriented Functions

Function	Description
new mysqli(MySQL server name, username, password, database name)	Opens a connection to a MySQL server. The MySQL server name, username, password, and database name must be stated within the parenthesis. For example, *$link = new mysqli('localhost', 'root', 'mypassword', 'databasename');*
query(sql query)	Sends a query to the currently active database. It executes SQL commands. For example, *$rs = $link->query('SELECT * FROM mytable');*
fetch_array(resource resultset)	Returns an array that corresponds to the fetched row and moves the internal data pointer ahead. You can loop through the array to fetch individual records. Example is *$row = $rs-> fetch_array();*
num_rows	Gets the number of rows in a query result. For example *$count = $rs->num_rows;*
close()	Closes the result set. For example, *$link->close();*

Connecting to MySQL Database Using MySQLi Extension

Creating a connection to MySQL database from PHP using MySQLi Extension is easy. As will be the format for this chapter, we will see both the Procedural and Object Oriented style of applying the MySQLi extension.

Procedural Style

Let us observe how the MySQLi extension is used to connect to the MySQL Server in the syntax below:

mysqli_connect('localhost', 'root', 'mypassword', 'databasename');

The Listing 20.1 shows the Procedural style of connecting to the MySQL Server using the MySQLi extension.

Listing 20.1: mysqli_p_conn.php

```
<?php

// set connection variables
$dbhost = 'localhost';
$dbuser = 'root';
$dbpassword = '';
$dbname = 'studentdb';

// connect to mysql server
$link = mysqli_connect($dbhost, $dbuser, $dbpassword,
$dbname);

// check if any error has occurred during connection
if(mysqli_connect_errno()) {
    echo "Error: Could not connect to database.";
    exit();
}

?>
```

In this example, **$dbhost** is the variable that holds the name of your MySQL server. When your webserver is on the same machine with the MySQL server you can use **localhost** or **127.0.0.1** as the value for **$dbhost**.

Hence

```
$dbhost = 'localhost';
```

or

```
$dbhost = '127.0.0.1';
```

The **$dbuser** and **$dbpass** are valid MySQL user name and password respectively. In this case

```
$dbuser = 'root';

$dbpassword = '';
```

Here the password is empty which suggests that there is no password set on the MySQL server.

In the example (**Listing 20.1**), the database name is stored in a variable called **$dbname**. In this case:

```
$dbname = 'studentdb';
```

Notice that here the database connection string is saved into a variable called **$link**. Also, the database name is part of the parameter of the mysqli database connection function.

```
$link = mysqli_connect($dbhost, $dbuser, $dbpassword,
$dbname);
```

After the above command is executed, we would like to know if the connection was successful. Hence:

```
mysqli_connect_errno()
```

If the connection to the server was **not successful** the above function will return a **true** value.

Object Oriented Style

As mentioned earlier, the common terms that were explained above in the Procedural Style may not have their explanations repeated in this style.

Now let us observe how the MySQLi extension is used to connect to the MySQL database in the syntax below:

```
new mysqli( "host", "username", "password", "databasename" );
```

The **Listing 20.2** shows the Object Oriented style of connecting to the MySQL database using the MySQLi extension.

Listing 20.2: mysqli_o_conn.php

```
<?php

// set connection variables
$dbhost = 'localhost';
$dbuser = 'root';
$dbpassword = '';
$dbname = 'studentdb';

// connect to mysql server
$link = new mysqli($dbhost, $dbuser, $dbpassword, $dbname);

// check if any error has occurred during connection
if($link->connect_errno) {
    echo "Error: Could not connect to database.";
    exit();
}

?>
```

Notice that here the database connection string is saved into a variable called **$link**. Also, the database name is part of the parameter of the mysqli database connection function.

```
$link = new mysqli($dbhost, $dbuser, $dbpassword, $dbname);
```

After the above command is executed, we would like to know if the connection was successful. Hence:

```
$link->connect_errno
```

If the connection to the server was **not successful** the above function will return a **true** value.

Using MySQLi Extension with a Port Number

Sometimes a web server will require you to specify the MySQL server name and port number, particularly where the default port number has been changed. For example if the MySQL server's host name is **db.hightel.com** and the port number is **3306** (the default port number for MySQL) then you can modify the above code to read:

Procedural Style

Listing 20.3: mysqli_p_portno.php

```
<?php

// assign values that connect to the mySQL server
$dbhost = 'db.hightel.com:3306';
$dbuser = 'root';
$dbpassword = '';
$dbname = 'studentdb';

// connect to mysql server
$link = mysqli_connect($dbhost, $dbuser, $dbpassword, $dbname);

// $link is now the connection identifier
// check if any error has occurred during connection
if(mysqli_connect_errno()) {
    echo "Error: Could not connect to database.";
    exit;
}

?>
```

Object Oriented Style

You will notice that the variable **$dbhost** in **Listing 20.3** and **Listing 20.4** holds both the host name and port number of the MySQL server. See also the colon ':' separating them.

```
$dbhost = 'db.hightel.com:3306';
```

Listing 20.4: mysqli_o_portno.php

```
<?php

// assign values that connect to the mySQL server
$dbhost = 'db.hightel.com:3306';
$dbuser = 'root';
$dbpassword = '';
$dbname = 'studentdb';

// connect to mysql server
$link = new mysqli($dbhost, $dbuser, $dbpassword, $dbname);

// $link is now the connection identifier
// check if any error has occurred during connection
if($link->connect_errno) {
    echo "Error: Could not connect to database.";
    exit;
}

?>
```

Closing MySQLi Connection

Normally, the connection opened in a script will be closed as soon as the execution of the script ends. But it is better if you close it explicitly by calling the MySQLi function to close. Let's take a look at how it is done in both the Procedural and Object Oriented style in the code below:

Procedural Style

Syntax

mysqli_close(connection identifier);

Example

Listing 20.5: mysqli_p_closedb.php

```
<?php
... series of codes go in here

// now, close the connection, $link (connection identifier)
mysqli_close($link);

?>
```

Object Oriented Style

Syntax

connection_identifier -> close();

Example

Listing 20.6: mysqli_o_closedb.php

```
<?php
 ... series of codes go in here

 // now, close the connection, $link (connection identifier)
 $link ->close();

?>
```

Including the Connection and Closing Scripts in PHP file

It is a common practice to place the database connection and closing scripts in separate files. In this case any time you want to open or close a connection, just **include** the files.

In the above examples, we have a **.php** file that stores the connection configuration and a **.php** file that closes the connection. These are kept in separate files. Now we can include these files in our scripts as shown in the script segment below. The advantage of doing this is to avoid having to re-code the connection and closing scripts for each **.php** file you write.

Procedural Style

Listing 20.7: mysqli_p_closeopendb.php

```
<?php
    // including the connection script
    include 'mysqli_p_conn.php';


    ... series of codes go in here


    // including the closing script
    include 'mysqli_p_closedb.php';

?>
```

Object Oriented Style

Listing 20.8: mysqli_o_closeopendb.php

```
<?php
    // including the connection script
    include ' mysqli_o_conn.php';


    ... series of codes go in here


    // including the closing script
    include ' mysqli_o_closedb.php';

?>
```

Execute a Query in MySQLi

Executing a script in MySQLi is not difficult. Let us take a look at how statements are executed in MySQLi below:

Procedural Style

Syntax

mysqli_query (connection identifier , sql query);

Example

Listing 20.9: mysqli_p_execute.php

```
<?php

// including the connection script
include 'mysqli_p_conn.php';

// here we make execute a query!
$rs =  mysqli_query($link,'SELECT * FROM subjects');

// $rs holds the resultset after the query
// check if the executed query was successful
if($rs) {
     echo "Query successfully executed";
}
else
{
    echo "Error executing query";
    exit();
}

// including the closing script
include 'mysqli_p_closedb.php';

?>
```

As you may have observed in the **mysqli_query()** function above there are two necessary parameters. The first parameter is the variable **$link** which is holding the connection string (you can reference in **Listing 20.1 mysqli_p_conn.php**) to the MySQL Server (also specifying the database to be used). The second parameter has to do with the MySQL statement you want executed. In this case '**SELECT * FROM subjects**'.

Notice in **Listing 20.9** the php condition below:

```
if($rs)
```

If the query executed was **successful** the above condition will return a **true** value. Thus it will display "Query successfully executed".

Object Oriented Style

Syntax

```
connection_identifier -> query ( sql query );
```

Example

Listing 20.10: mysqli_o_execute.php

```
<?php

// including the connection script
include 'mysqli_o_conn.php';

// here we make execute a query!
$rs = $link->query("SELECT * FROM subjects");

// $rs holds the resultset after the query

// including the closing script
include 'mysqli_o_closedb.php';

?>
```

In the **mysqli_query()** function above there are two necessary parameters you need to take note of. The first parameter is the variable **$link** which is holding the connection string (you can reference in **Listing 20.2 mysqli_o_conn.php**) to the MySQL Server (also specifying the database to be used). The second parameter has to do with the MySQL statement you want executed. In this case '**SELECT * FROM subjects**'.

Count the Number of Rows Fetched in a Query

Knowing the number of rows in a result set after a query is executed is sometimes necessary information to know the kind of action to take on that data. To achieve this let us consider the following scripts:

Procedural Style

Syntax

mysqli_num_rows (resource resultset)

Example

Listing 20.11: mysqli_p_numrows.php

```
<?php

// including the open connection script
include 'mysqli_p_conn.php';

// here we make execute a query!
$rs = mysqli_query($link,"SELECT * FROM subjects");

// now, how many rows in the subjects table!
echo "Total Number of Subjects: " . mysqli_num_rows($rs) . "<br
/>";

// including the closing connection script
include 'mysqli_p_closedb.php';

?>
```

From the above example you would observe that the variable **$rs** is holding the result of the query that was executed. The **mysqli_num_rows($rs)** only counts the number of rows in the result which is in the **$rs** variable.

Object Oriented Style

Syntax

resource_resultset -> num_rows

Example

Listing 20.12: mysqli_p_numrows.php

```
<?php

// including the open connection script
include 'mysqli_conn.php';

// here we make execute a query!
$rs = $link->query("SELECT * FROM subjects");

// now, how many rows in the subjects table!
echo "Total Number of Subjects: " . $rs->num_rows . "<br />";

// including the closing connection script
include 'mysqli_closedb.php';

?>
```

As you would see in the above listing, the variable **$rs** is holding the result of the query that was executed. The **$rs->num_rows()** only counts the number of rows in the result which is in the **$rs** variable.

Display a Query Result Using MySQLi Fetch Array

After a query is executed, it is expected that the results of the query be displayed. In this section we will see how to display those resulting records with MySQLi Fetch Array.

Procedural Style

Syntax

mysqli_fetch_array(resource resultset)

Example

Listing 20.13: mysqli_p_display.php
```
<?php

// including the connection script
include 'mysqli_p_conn.php';

// here we make execute a query!
$rs = mysqli_query($link,"SELECT * FROM subjects");

// now, how many rows in the subjects table!
echo "Total Number of Subjects: " . mysqli_num_rows($rs) .
"<br />";

// display values in the result set, $rs
while($rows = mysqli_fetch_array($rs))
{
    echo "Subject Description: " . $rows['SubjectName'] .
    "<br />";
}
// including the closing script
include 'mysqli_p_closedb.php';
?>
```

When a query to select some records from a table is executed the MySQL Server sends back the result in a series of records. Together, all the records that are returned after a query is executed is called a Recordset. In description the Recordset is like a table holding the results of an executed SQL select command that is created in the memory of the MySQL Server. This so-called table contains all the rows of data returned by the query. Each row of data (record) is also subdivided into its own columns. In PHP we can use a loop to retrieve each record in the recordset one at a time. In this case the while loop fetches each row of data into the $rows variable as an array. Hence

```
while($rows = mysqli_fetch_array($rs))
```

To access the data held in the $rows array from the SubjectName column we use this code:

```
$rows['SubjectName']
```

Object Oriented Style

Syntax

resource_resultset -> fetch_array()

Example

Listing 20.14: mysqli_o_display.php

```
<?php
// including the connection script
include 'mysqli_o_conn.php';

// here we make execute a query!
$rs = $link->query("SELECT * FROM subjects");

// now, display how many rows in the subjects table!
echo "Total Number of Subjects: " . $rs->num_rows . "<br />";

// display values in the result set, $rs
while($rows = $rs->fetch_array())
{
  echo "Subject Description: " . $rows['SubjectName'] . "<br />";
}
// including the closing script
include 'mysqli_o_closedb.php';

?>
```

As you will observe, the code loops through all records in the resultset. In this case:

```
while($rows = $rs->fetch_array())
```

Display a Query Result Using MySQLi Fetch Object

After a query is executed, it is expected that the results of the query be displayed. In this section we will see how to display those resulting records with MySQLi Fetch Object. The difference between this function and the MySQLi Fetch Array function is that after a query is executed, this function returns the current row of a resultset as an **object** and not an **array**. Let's consider below:

Procedural Style

Syntax

mysqli_fetch_object(resource resultset)

Example

Listing 20.13: mysqli_p_display.php

```
<?php

// including the connection script
include 'mysqli_p_conn.php';

// here we make execute a query!
$rs = mysqli_query($link,"SELECT * FROM subjects");

// now, how many rows in the subjects table!
echo "Total Number of Subjects: " . mysqli_num_rows($rs) .
"<br />";
```

Continuation of Listing 20.13: mysqli_p_display.php

```
// display values in the result set, $rs
while($rows = mysqli_fetch_object($rs))
{
    echo "Subject Description: " . $rows->SubjectName . "<br />";
}

// including the closing script
include 'mysqli_p_closedb.php';

?>
```

To access the data held in the $rows object from the SubjectName column we use this code:

```
$rows -> SubjectName
```

Object Oriented Style

Syntax

resource_resultset ->fetch_object()

Example

Listing 20.14: mysqli_o_display.php

```
<?php

// including the connection script
include 'mysqli_o_conn.php';

// here we make execute a query!
$rs = $link->query("SELECT * FROM subjects");

// now, display how many rows in the subjects table!
echo "Total Number of Subjects: " . $rs->num_rows . "<br />";
```

Continuation of Listing 20.14: mysqli_o_display.php

```
// display values in the result set, $rs
while($rows = $rs->fetch_object())
{
    echo "Subject Description: " . $rows->SubjectName . "<br />";
}

// including the closing script
include 'mysqli_o_closedb.php';

?>
```

Create a Database Using MySQLi

Creating a database is as easy as executing a query. Let us see how it is done in both the Procedural and Object Oriented style of MySQLi. Observe Listing 20.15 and Listing 20.16.

Listing 20.15 and Listing 20.16 will both create **testingdb** database. If an error occurs during the process of database creation, the script execution is terminated and an error message "**Error creating database**" will be displayed.

Procedural Style

Listing 20.15: mysqli_p_createdb.php

```
<?php
// including the connection script
include 'mysqli_p_conn.php';

// here we make execute a query!
$rs = mysqli_query($link,"CREATE DATABASE testingdb");

// check if the database is created
if($rs)
{
        echo "Database successfully created";
}
```

Continuation of Listing 20.15: mysqli_p_createdb.php

```
else
{
    echo "Error creating database";
    exit();
}
// including the closing script
include 'mysqli_p_closedb.php';

?>
```

Object Oriented Style

Listing 20.16: mysqli_o_createdb.php

```
<?php

// including the connection script
include 'mysqli_o_conn.php';

// here we make execute a query!
$rs = $link->query("CREATE DATABASE testingdb");

// check if the database is created
if($rs) {
      echo "Database successfully created";
}else{
    echo "Error creating database";
    exit();
}

// including the closing script
include 'mysqli_o_closedb.php';

?>
```

Creating a Table in an Existing Database

To create tables in an existing database, we need to do a similar thing as we did when we were creating the database. Let us do this by first issuing a SQL table creation statement and assigning it to a variable (**$query**). After the assignment, we will now execute the command to create the table. Observe this in **Listing 20.17** and **Listing 20.18** below:

Procedural Style

Listing 20.17: mysqli_p_createtable.php

```
<?php

// including the connection script
include 'mysqli_conn.php';

// define the table structure
$query = 'CREATE TABLE contact('.
         'Id BIGINT(10)AUTO_INCREMENT, '.
         'MemberId VARCHAR(20), '.
         'FirstName VARCHAR(20) NOT NULL, '.
         'LastName VARCHAR(20) NOT NULL, '.
         'City VARCHAR(50) NOT NULL, '.
         'Region VARCHAR(30) NOT NULL, '.
         'Comment TEXT NOT NULL, '.
         'PRIMARY KEY(Id))';

// here we execute a query to create the table
$rs = mysqli_query($link,$query);

// check if the table is created
if($rs) {
      echo "Table successfully created";
} else{
    echo "Error creating table";
    exit();
}

// including the closing script
include 'mysqli_p_closedb.php';

?>
```

Object Oriented Style

Listing 20.18: mysqli_p_createtable.php

```
<?php

// including the connection script
include 'mysqli_conn.php';

// define the table structure
$query = 'CREATE TABLE contact('.
         'Id BIGINT(10)AUTO_INCREMENT, '.
         'MemberId VARCHAR(20), '.
         'FirstName VARCHAR(20) NOT NULL, '.
         'LastName VARCHAR(20) NOT NULL, '.
         'City VARCHAR(50) NOT NULL, '.
         'Region VARCHAR(30) NOT NULL, '.
         'Comment TEXT NOT NULL, '.
         'PRIMARY KEY(Id))';

// here we execute a query to create the table
$sql = $link->query($query);

// check if the table is created
if($rs) {
      echo "Table successfully created";
} else{
    echo "Error creating table";
    exit();
}

// close the result set, $sql
$sql->close();

// including the closing script
include 'mysqli_closedb.php';

?>
```

Drop a Database within PHP Script

If you have been following this chapter from the beginning I am sure you won't find truncating a database as a problem. All we would do is to execute the **SQL DROP DATABASE** statement. This statement drops (delete) the database with all tables in it. Observe below:

Procedural

Listing 20.19: mysqli_p_dropdb.php

```
<?php

// including the connection script
include 'mysqli_p_conn.php';

// here we make execute a query!
$sql = mysqli_query($link,"DROP DATABASE testing");

// check if the database is truncated
if($rs)
{
        echo "Database successfully dropped";
}
Else
{
     echo "Error dropping database";
     exit();
}
// including the closing script
include 'mysqli_p_closedb.php';

?>
```

Object Oriented Style

Listing 20.20: mysqli_o_dropdb.php

```
<?php

// including the connection script
include 'mysqli_o_conn.php';

// here we make execute a query!
$rs = $link->query("DROP DATABASE testing");

// check if the database is truncated
if($rs)
{
      echo "Database successfully dropped";
}
Else
{
    echo "Error dropping database";
    exit();
}

// including the closing script
include 'mysqli_o_closedb.php';

?>
```

Programming Challenge

Basic Interactions between PHP and MySQL Database Using MySQLi Class

a. In this exercise you will write PHP data-driven scripts to do the following:

b. Check and write down your MySQL server's name, username, and password.

c. Write a connection script and name it mysqli_config.php.

d. Write a script that closes the connection to the server and call it mysqli_close_conn.php.

e. Write a script to create a database known as student_details_db. Your script should include the database connection and closing scripts in (b) and (c) respectively.

f. Write a script to create the transcript and program tables which are made up of the following structures:

Transcript Table

Field Names	Data Type and Size	Constraint
Record Key	Bigint (20)	Primary Key, Not Null
AdmissionNo	Varchar (20)	Not Null
StudentName	Varchar (100)	Null
SubjectID	Varchar (20)	Null
SubjectName	Varchar (100)	Null
ClassScore	Float (15,0)	Null
ExamScore	Float (15,0)	Null
TotalScore	Double (7,0)	Null
Grade	Varchar (10)	Null
AcademicYear	Varchar (20)	Null
ProgrammeID	Varchar (20)	Foreign key, Not Null
GPA	Double (7,2)	Null
Remarks	Varchar (20)	Null

Program Table

Field Names	Data Type and Size	Constraint
ProgrammeID	Varchar (20)	Primary Key, Not Null
ProgrammeName	Varchar (100)	Not Null
DepartmentID	Varchar (20)	Not Null

g. Write a script to truncate student_Details_db database.

h. Write a script to drop student_Details_db database.

21

Insert, Update, Select, Delete Records

Considering the current sad state of our computer programs, software development is clearly still a black art, and cannot yet be called an engineering discipline.
- Bill Clinton

Learning Objectives

After studying this chapter, you should be able to:

- Understand how to use record insertion, updating, retrieving, and deletion together with HTML form.
- Solve problems involving MySQL and PHP commands for insertion, updating, retrieving, and deletion on the same HTML form.

Integrating Insert, Update, Select, and Delete of Records

You can design a single form to carry out record insertion, updating, retrieving, and deletion as shown in Figure 21.1.

The database manipulation commands are put together on the following form. These are INSERT, SELECT, UPDATE and DELETE.

Membership Registration Form

A typical input form for interacting with **contact** table is shown below. The form fields are named accordingly:

Contact (Id, memberid, lastname, firstname, city, region, comment)

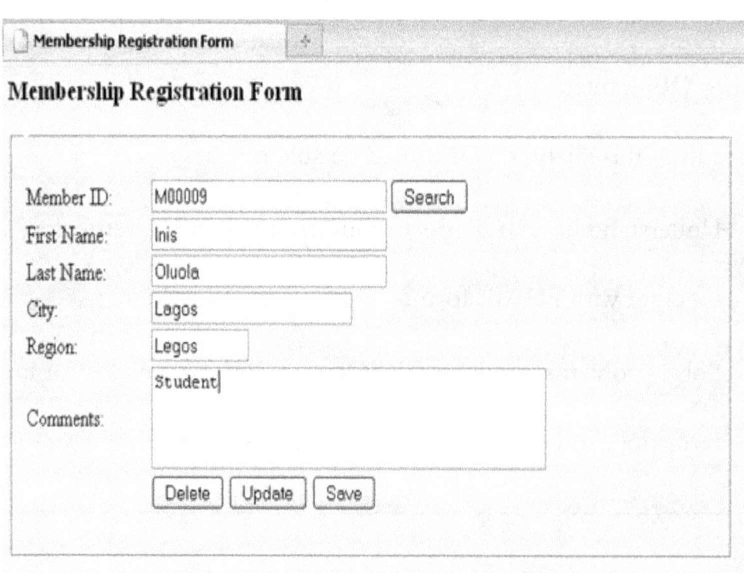

Figure 21.1: Insert, Select, Update and Delete Records

The scripts to undertake the insert, select, update and delete are presented below. The database connection and closing scripts are listed in Listing 21.1 and Listing 21.2 respectively. These file are included Listing 21.3.

Listing 21.1 logon_mysqlioop.php

```
<?php

$hostName = "localhost";          // Host (server) name
$userName = "root";               // DB username
$pass = " ";                      // DB password
$dbName   = "accountdb";          // Database name

$myoop_conn = new mysqli($hostName, $userName, $pass,
$dbName);

?>
```

Listing 21.2 close_mysqlioop.php

```
<?php

mysqli_close($myoop_conn);

?>
```

Listing 21.3: db_altogether.php

```
<?php

// open connection to database
include 'logon_mysqlioop.php';


/* saving record. Check whether the user clicks on the Save
button */
if(isset($_POST['submit']))
{
  // assign the values on the form to the following variables
  $memberid = $_POST["MemberId"];
  $fname = $_POST["Fname"];
  $lname = $_POST["Lname"];
```

Continuation of Listing 21.3: db_altogether.php

```
  $city = $_POST["City"];
  $region = $_POST["Region"];
  $comment = $_POST["Comment"];

  // save the values on the form into the table
  $sql = "INSERT INTO contact (memberid, firstname, lastname,
  city, region,comment) VALUES ('$memberid','$fname',
  '$lname','$city','$region','$comment')";

  $rs = $myoop_conn -> query($sql) or die('Error, record not saved!');

   // give a message when the save is successful
  if($rs)
  {
     echo "Record successfully added";
  }
}


/* Retrieving record. Check whether the user clicks on the
Search button */
if(isset($_POST['search']))
{
  // assign member ID value on the form to a variable
  $memberid = $_POST["MemberId"];

   /* select record that meets member id value typed into the
       text box */
  $sql = "SELECT * FROM contact WHERE memberid='$memberid'";
  $rs = $myoop_conn -> query($sql) or die('Error, cannot insert record');

  // hold the recordset in a variable
  $row = $rs->fetch_array();

  /* assign individual values fetched from the table to
  their corresponding textbox fields on the form */
  $memberid = $row['memberid'];
  $fname = $row['firstname'];
  $lname = $row['lastname'];
  $city = $row['city'];
  $region = $row['region'];
  $comment = $row['comment'];
}
```

Continuation of Listing 21.3: db_altogether.php

```
/* Updating record. Check whether the user clicks on the
Update button */
if(isset($_POST['update']))
{
  // assign form fields to variables
  $memberid = $_POST["MemberId"];
  $fname = $_POST["Fname"];
  $lname = $_POST["Lname"];
  $city = $_POST["City"];
  $region = $_POST["Region"];
  $comment = $_POST["Comment"];

  /* update record that meets memberId value in the searched
  textbox */
  $sql = "UPDATE contact SET firstname='$fname',
  lastname='$lname',city='$city',region='$region',
  comment='$comment' WHERE memberid='$memberid'";

  $rs = $myoop_conn -> query($sql) or die('Error, cannot update
       record');

  // give a message when the update is successful
  if($rs)
  {
      echo "Record successfully updated";
  }
}

/* Deleting record. Check whether the user clicks on the
delete button */
if(isset($_POST['delete']))
{
  // assign form fields to variables
  $memberid = $_POST["MemberId"];
  $fname = $_POST["Fname"];
  $lname = $_POST["Lname"];
  $city = $_POST["City"];
  $region = $_POST["Region"];
  $comment = $_POST["Comment"];
```

Continuation of Listing 21.3: db_altogether.php

```
   //delete record that meets memberid in the searched textbox
  $sql = "DELETE FROM contact WHERE memberid='$memberid'";
  $rs = $myoop_conn -> query($sql) or die('Error, cannot update record');

  // clear the form fields in the textboxes
  $memberid = " ";
  $fname = " ";
  $lname = " ";
  $city = " ";
  $region = "";
  $comment = " ";

  // give a message when the delete is successful
  if($rs)
  {
     echo "Record successfully deleted";
  }
}

//close connection to database
include 'close_mysqlioop.php';
?>

<html>
<head>
<title>Membership Registration Form</title>
</head>
<body bgcolor="#F3F3F3">

<h3> Membership Registration Form </h3>

<!-- html tags to create the form -->
<pre>
<form action="db_altogether.php" method="post">

Member ID: <input type text" name="MemberId" size="30" value =
           "<?php echo $memberid ?>"/>
         <input type="Submit" name="search" value="Search"/>

First Name: <input type="text" name="Fname" size="30" value  =
           "<?php echo $fname ?>"/>

Last Name: <input type="text" name="Lname" size="30" value =
           "<?php echo $lname ?>"/>
```

Continuation of Listing 21.3: db_altogether.php

```
City:     <input type="text" name="City" size="25" value="
          <?php echo $city ?>"/>

Region:  <input type="text" name="Region" size="30" value =
          "<?php echo $region ?>"/>

Comments:  <textarea name="Comment" cols="40" rows="5">
            <?php echo $comment ?></textarea>

          <input name="delete" type="Submit" id="delete"
                 value="Delete"/> 
                 <input type="Submit" name="submit"
                 value="Save"/> 
                 <input name="update" type="Submit" id="update"
                 value="Update"/>
</form>
</pre>
</body>
</html>
```

Programming Challenge

Q1. Inserting and Multiple Records Update

In this project you will write scripts to insert and update records. You will use SQL commands and MYSQL PHP functions extensively in this project. You will use arrays to perform multiple records update.

a) Create a database called **Members** in MySQL.

b) Create a table called **membership**. The table will consist of the fields indicated on the form below.

c) Write a PHP scripts and HTML tags to create and display **Form 1** below. The file name should be **membership.php**.

d) Create a database connection file called **config.php**. In your **membership.php** script, use appropriate commands to include the **config.php** file.

e) Enter at least **5** records into the database.

Form 1:

Membership Registration Form

Member Registration Form

Member ID: M00006

First Name: Jane

Last Name: Tutuolla

City: Accra

Region: Greater Accra

Comments: PHP is fun

Register

f) Create another file called **display_membership.php**. Your file should make use of textboxes to display the data and all the data on the screen should be editable apart from the **MemberId** which is readonly. It should look like **Form2.**

g) Once the form is displayed, the user can edit any field on the form. The user then clicks the **Save All** button to carry out the multiple update of records.

Form2:

Update Multiple Records

Update Multiple Records

Multiple Record Update

MemberId	FirstName	Lastname	City	Region	Comment
M00001	John	Baba	Accra	Greater Accra	Student
M00002	Rebecca	Zila	Tema	Greater Accra	Worker
M00003	Amos	Mensah	Tema	Greater Accra	Worker

Save All

Q2. Searching, Inserting, Deleting, and Updating

The HTML form controls allow users to input data, make selections and provide a mechanism by which users interact with a web page. A form is useful to the extent that it is backed by a processing script coded on a web page or by a program running on the Web server. In this question, you will write PHP data-driven applications for retrieving, updating, inserting, and deleting data.

Use the information on the form below to answer the following questions:

a) Use MySQL command to create a database **Customer.**

b) With the form fields named accordingly, as
Register (IDNumber, FirstName, LastName, City, State, Message)
you are required to create the table **Register** in the **Customer** database. Choose

appropriate field sizes and types.

c) Write HTML tags to display the Online Membership Form shown below.

d) Write a PHP script that will contain the login parameters to the database. Assume that your database has ***root*** as the user name and ***lukb4uleep*** as the password. The login filename should be ***login.php***

e) When the user clicks on the **Save** button, the input data collected on the form are saved into the **Register** table. Write a script segment to perform the saving.

f) When the user clicks on the **Search** button, the data saved into the **Register** table should be displayed on the form. Write a script segment to perform the record retrieval.

g) After the record has been retrieved in (f) above the user makes changes to it and clicks on the **Update** button to save the modified record. Write a script segment to perform the record updating.

h) After the record has been retrieved in (f) above the user clicks on the **Delete** button to delete the record. Write a script segment to perform the record deletion.

Online Membership Form

ID Number: [ ] Search

First Name: [ ]

Last Name: [ ]

City: [ ]

State: [ ]

Message: [ ]

Save | Search | Update | Delete

3. User Management, Sessions, Audit Trails

In this project you will write scripts to insert users, encrypt password, and authenticate user login. You will use SQL commands, Session management commands, and MySQL PHP functions extensively in this project.

a. Create a database called **LoginDb** in MySQL.

b. Create two tables namely **users** and **audit_trails**. The tables will consist of the following fields indicated on **Form 1a** and **Form 1b** below respectively.

c. Write an HTML tags to create the **Form 1a**. The file name should be **users.php**.

d. Create a database connection file called **config.php**. In your **users.php** script, use appropriate command to include the **config.php** file.

e. When the form is submitted, create a new script **userprocessing.php** that carries out the processing of the form. The file processing will involve insertion of records into the **users** table. The password field is to be *encrypted* before it is added to the table.

f. Enter 2 users into **users** table.

g. Create a login form (**login.php**) similar to **Form 2** below and write a script to allow authorized users to gain access to the system.

h. When access is allowed the user's information from the **user** table should be added to the **audit_trails** table. The session Id, time logged in, user's name, the URL of the page visited should all be included in the **audit_trails** table.

i. Now, display the records of the **audit_trails** table on the screen. Name the file **audit_monitoring.php.** The file should refresh itself every 30 seconds.

Form 1a:

Registration Form

Fields marked with a (*) are required.

Username	*
Password :	*
Re-type Password :	*
Email	*
Full Name :	
	Register

Form 1b:

Field Name	Datatype	Len
ID	int	10
aud_SessionID	varchar	50
aud_User	varchar	50
aud_Date	varchar	25
aud_Form	varchar	50
time_in	varchar	25
time_out	varchar	25

Form 2

Please enter your username and password to login.

Username :

Password :

Login

Appendix A:

Reprecated Extensions, Functions, and SAPIs

Reprecated Extensions, Functions, and SAPIs

Deprecated	Replacement With
Deprecated Extensions	
ext/ereg	ext/pcre
ext/mysql	ext/pcre or ext/pdo_mysql
ext/mssql	
ext/ sybase_ct	
Deprecated Functions	
set_magic_quotes_runtime and magic_quotes_runtime	
set_socket_blocking	stream_set_blocking
mcrypt_generic_end	mcrypt_generic_deinit
mcrypt_ecb, mcrypt_cbc, mcrypt_cfb and mcrypt_ofb	mcrypt_encrypt and mcrypt_decrypt
datefmt_set_timezone_id and IntlDateFormatter::setTimeZoneID	datefmt_set_timezone or IntlDateFormatter::setTimeZone
Deprecated SAPIs	
aolserver	
apache	
apache_hooks	
apache2filter	
caudium	
continuity	
isapi	
milter	
nsapi	
phttpd	
pi3web	
roxen	
tux	
webjames	

Appendix B

Installation of XAMPP server

Table 1.1: Installation of XAMPP server

Procedure	Image/Icon/Window
1. Locate the setup folder on the setup CD or the device that contains the setup files. Double click to open the file (XAMPP setup executable).	 **Setup Icon**
2. Select the language you prefer when the language menu appears and click **OK**.	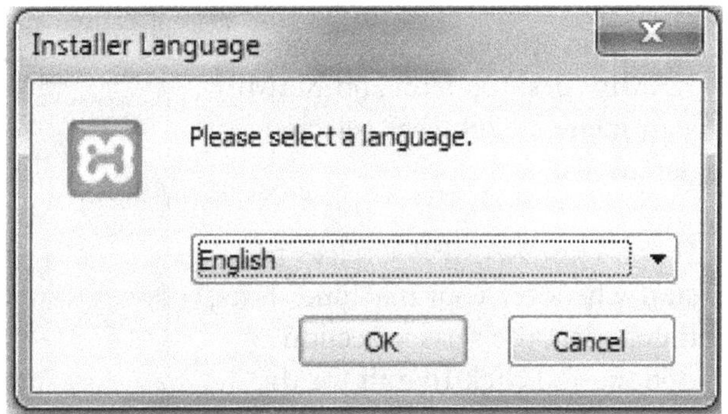
3. A pop-up menu appears asking you to close all applications. Therefore, close all applications and click **Next** to continue.	

4. Select the drive on which you want to install the application. Thus, select destination, then click **Next** to continue.

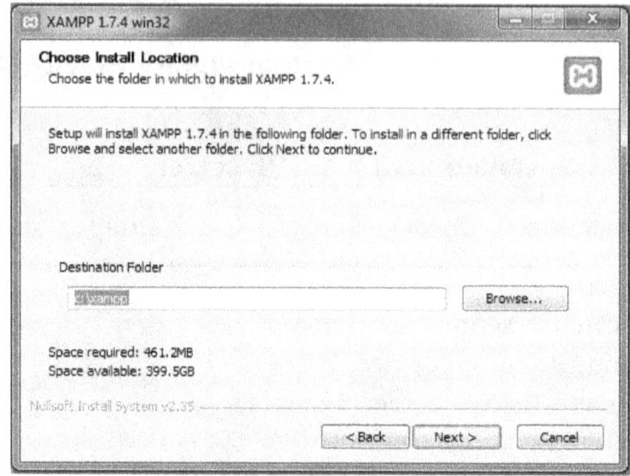

5. Select the options of installation. XAMPP desktop icon and XAMPP start menu creation are selected by default.

   If you want XAMPP services to start whenever your machine starts, then, select the service section options and click **Install** for the application to be installed.

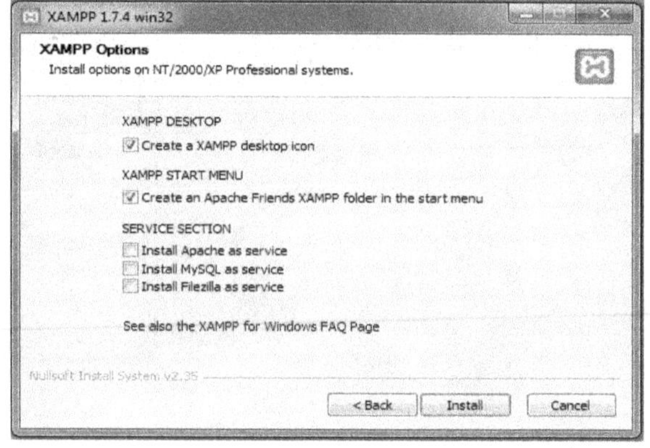

6. Wait while the application is installed. This takes less than three minutes.

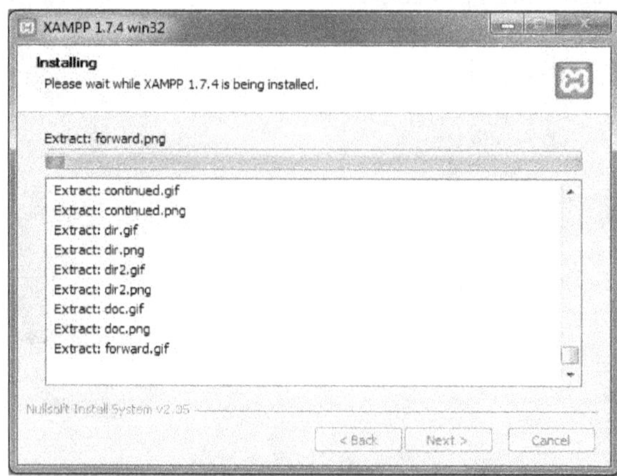

7. After the installation is over, click on **Finish** to close window when the Complete Setup menu appears as shown.

8. A congratulation menu appears when the installation is successful. Click **Yes,** if you want to start xampp control panel immediately or **No**, if you want to start it later.

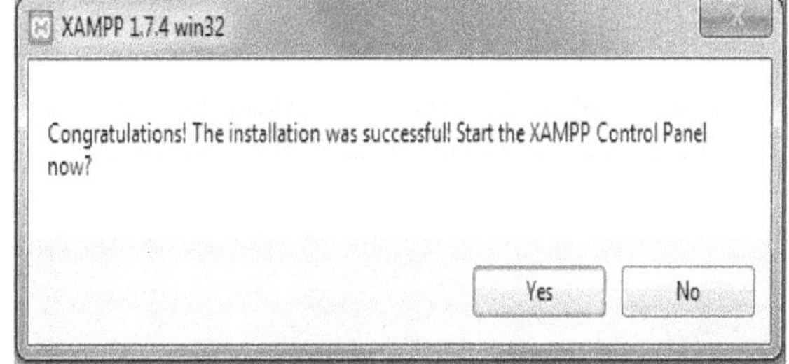

9. If Yes was selected at step 8, then, the XAMPP Control Panel will display as shown.

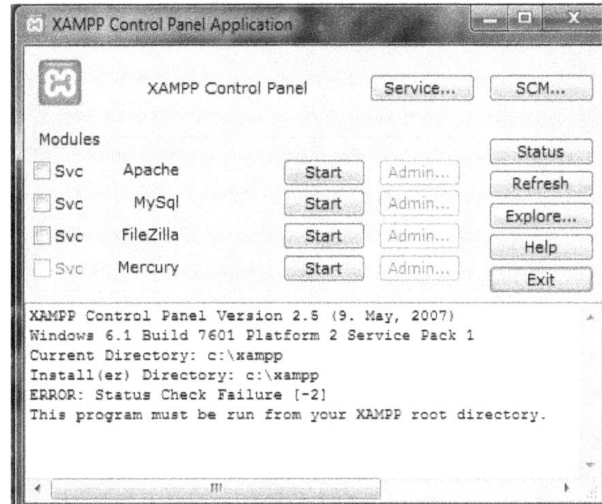

10. You can now click on the Start button against any of the servers to be run. Also if you want XAMPP to run as service from the Control Panel, select the respective checkbox.

    For instance, if I want to start Apache and MySql servers and at the same time run Apache as service. See the figure.

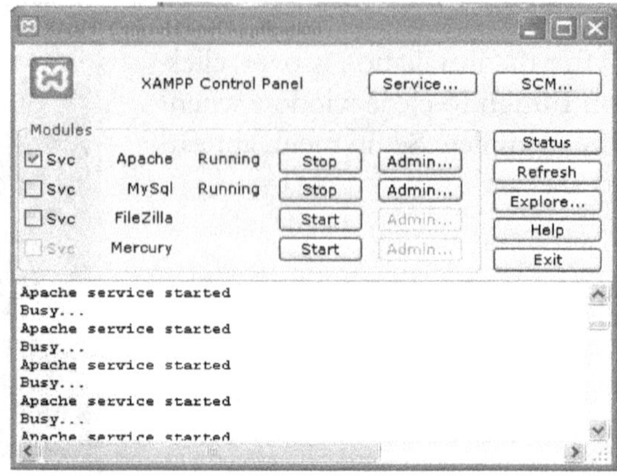

Bibliography

Book Sources

Bloch, J. (2008). *Effective Java (2 ed).* Prentice Hall.

Dowek, G. (2009). *Principles of Programming Languages (Undergraduate Topics in Computer Science)*, Springer.

Doyle, M (2010). Beginning PHP 5.3 (Wrox Programmer to Programmer). Wiley Publishing Inc, Indiana, USA.

Duckett, J. (2009), *Beginning HTML, XHTML, CSS, and JavaScript (Wrox Programmer to Programmer),* Wrox.

Foxall, J. D. (2010). *Sams Teach Yourself Visual Basic 2010 in 24 Hours Complete Starter Kit (Sams Teach Yourself 24 Hours),* Sams.

Gaddis, T., Irvine, K., & Denton, B. (2003). Starting Out with Visual Basic.NET (2 ed). Scott Jones Publishing, California, USA

Goodrich, M. T., & Tamassia, R. (2010). *Data Structures and Algorithms in Java*, Wiley.

Jeffrey, E. F. (2006) Mastering Regular Expressions. O'Reilly Media Inc, CA, USA.

Johnston, B. (2007). *C++ Programming Today (2nd Edition),* Prentice Hall.

Karumanchi, N. (2011). *Data Structures and Algorithms Made Easy: 700 Data Structure and Algorithmic Puzzles*, CreateSpace.

Lavin, P. (2006) Object-Oriented PHP: Concepts, Techniques, and Code. No Starch Press, Inc. CA, USA.

Liang, Y. D. (2010). *Introduction to Java Programming, Comprehensive (8th Edition)*, Course Technology.

Louden, K,. C., & Lambert (2011). *Programming Languages: Principles and Practices*, Brooks/Cole.

Malik, D. S. (2010). *C++ Programming: From Problem Analysis to Program Design*, Course Technology.

Mann, A. T. (1995). Real-World Programming with Visual Basic 4 (2 ed). SAMS Publishing, Indiana, USA.

Meloni, J. C.(2010). *Sams Teach Yourself HTML, CSS, and JavaScript All in One,* Sams Publishing.

Meloni, J. C. (2008). Sams Teach Yourself PHP, MySQL and Apache in 24 Hours. SAMS Publishing 2008, USA.

Meyer, B (1997). *Object-Oriented Software Construction (2 ed).* Prentice Hall, New Jersey, USA.

Murach, J., & Harris, R. (2010). *Murach's PHP and MySQL (Murach: Training & Reference),* Murach and Associates, Inc.

Nixon, R. (2009). Learning PHP, MySQL, and JavaScript: A Step-By-Step Guide to Creating Dynamic Websites (Animal Guide). O'Reilly Media Inc, CA, USA.

Nixon, R. (2009), *Learning PHP, MySQL, and JavaScript: A Step-By-Step Guide to Creating Dynamic Websites (Animal Guide),* O'Reilly Media.

Norman, R. J. (1996). Object-Oriented System Analysis and Design. Prentice Hall, Inc.

Northrup, N., & Snell,M. (2010). *MCTS Self-Paced Training Kit (Exam 70-515): Web Applications Development with Microsoft .NET Framework 4 (Mcts 70-515 Exam Exam Prep),* Microsoft Press

Powers, D. (2010). PHP Solutions: Dynamic Web Design Made Easy. Springer, USA.

Skiena, S.S. (2008). *The Algorithm Design Manual*, Springer.

Steelman, A,. & Murach, J. (2008), *Murach's Java Servlets and JSP, 2nd Edition,* Murach and Associates, Inc.

Stephens, R. (2010). Visual *Basic 2010 Programmer's Reference (Wrox Programmer to Programmer),* Wrox.

Surfas, M., Brown, M., & Jung. J. (1996). Using Intranet HTML. QUE Corporation, IN, USA.

Ullman, L. E. (2007). PHP 6 and MySQL 5 for Dynamic Web Sites: Visual QuickPro Guide. Peachpit Press, Berkeley, CA.

Weiss, M. A. (2006). *Data Structures and Algorithm Analysis in C++ (3rd Edition),* Addison Wesley.

Welling, L. & Thomson, L. (2009). PHP and MySQL Web Development (4th ed). Pearson Education Inc.

Willis, T., & Newsome, B. (2010). *Beginning Visual Basic 2010 (Wrox Programmer to Programmer)*, Wrox.

Zak, D. (2010). *An Introduction to Programming With C++*, Course Technology.

Internet Sources

1keydata.com. (2007). PHP Variables, PHP Commands, PHP String Functions. Retrieved from http://www.1keydata.com/php-tutorial/variables.php.

Abel Angel Rodriguez (n.d). Visual Basic.NET Programming. Retrieve from http://websupport1.citytech.cuny.edu/Faculty/arodriguez/Downloads%5CCS608%5CLecture%201A%20-%20CS608VBNETIntro_Part%20I%20of%20IV.pdf

Apeldoorn, R. (copyright 2005). Easy PHP Install Guide 1.8. Retrieved from http://www.canowhoopass.com/guides/easyphp/getting.php

Answerbag.com (2009). What is Cookie. Retrieved from http://www.answerbag.com/q_view/646698

Answers.com (2009). Whats the difference between cache and cookies? Retrieved from http://answers.yahoo.com/question/index?qid=20090401215635AAFepHB

Bakken et al.(2002). PHP Manual. Retrieved from http://www.uvm.edu/~fcs/Doc/php_manual_en.html

Bradley, A.(n. d.). PHP Login Scripts, Using PHP With MYSQL, Basic PHP Sessions. Retrieved from http://php.about.com/od/learnphp/qt/session_cookie.htm

Bradley, A. (n. d.). PHP / MySQL, PHP Basics, MySQL Basics, Advanced Skills. Retrieved from http://php.about.com/od/learnphp/qt/session_cookie.htm

CareerRide.com. PHP creating & deleting directories. Retrieved from http://www.careerride.com/PHP-creating-deleting-directories.aspx

Claiborne, S. (n.d). Simple Server-Side Include. Retrieved from http://www.frugalmarketing.com/dtb/simple-ssi.shtml

Codewalkers. (2002, July 26). PHP Debugging Tutorial. Retrieved from http://www.codewalkers.com/c/a/Miscellaneous/PHP-Debugging-Tutorial/

Coditel.net (2008). PHP Tutorial – Introduction. Retrieved from http://users.coditel.net/lpgc/php/mysql/tips/php.htm

Dahurfar (2011). Php5 and mysql_bible. Retrieved from http://www.slideshare.net/dahurfar/php5-and-mysqlbible

Developer.mozilla.org. Block Statement. Retrieved from https://developer.mozilla.org/en/JavaScript/Guide/Statements

DigitalOcean (2015). Getting Ready for PHP 7. Retrieved from https://www.digitalocean.com/company/blog/getting-ready-for-php-7/

Docstoc.com. Learn PHP. Retrieved from http://www.docstoc.com/docs/4357936/learn-php

Dream.In.Code (2010). Database Error Handling in PHP 5. Retrieve from http://www.dreamincode.net/forums/topic/185726-database-error-handling-in-php-5/

Duckett, J. (2008). Beginning Web Programming with HTML, XHTML, and CSS, (2nd ed.). Retrieved from http://www.docstoc.com/docs/28614079/Beginning-Web-Programming-with-HTML_-XHTML_-and-CSS_-2nd-ed

Fletcher, A. (2009, September 3). PHP: Sending Email (Text/HTML/Attachments). Retrieved from http://webcheatsheet.com/php/send_email_text_html_attachment.php

Fulghum, E. (2002). Functions in PHP. Retrieved from http://www.developer.com/lang/php/article.php/956891/Functions-in-PHP.htm

Gagandeep Singh, T. (2007, October 1). Using PHP Variables. Retrieved from http://www.opensourcetutorials.com/tutorials/Server-Side-Coding/PHP/php-variables/page1.html

Garrett (2004). Why Use Object Oriented Programming? Retrieved from http://liquidphp.net/why-use-object-oriented-programming

Geek Files(2007). PHP5 Tutorial – Defining Attributes of a PHP5 Class. Retrieve from http://www.sunilb.com/php/php-tutorials/php5-oops-tutorial-defining-attributes-of-a-php5-class

Geek Files (2008). PHP 5 Tutorial – Handling Exceptions in PHP5. Retrieve from http://www.sunilb.com/php/php-5-tutorial-handling-exceptions-in-php5

Gertjan (2009). Exception Handling In PHP5- php tutorial. Retrieve from http://www.ineedtutorials.com/code/php/exception-handling-in-php5-php-tutorial

Gervasio, A. (2006). Error Handling in PHP: Introducing Exceptions in PHP 5. Retrieve from http://www.devshed.com/c/a/PHP/Error-Handling-in-PHP-Introducing-Exceptions-in-PHP-5/

Globalguideline.com (2009). Basic and Advance PHP Programming Updates and Articles. Retrieved from http://www.globalguideline.com/articles/analysis.php?k=Functions_in_PHP

Gowans, D. (1999 – 2001). Introduction to Cookies, PHP and Cookies. Retrieved from http://www.freewebmasterhelp.com/tutorials/cookies

Gowans, D. (2001). Cookies Tutorial Part 1 - Introduction to Cookies. Retrieved from http://www.freewebmasterhelp.com/tutorials/cookies

Gowans, D. (2001).Cookies Tutorial Part 2 - PHP and Cookies. Retrieved from http://www.freewebmasterhelp.com/tutorials/cookies/2

Guest Contributor (2004). A tour of the PHP.INI configuration file. Retrieve from http://www.techrepublic.com/article/a-tour-of-the-phpini-configuration-file-part-1/5268948

Home.cogeco.ca. Tutorial 5 - Inheritance & Polymorphism. Retrieved from http://home.cogeco.ca/~ve3ll/jatutor5.htm

Hscripts.com. File Upload in PHP. Retrieved from http://www.hscripts.com/tutorials/php/variables/files.php

Hudson, P. (2006).PHP in a Nutshell (In a Nutshell (O'Reilly)). Retrieved from http://searchsoftwarequality.techtarget.com/sDefinition/0,,sid92_gci211838,00.html

Internet.com. (2007). Learn PHP by examples. Retrieved from http://www.webopedia.com/TERM/V/validation.html.

iStock (2015). Human finger. Retrieved from http://www.istockphoto.com/vector/

John, WebCheatSheet.Com (2006, November 1). PHP Constants. Retrieved from http://webcheatsheet.com/php/constants.php

Kumar, A. (2011). PHP Tutorial – Learn PHP. Retrieved from http://www.slideshare.net/anilpulla/php-tizag-tutorial-6819400

Laurellion, (2008). PHP and MySQL, PHP Variable. Retrieved from http://php-and-mysql.learnhub.com/lesson/2029-php-variables

Mike Steward (2011). Exception handling in PHP: Part 1. Retrieve from http://www.c-sharpcorner.com/UploadFile/c8aa13/working-with-php-exception-handling-part-1/

Organic-Intelligence.com.. (Copyright 2008). PHP Server-Side Include. Retrieved from http://www.organic-intelligence.com/ssi.php

PHP – Learn – It.com. (2007). Creating files in PHP. Retrieved from http://www.php-learn-it.com/php_files/php_files_intro.html.

PHP – Learn – It.com. (2007). PHP File Handling. Retrieved from http://www.php-learn-it.com/php_files/php_files_intro.html.

PHP – Learn – It.com. (2008). How to create a folder in PHP. Retrieved from http://www.php-learn-it.com/php_date.html, http://www.php.net/manual/en/function.mk…,

PHP – Learn – It.com. (n. d.). PHP Tutorials – Arrays. Retrieved from http://www.learnphp-tutorial.com/Arrays.cfm#h1.3.

Php.net. (2009, 23 March). Sessions. Retrieved from http://www.php.net/manual/en/intro.session.php.

Php.share.org. (2007). Cookies versus PHP Sessions. Retrieved from http://www.phpshare.org/articles/Cookies-versus-Sessions.html.

Phpjabbers.com. PHP validation and verification. Retrieved from http://www.phpjabbers.com/php-validation-and-verification-php27.html

PHpKnowHow (2012). Working with XAMPP. Retrieved from

http://www.phpknowhow.com/basics/working-with-xampp/

Phpmysqlquestion.blogspot.com(2011). PHP MYSQL Interview Question & Books download. Retrieved from http://phpmysqlquestion.blogspot.com/feeds/posts/default?orderby=updated

plus2net.com. (copyright 2000 - 2009). String Functions, Sections. Retrieved from http://www.plus2net.com/php_tutorial/strtolower.php

Poole, E. (2005, January 30). PHP Variable and Operators. Retrieved from http://www.lowter.com/article/php-variables-operators

Programming and SEO Forum. (2005, Sept. 5) Form validation with PHP & JavaScript. Retrievedfrom http://www.go4expert.com/forums/showthread.php?t=438

Saini, V. K. (2012). Types of Errors in PHP. Retrieve from http://www.c-sharpcorner.com/UploadFile/051e29/types-of-error-in-php/

Salleh,M. K.(2008). PHPTutorial –Learn PHP. Retrieved from http://www.scribd.com/doc/3211152/Pengenalan-Kepada-Bahasa-PHPII

Santos, S. (n.d). PHP Basics - Part 2. Retrieved from http://www.php-tutorials.info/phpBasicsP2.php

Scribd.com. Part I. Getting Started. Retrieved from http://www.scribd.com/doc/13104643/Php-Documents-Oops

Seiller, S. (2009, June 9). PHP Graphs & Charts On-The-Fly. Retrieved from http://www.communitymx.com/abstract.cfm?cid=2AB8E

Shannon, R. (2000). Form Validation. Retrieved from http://www.yourhtmlsource.com/javascript/formvalidation.html

Sharing PHP (2011). PHP: Cookies. Retrieved from http://sharingphp.blogspot.com/

Sweat, J.E. (2002, May 8). Developing Professional Quality Graphs with PHP. Retrieved from http://devzone.zend.com/article/1260-Developing-Professional-Quality-Graphs-with-PHP

Tech Target. (2006). Cookie. Retrieved from http://searchsoftwarequality.techtarget.com/sDefinition/0,,sid92_gci211838,00.html

Till, I.(1996, May 20). PHP Form Validation. Retrieved from http://www.htmlcenter.com/blog/php-form-validation/

Tizag.com. (2003-2005). Beginner's Tutorial, HTML Tutorial, CSS Tutorial. Retrieved from http://www.tizag.com/about/contact.php.

Tizag.com. (2007). Learn PHP by examples, PHP Date Function. Retrieved from http://www.php-learn-it.com/php_date.html.

TutorialPoint.com (2012). What is HTML? Retrieved from http://www.tutorialspoint.com/html/what_is_html.htm

TutorialPoint.com (2012). PHP Variable Types. Retrieved from http://www.tutorialspoint.com/php/php_variable_types.htm

Tutorials Point.com. (copyright 2000). PHP Operator types. Retrieved from http://www.tutorialspoint.com/php/php_operator_types.htm.

Tutorialspoint.com. PHP File Uploading. Retrieved from http://www.tutorialspoint.com/php/php_file_uploading.htm

Tutorialspoint.com. PHP - Sending Emails. Retrieved from http://www.tutorialspoint.com/php/php_sending_emails.htm

Tutorials Point.com. (n. d.). PHP File Uploading. Retrieved from http://www.tutorialspoint.com/php/php_file_uploading.htm.

Ulysses (2009). Understanding PHP Exception Handling. Retrieve from http://ulyssesonline.com/2009/10/18/understanding-php-exception-handling/

Vaswani, V. (2010, March 5). Creating Scalable Vector Graphs with PHP. Retrieved from http://devzone.zend.com/article/11915-Creating-Scalable-Vector-Graphs-with-PHP

W3schools. PHP Error Handling. Retrieve from http://www.w3schools.com/php/func_error_trigger_error.asp

W3schools.com. PHP Exception Handling. Retrieve from
http://www.w3schools.com/php/php_exception.asp

Ward, K. (1998). Basic String Functions. Retrieved from
http://www.trans4mind.com/personal_development/phpTutorial/strings.htm

Weaver, D. (2003) Error Handling. Retrieve from
http://www.tutorials-expert.com/tutorial/4310/Error-Handling.html

WebCheatSheet.com(2007). PHP: Sending Email (Text/HTML/Attachments). Retrieved from
http://webcheatsheet.com/php/send_email_text_html_attachment.php?print=Y

Web Development tutorial.com. (n. d.). HTML Tutorial. Retrieved from
http://webdevelopmenttutorials.com.

Webmaster Geek.com. Reusing Code and Functions – Using Functions. Retrieved from
http://webmaster-geek.com/

Webopedia . Apache Web server. Retrieve from
http://www.webopedia.com/TERM/A/Apache_Web_server.html

Wiesendanger, S. (2000, December 18). Bar Charts With GD. Retrieved from
http://www.phpbuilder.com/columns/wiesendanger20001218.php3

Wikipedia. (2009, March). HTTP cookie. Retrieved from
http://en.wikipedia.org/wiki/HTTP_cookie.

Wikipedia. (n. d.). JavaScript Form Validation. Retrieved from
http://www.tizag.com/javascriptT/javascriptform.php.

Williams, N., CodeHelp.co.uk. (1998 – 2004). PHP String Functions. Retrieved from
http://www.codehelp.co.uk/php/string.php

Williams, R. (2007, February 8). Sever-Side Include in PHP – Part 1. Retrieved from
http://www.communitymx.com/abstract.cfm?cid=80E95

WordPress.com (2011). PHP Sessions – Why Use Them? Retrieved from
http://rplclass.wordpress.com/2011/05/03/php-sessions-why-use-them/

www.apache.org. The official website of The Apache Software Foundation

www.mysql.com. The official website of MySQL Database.

www.php.net. The official website of PHP (Hypertext Preprocessor).

Zend Developer Zone. (2008, August 14). Dynamically Creating Graphs and Charts with PHP and GDChart. Retrieved from http://devzone.zend.com/article/3774.

Index

www.ingramcontent.com/pod-product-compliance
Lightning Source LLC
Chambersburg PA
CBHW060638060326
40690CB00020B/4441

* 9 7 8 1 5 4 1 2 0 3 7 2 3 *